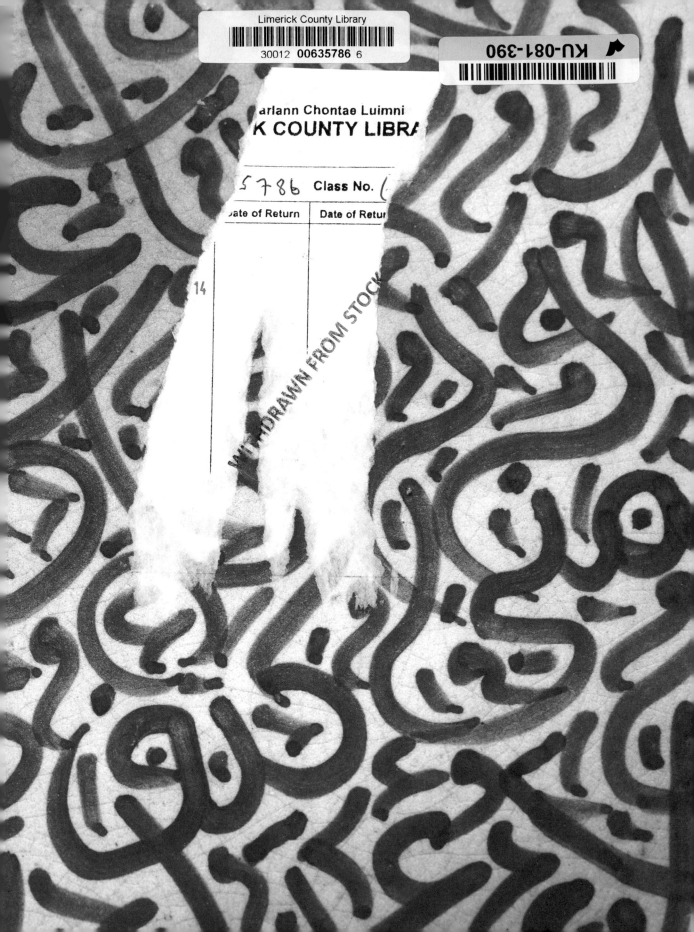

Claudia Roden Arabesque

Claudia Roden Arabesque

A taste of Morocco, Turkey & Lebanon

MICHAEL JOSEPH
an imprint of PENGUIN BOOKS

For my children Simon, Nadia and Anna, grandchildren Cesar, Peter, Sarah, Ruby and Nell and also for Clive and Ros

MICHAEL JOSEPH

Published by the Penguin Group
Penguin Books Ltd, 80 Strand, London WC2R 0RL, England
Penguin Group (USA) Inc., 375 Hudson Street, New York, New York 10014, USA
Penguin Books Australia Ltd, 250 Camberwell Road,
   Camberwell, Victoria 3124, Australia
Penguin Books Canada Ltd, 90 Eglinton Avenue East, Suite 700, Toronto, Ontario, Canada M4P 2Y3
Penguin Books India (P) Ltd, 11 Community Centre,
   Panchsheel Park, New Delhi - 110 017, India
Penguin Group (NZ), cnr Airborne and Rosedale Roads, Albany,
   Auckland 1310, New Zealand
Penguin Books (South Africa) (Pty) Ltd, 24 Sturdee Avenue,
   Rosebank 2196, South Africa

Penguin Books Ltd, Registered Offices: 80 Strand, London WC2R 0RL, England

www.penguin.com

First published 2005
9

Text © Claudia Roden 2005
Photographs © Jason Lowe 2005
except for those pictures on pages 2, 9, 12, 128, 248, 298 © Noel Murphy 2005

Set in Quadraat and Quadraat Sans
Designed and typeset by Smith & Gilmour, London
Printed and bound by Graphicom, Italy

A CIP catalogue record for this book is available from the British Library

ISBN- 13: 978-0-718-14581-1

Contents

Introduction

Three great cuisines – of Morocco, Turkey and Lebanon – developed around the Mediterranean where the Occident meets the Orient and where, long ago, medieval *jihadis* and crusaders clashed. The three are part of the Mediterranean culinary culture that the West has come to love and also share legacies from the Islamic world, with echoes from ancient Persia and medieval Baghdad, Moorish Spain and the Ottoman Empire.

The three countries have been centres of empire (Lebanon as part of historic Syria) with imperial capitals where high culinary styles developed. Damascus was the first capital of the Islamic Arab Empire during the Umayyad dynasty from the seventh to the eighth century when the empire spread all the way to Spain. Morocco was the centre of the Almoravide and Almohad dynasties that ruled over Spain and North Africa from the eleventh to the thirteenth century. And Istanbul was, for more than 400 years, the glittering capital city of the huge Ottoman Empire. Empires had a way of drawing in culinary riches from distant lands, and court kitchens were places of creativity and refinement. Something of the old grandeur and sophistication of their golden ages has passed down into the kitchens of today.

The cuisines, especially Moroccan cooking, are known for their aromatic flavourings, for the subtlety of combinations and the harmonious equilibrium. Since early times, the countries were transit areas on the spice routes between the Far East, Central Africa, the Spice Islands and Europe. (My ancestors were involved in the camel-caravan trade through Àleppo in Syria.) Today, practically every main town has its spice shops in the souk or bazaar and each country has its own characteristic spices and aromatics. If you travelled with your eyes closed, you could know where you were by the taste of the food.

Lately there has been a renaissance of interest in the culinary past. Restaurants in Istanbul are recreating Ottoman cuisine; Fez recently had a festival dedicated to medieval dishes from a thirteenth-century manuscript, and Lebanese gastronomes regularly quote medieval Arab recipes. And at the same time, in each of these countries, the rural regional cuisines have become immensely popular.

There have been great social and technological changes which have affected the way people cook and eat. Until not very long ago, most cooked on braziers and primus stoves and in outside clay ovens, or they sent dishes to the public oven to be cooked. The modern generation has less time to spend in the kitchen and is part of the global society with the same interests in new trends and concerns about healthy eating as we have in the west. They feel they can do things in a different way without losing their age-old traditions, and that the new approaches do not have to kill the old. I love tradition and respect cuisines that have a past and are part of an old civilization – that is what this book is about. But cooking does not stand still, it evolves, and I want to celebrate tradition whilst reflecting the changes. For me, what matters is what makes the food more delicious and appealing and also easier and more accessible.

In the 1960s, when I began researching the cooking of the Middle East and North Africa, the dishes were entirely strange in this country. Now they are fashionable and some have been adopted as our own. The aim of this book was to offer what were for me new, recently discovered recipes, and variations on those already known, with some of the more famous classics that I have featured in previous books. I have picked dishes that have given me the most pleasure – exciting, delicious, healthy and easy to make – that I know you will love.

Using the Book

Trust your taste and allow yourself a certain freedom in the preparation of the dishes. This is in the spirit of these cuisines which, although faithful to tradition, have no absolute rules and are rich in variations and poor in precision. You are told to 'weigh with the eye' and to taste as you go along. And that is what cooking is about. We are dealing with products of nature and these vary. You can have a small lemon that has more juice and is sharper than a larger one. Garlic cloves vary in size and flavour; there are many varieties and they can be young or old and more or less strong. Many of the vegetables available to us come from different countries and are grown in different soils, under a different sun. They have a different taste and respond differently to cooking. Rice, even of the same variety and the same provenance, varies from one year to the next and, depending on whether it is new or old, in the amount of water it absorbs. Once upon a time the recommendation for many rice recipes (also those using flour) was to add 'as much water as it takes' and there was much sense in that.

The flavour of fresh herbs varies as do spices, depending on where they come from and the particular harvest. There are different grades and qualities. If spices or dry herbs are old they lose their strength, which is why you may have to use more or less and why you should buy small quantities at a time. Even rose and orange blossom waters, which come in bottles, can be more or less diluted according to the producer and depending on whether they were the first or last batch in the distillation process. I do not generally give precise quantities of salt in my recipes, because I believe salting is so much a matter of personal taste and it is the one seasoning that people know how to use and have an 'eye' for, even before tasting. It is best to start with less and add more later. It is quite possible to substitute oil for butter in dishes without spoiling them; and onions and garlic may be used abundantly or omitted entirely if you don't like them.

The book is divided by country, so that you can choose to have dishes of the same country in one meal. But you can also have a mixed menu, which is what I often do. Each country is divided into first, main and dessert courses to make it easier to plan a menu. Ours is a different society from the ones whose dishes we are adopting, so we can be flexible and we can plan around our own ways of eating and entertaining. For instance, you can feel free to serve appetizers – *mezze* or *kemia* – with drinks, as starters, or as side dishes. You can make a casual meal out of two or three, accompanied by bread and perhaps cheese or yoghurt and olives, while a large assortment can be produced for a buffet party. You can make a meal out of a soup accompanied by bread. A pie or an omelette – both of which can be quite substantial – can also serve as a one-course snack. For most of the fish dishes you may use alternative kinds of fish. Lamb is the traditional meat of the three countries, but beef or veal can be used instead; and in many recipes, such as stews, meat and poultry are interchangeable. Rice, couscous and bulgur are staples that make good accompaniments to many dishes.

It is important to use good ingredients – free-range, corn-fed or organic chickens, natural (full-fat) yoghurt, full fat cheese, good extra virgin olive oil. A mild-tasting olive oil is best with all the dishes. You will find the ingredients you need in Middle Eastern (Turkish, Lebanese, Persian), North African, Greek and Asian food stores and many of our own best food stores now also stock most of what you require.

About Aromatics

A certain magic surrounds the use of spices and aromatics, which are used not only for their flavour but also for their medicinal, therapeutic and even sometimes aphrodisiac value. They are variously believed to increase the appetite, help digestion or calm the nerves, to be good for the heart and circulation, to be anti-toxic or sexually stimulating and even to kill microbes. Attributes may be well founded or romantic; ginger is said to make people loving, rose water to give a rosy outlook, dill and aniseed to have digestive qualities, and garlic to be both health-giving and antiseptic. Herbs are so popular in the three countries that they are sometimes placed in a bunch on the table for people to pick at. The most commonly used are flat-leaf parsley, coriander and mint.

Gum mastic has nothing at all to do with the waterproof filler called mastic, nor with the glue called 'gum Arabic' sold in the building trades. It is an aromatic resin from the lentisc tree or bush, a small evergreen tree that grows on the Greek island of Chios. When tiny incisions are made in the stems in the summer, sticky oval tears of resin appear. It is pronounced *miskeh* in Lebanon and some London restaurants misleadingly spell it 'musk'.

It is sold in tiny hard, dry translucent lumps. To use them, you must first pound them and grind them to a fine powder with a pestle and mortar, together with a pinch of sugar, or use a spice grinder. Use very little otherwise the taste can be quite unpleasant.

Olive oil is native to all three countries. Although other oils such as sunflower and groundnut oil are also used, olive oil has come to be seen as the oil of choice for gourmets. Use mild-tasting extra virgin oil for all the recipes and refined non-virgin for deep-frying.

Orange blossom water, produced by boiling the blossom of the bitter orange tree and condensing the steam in an alembic or still, lends a delicate perfume to syrups, pastries and puddings. As the flavour is rather powerful and because the distilled water comes in varying degrees of strength, it is worth adding a little less than the amount stated to begin with, and adding more to taste.

Pomegranate molasses, also called concentrate and syrup, is made from the juice of sour (not sweet) pomegranates boiled down to a thick syrup. Some varieties are a bit too sweet for my liking. A little added lemon juice or wine vinegar can improve on the sweet-and-sour flavour.

Preserved (or pickled) lemons lend a unique and distinctive flavour to Moroccan dishes. (Some British importers call them 'pickled', claiming that 'preserved' here denotes a 'sweet' preserve.) Pickled in salt, they loose their sharpness. To make them yourself, *see* p.46.

Rose water, produced by boiling rose petals and condensing the steam in an alembic or still, is used to perfume syrups, pastries and puddings. It is weaker than orange blossom water and can be used less sparingly. The two are often used together.

Saffron: the highly prized red saffron threads – the pistils of the purple *Crocus sativus* – are much used in Moroccan cooking. There are various grades. The highest have an incomparable flavour. It is better to buy the threads than the powders but in certain dishes a powder is more useful. Some commercial powdered saffron is very good and worth buying (it is cheaper than the threads) but many brands are adulterated.

Sumac, the dark wine-coloured spice with an astringent sour flavour, is made from the coarsely ground dried berries of the sumac shrub. Turks and Lebanese use it frequently to sprinkle on grills and salads or on fish. It can be used instead of lemon.

Tahini is a paste made of ground sesame seeds. It is used extensively in Lebanon where it is spelled *tahina*. (We call it *tahini* because it first came to this country from Cyprus.) Because it separates, with the oil rising to the top and the thick paste remaining at the bottom, it needs to be stirred with a spoon before use.

Preparing Vegetables

To Prepare Artichoke Bottoms: Choose large globe artichokes and cut off the stems at the base. With a pointed knife, trim off all the outer leaves and any hard bits round the base, cutting round it spirally. Putting the artichoke on its side, cut away the top inner leaves, then remove the chokes. Rub each prepared artichoke bottom with a squeezed lemon half, and throw it into a bowl of water acidulated with 2–3 tablespoons vinegar or lemon juice to keep them from discolouring.

Salting Aubergines: It is the custom to salt aubergines to rid them of their bitter juices and to make them absorb less oil when they are fried. These days, aubergines are not bitter and even if they have been salted they absorb a lot of oil when they are fried. I now prefer to grill or roast aubergines, in which case salting is not necessary. But if you are frying, it is worth salting them. There are two traditional ways. One is to soak them in salted water for $1/2$–1 hour – this also stops them from discolouring if you have to wait for some time before you use them. Another is to sprinkle them with plenty of salt, leave them in a colander to disgorge their juices, then rinse them and pat them dry with kitchen paper.

To Roast and Mash Whole Aubergines: Prick the aubergines in a few places with a pointed knife to prevent them from exploding. Turn them over the flame of the gas hob or barbecue, or under a pre-heated grill on a sheet of foil on an oven tray, until the skin is charred all over and they feel very soft. Alternatively, place them on a sheet of foil on an oven tray and roast them in the *hottest* oven for 45–60 minutes until they are very soft. When cool enough to handle, peel the aubergines (you can do this under the cold tap), drop the flesh into a colander or strainer, then chop it with a knife and mash it with a fork, letting the juices escape. Adding a squeeze of lemon juice helps to keep the purée looking pale and appetizing.

Garlic: Garlic cloves must be firm, not soft or hollow. If the garlic has begun to sprout inside a clove, cut into the middle of the clove and remove the pale green sprout which has a bitter taste. To crush it, bash it on a board under the flat blade of a large knife, then chop it or scrape it to a mush on the board. Or use a garlic press – I have nothing against them but so many are useless. My own works very well and dates from my schooldays in Paris.

To Roast and Peel Bell Peppers: Grill them over the flame of the gas hob or barbecue, or put them on a sheet of foil on an oven tray under a pre-heated grill. Turn them until their skins are black and blistered. Alternatively, roast them in the hottest oven for 30 minutes, turning them once, until they are soft and their skins blistered and blackened. To loosen the skins further, put them into a plastic freezer bag, twist it shut and leave for 10–15 minutes. When cool enough to handle, peel the peppers and remove the stems and seeds. Strain the juice that comes out since it can form part of the dressing.

To Peel Tomatoes: Pour boiling water over them, prick the skins with a pointed knife and leave for 1 minute before draining and peeling off the skin.

About Filo Pastry

Filo is used in Turkey and Lebanon. In Lebanon, another pastry called *rakakat*, like a very thin, soft, large round pancake, softer and more malleable and also tougher than filo, is used to make savoury pies. I have used filo instead of *rakakat* and instead of the Moroccan paper-thin pancake called *warka* or *brick* with perfect results.

Filo is widely available here both fresh and frozen. Commercial brands generally weigh 400g (packets used to be 500g) but vary in the size of sheets and their fineness. I have come across the following sizes: 50cm x 30cm, 48cm x 30cm, 46cm x 35cm, 46cm x 31cm, 30cm x 18cm and 29cm x 12cm, and they will often vary by a centimetre or two even within the same brand. Sizes are not given on the packaging. Supermarket brands usually contain fresh sheets in the smaller size, while packets containing large-sized sheets are usually sold frozen, in specialist stores. If you are using a frozen brand, it is important to find a reliable one, as some are totally unsatisfactory, with damp sheets sticking together when defrosted and tearing when you try to use them.

Frozen filo must be allowed to defrost slowly for 2–3 hours. Packets should then be opened just before using and the sheets should be used as quickly as possible as they become dry and brittle when exposed to the air. Keep them in a pile as you work, always brushing the top one with melted butter so the air has no opportunity to dry them out. If you have to leave them for a few minutes, cover them with cling film. Any leftover pieces can be wrapped in cling film and kept in the refrigerator for later use.

Filo pies with any filling except one that is very moist can be frozen and put straight from the freezer into the oven without thawing, but they will need a little more cooking time.

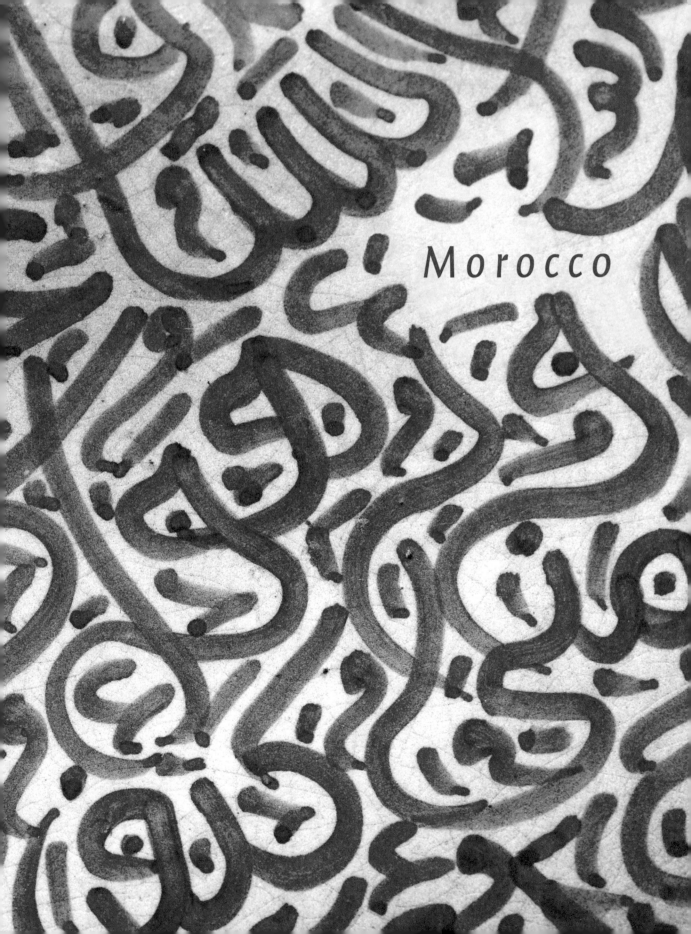

Morocco

Moroccan cooking is the most exquisite and refined of North Africa, famous for its couscous, its crispy multilayered pies and delicately flavoured tagines, its marriages of meat with fruit, and its extraordinary combinations of spicy, savoury and sweet. In a society based around the family, where the oldest generation of women is still mostly illiterate, cooking is a woman's art and still an oral tradition with its secrets passed down from mother to daughter. It is the lore learnt in the kitchen, a precious heritage, which a bride brings to her husband's home. It is an all-important activity, central to every aspect of life. In Morocco, any reason, any event, happy or sad, is an occasion for meeting around the table.

Styles of cooking go back hundreds of years. Some are rooted in the rural traditions of the indigenous Berber populations of Morocco, while an important grand style is a legacy from the royal kitchens of the great Moroccan dynasties – the Almoravides, Almohads, Merinids, Saadians and Alaouites – which has echoes from medieval Baghdad and Muslim Spain. Morocco was invaded by the Arabs in several waves from the seventh until the fourteenth century. More than any other country that adopted Islam, it inherited most directly the high culinary culture of Baghdad in the time of the Abbasid caliphs when that city was the capital of the Islamic Empire and its court cuisine was influenced by Persian styles. In 711, the Arabs invaded Spain with North African Berber foot soldiers. They conquered half the country and remained in the south, which became known as Al Andalus, for almost 800 years. From the eleventh to the thirteenth century, the ruling dynasties in Muslim Spain – the Almoravides and the Almohads – were Berber. The capital cities of their vast empire that spread through Spain, Tunisia, Algeria and into Senegal, were in Morocco, this country becoming a centre of excellence and sophistication.

Until the final expulsion of the Moors from Spain in 1492, there was constant cultural exchange between Spain and Morocco. A new eclectic style of cooking developed in the part of Spain that was under Muslim occupation. It was a multicultural civilization with people from various parts of the Muslim and Mediterranean world, including Jews and the indigenous Christians. A Kurdish lute player known as Ziryab, a freed slave from the court of Harun al Rashid in Baghdad who joined the court of Cordoba, is credited in particular for transforming the 'art of living' and cooking in Andalusia. He introduced new music and taught people how to dress and wear make-up. He established rules of etiquette, table manners and table setting, the order of serving three different courses, and encouraged refinements in the kitchen.

When the Moors were finally thrown out of Spain, many found refuge in Morocco, where they settled mostly in Tangier, Tetouan and Fez. These 'Andalusians', as they were called, brought with them the exuberant and convivial lifestyle that had blossomed in Spain. They also started a culinary renaissance. You can see their influence in the country's architecture, you can hear it in the music, and you can taste it in the food.

Other influences on Moroccan cuisine are through the influx of thousands of black slaves from central Africa in the seventeenth century, and also Ottoman influences via refugees from Algeria and Tunisia who migrated while those countries were under Ottoman rule.

Regional Cooking

Some years ago I was invited to a festival celebrating the regional cooking of Morocco, held in Fez. Each night, we were offered a taste of at least twenty-five dishes coming from two or three cities, while musicians, singers and dancers entertained us. It was an enthralling experience. In Moroccan cooking, there are traditions which come from both the countryside and the mountains, and from the sea – both of the Atlantic and the Mediterranean – and there is urban cooking which varies from one city to another. Some dishes are common throughout Morocco, varying only in the spicing and one or two ingredients, but every city also has its own special dishes and distinctive style which reflects its geographic position and climate as well as its past. In Tangier and Tetouan in the north, the influences are Andalusian and Mediterranean and there is also, unusually for Morocco, an Ottoman influence, especially in the pastries such as *ktaief* and *baklava*. In the south, in Marrakesh, Safi and Essaouira, the influences come from Africa and the Atlantic. The cooking of Fez reflects the mix of its past inhabitants, Arab, Andalusian, Berber and Jewish (the old Jewish quarter, the Mellah, situated in the medina, backs on to the Royal Palace), as well as the city's position on the camel-caravan spice route. A particularly refined and sophisticated bourgeois cuisine emanates from cities like Fez, Meknès and Marrakesh that were once imperial capitals and are now gastronomic rivals with very distinctive styles of cooking.

A Festive Meal in a Traditional Moroccan Home – a Riad

You arrive at the traditional Moroccan house from a narrow street in the medina. There is a blank wall, with a tiny window. You enter by a heavily-studded wooden door through a dark narrow corridor carpeted with fragrant rose petals and arrive in a glorious inner patio filled with little fruit trees and scented flowers. The floor and arched walls around it are lined with cobalt blue, turquoise and yellow mosaics called zeligs. Water trickles from a fountain. Alcoves around the courtyard are ornately decorated. Brilliantly coloured hangings line the walls of the living area. Placed against them are low sofas with embroidered cushions. The meal is served in the patio. The scent of jasmine hangs in the air. A band plays Andalusian music. The tables are large brass trays on low folding legs. You sit on cushions around them. The crockery is classic Chinese. Long ago, Morocco fell in love with Chinese porcelain with blue designs; now they make it themselves.

You wash your hands in water poured from a jug and then rose water sprinkled from a silver flagon. Dishes follow one another. A multitude of appetizers (*kemia*): pickles, spiced vegetable purées, fried fish in a sauce flavoured with cumin, chilli and green coriander; pastry 'cigars' filled with chopped meat and with prawns. Then pigeon pie or baby pigeons stuffed with nutty couscous in a saffron and ginger honey sauce; followed by a tagine of lamb with wild artichokes, broad beans and preserved lemon, and another with quinces. And next, couscous, mountains of it, crowned with meat cooked to melting tenderness, and with vegetables pressed into the sides of the mountains of grain. Then platters of fruit, followed by mint tea and almondy pastries. You might be worried by how much food is left uneaten. But the next day, family, friends and neighbours have their feast; and what is left – every bit of it – is eaten by the cooks, staff and helpers. That too is part of the ritual.

The Dadas, and their Secrets

Men are excluded from all kitchens. The great cooks – family cooks, professional cooks, those who cook for weddings and parties, the guardians of the great culinary traditions – are the dadas. They are all women and most of them are black. Who they are is a taboo subject, the hidden face of Morocco. The women are descended from African slaves who were brought from the Sudan which was once part of the

Moroccan empire. In the seventeenth century, the sultan Moulay Ismail recruited 150,000 slaves from the Sudan and the states of the African Sahel. The men became the origin of the Sherifan black guard. The women became domestics in people's homes. Some became concubines, some wives, some were freed and became midwives. In imperial Fez, it was not uncommon for men of great families to chose young dadas as their fourth wives so that they would look after their children and cook. Their children were often formally recognized and took on the father's name. A form of bondage went on until not so long ago, and the women remained illiterate. That is why it is still a taboo subject. I heard this from Fatema Hal, anthropologist, food writer and owner of the restaurant La Mansouria in Paris.

In more recent times dadas have joined cooks' corporations, catering for great occasions such as weddings, circumcisions and receptions. A man is in overall charge on such occasions, an amine or chief. It is he who discusses the menu with the host, who works out quantities, and hires the giant saucepans and piles of crockery, the silver teapots, ornate tea glasses and the trays.

The women arrive, heads tied in fringed and floral scarves, with their helpers and their pots and pans, and stay several days with the families. They shop, slaughter sheep and pigeons, prepare the warka for *bstilla*, set up the big copper pans on braziers, and prepare all the dishes while the ladies of the house and their relatives busy themselves with the sweet pastries. These dadas pass on the oral traditions of grand cooking to one another. They also pass from one kitchen to another, the inside stories and scandals of the top families. Their stories of sorcerers and devils frighten the children who gather to watch the activities around the giant pans and to see the dadas throw a grain of incense in the fire to drive away the *jnoun* (devil). They are paid little but they are fed and they can take away offals and leftovers.

Some dadas have become famous itinerant specialists of one dish only or a culinary style. A few lead the battalions of women in the kitchens of the best hotels. Most of the great ones who lived all their lives with families are old now. They are disappearing, and people have had to learn to do without them. Some of their specialities, like the paper-thin pancakes called *warka* (or *brick*) can now be bought loose at the souk and vacuum-packed in supermarkets.

Street Food

Donkeys carry produce from the country – great bundles of fresh green mint and coriander, baskets of fat tomatoes, little wild purple artichokes, long fleshy cardoon stalks – into the heart of the medina through the narrow meandering streets and into the souk. Powerful aromas emanate from the mounds of red, gold and brown powders, curious-looking roots, bits of bark, shrivelled pods, seeds, berries, bulbs, rose buds and orange blossoms which are on display in the spice shops. Vendors pack the spices into tightly rolled cones of newspaper and offer them as though they were magic potions. Some of the spice merchants are also magic men. I got to know one who said he was a white magic man who defeated the evil eye and black magic spells. Mostly it meant he dealt with any mischief from co-wives and restored potency to men.

In every town, in the souks, in the old medinas, the squares where weekly markets set up, at bus stops on inter-city roads, there are street vendors. From tiny cafés and boutiques as small as a cupboard, from carts or stands or sometimes from an upturned box with a chair for customers, they offer their specialities: boiled carrot salad with cumin, *harira* (soup with meat or chicken, chickpeas, lentils or other beans), tiny spicy snails, grilled minced meat on skewers, spongy pancakes, fritters in sugar syrup.

Place Djemaa-el-Fna in Marrakesh is the most enthralling gastro-theatre. One of my friends has a medical clinic there. I stayed in the family home and hung around the square day and night. During the day, musicians and dancers from the mountains, snake charmers, fire eaters, letter writers, story tellers, fortune tellers, have possession of the huge square. As the sun begins to fall, the entire area is taken over by hundreds of cooks. They set up stands and trestle tables, and start charcoal fires. Clients sit on benches around each stand. All night long the vendors serve soups from huge pots, often accompanied by dates. The smoke of fish frying and meat grilling on braziers and the mingled aromas of mint and coriander, cumin and turmeric fill the air.

Restaurants

There have always been small, modest establishments where travellers and country folk who bring their products to market can find something to eat – soups simmering in large copper pans, fried fish, mountains of couscous, pancakes oozing with honey and melting butter. But it is only in the last decade or two that grand restaurants serving traditional local foods have opened. Moroccans are not used to eating out. They are used to entertaining at home. The local hospitality is legendary. Even strangers, poor travellers knocking at the door of a home in the medina, will be offered at least soup and a piece of bread.

Tourist hotels used to serve French cuisine, now they mostly serve international food. Recently, grand restaurants that employ family cooks or dadas who can make exquisite, refined dishes have opened in old riads – palaces that were family homes. It is an extraordinary experience to eat in one of those restaurants with their fabulous décor. The best meal I had on a recent visit to Fez was in one such riad built in the eighteenth century, the *maison d'hôtes* Dar El Ghalia. It has been converted by descendants of the original owners into a restaurant with hotel rooms, but otherwise it has kept the reception area as it was, with inner patio and fountain, mosaics, alcoves with low sofas, and seating around huge brass trays. For me, it is a bit of heaven. In Morocco hospitality is an art, and this restaurant emulates the traditions of the home. The owners receive you with effusive warmth, offer you mint tea poured from a silver teapot held high into little glasses, and serve you the local dishes cooked in the traditional way.

Of Tagines, Qdras and Other Long-cooked Dishes

During a round-table discussion at a festival of culinary arts in 2001 entitled 'Saveurs d'hier et d'aujourd'hui' ('Flavours of Yesterday and Today'), there were heated arguments between those who did not accept any changes to tradition and those who wanted to be free to invent and do dishes their way. The latter were Moroccan restaurateurs abroad. Local restaurateurs were concerned about the loss of their beloved traditions and were prickly about every little detail. The 'modernizers' in between advocated making dishes lighter and healthier by using less fat.

One man regretted the passing of the time, not long ago, when people would walk down the street and know, by the smells, exactly what their neighbours were cooking, and what stage of readiness the stews had reached. I am not sure if this is because they have cars now and have moved out of the medina or because many cooks now use the *cocotte minute* or *mijotte* (pressure cooker). Years ago when I was travelling through Morocco I was told that I had to go and see a woman who had developed a new style of 'fast' Moroccan cuisine. I contacted her and she invited me to lunch. On the table was a pressure cooker in which she made her tagines. It was the start of a trend that, a long time later, has taken the country by storm.

The word tagine derives from the shallow round clay cooking pot with the pointed cone-shaped lid in which stews are traditionally cooked. The word has become so glamorous and prestigious in our western world, and so misused in restaurants in Morocco, that it has come to mean any kind of stew or braise. Cooking in a clay tagine, very gently over a brazier (*kanoun*) of constantly replenished embers, diffuses the heat all round the pot and produces at the end a reduced sauce sizzling in its fat. Tagines are distinguished by their cooking fats and spicing, although the distinctions have become blurred these days. *M'qualli* denotes those cooked in oil where there is saffron and ginger and the sauce is yellow. *M'hammer* refers to those cooked with olive oil or butter, and spiced with cumin and paprika, where the sauce is red.

For parties and great occasions it has never been possible to cook in tagines because they don't contain enough. The cooking then is done in giant pots. You see them in copper, aluminium or stainless steel in the souks, for sale or to rent. The word *qdra*, the name of the big pots used for the grand parties in the royal cities, has come to mean the kind of grand dishes with noble ingredients that are cooked in them on such occasions. The cooking fat is butter (although nowadays many substitute olive oil), the flavour is that of saffron, sometimes combined with ginger and cinnamon, and they nearly always include chickpeas or almonds. Huge quantities of chopped onions are reduced to melting softness to produce a rich, creamy sauce. There is often also a touch of honey. The varieties of stews cooked and sold in the streets and in the souks, and those cooked in the countryside, in ordinary saucepans with oil and turmeric instead of saffron, are called *marqa*. They are the poor man's *qdra*.

Until recently, people did not have ovens. Nowadays, most city families have every modern appliance and utensil. They can make life easier for themselves without betraying the memory of the old gastronomy. It is more convenient to cook in saucepans and casseroles over gas than in a tagine over a dying fire. The result can be as good if you cook slowly with very little water, adding more as it evaporates, and if you reduce the sauce until it is rich and unctuous. In restaurants stews are cooked in large pans and finished off and brought to the table in beautiful individual tagines decorated with blue, green, turquoise and yellow arabesques. People also do more roasting and baking in their ovens.

Moroccan dishes change little even when they are 'modernized'. As with legends that vary in small details as they travel from place to place and are passed from one person to another, the differences in cooking lie in the use of spices, fats and local seasonal produce, as well as in method. While in many places they brown the meat and soften the onions in oil or butter before adding water, in Fez they never fry first but put all the ingredients in together with the water. *Smen*, the 'matured' clarified butter that was once very common, is now little used. (To outsiders, including myself, and also to many local people these days, it appears to give the food an unpleasant rancid taste.) Some braise their chickens whole, others joint them. Although lamb and mutton are the traditional meat, beef and veal are now also used. There are also differences as to when to put in olives and preserved lemon – ten minutes before the end of cooking, or as a garnish just before serving.

About Couscous

Couscous is the national dish of Morocco. The name refers to the grain as well as to the combined dish of broth with meat, chicken or fish with vegetables over which the grain is traditionally steamed and which is served with the grain. The processed grain is semolina made from durum hard wheat which has been ground then moistened and coated or 'rolled' in flour. The resulting granules are cooked by steaming. Other grains – maize, millet and especially barley – are also used in the same way.

In Morocco, where all foods based on grain are considered sacred, couscous has a quasi-mystical character. It is served on all great occasions, both happy and sad – at weddings and at funerals. It is a celebratory dish served at the end of great feasts to make sure that no one is left hungry. It is usually the musicians and the *tolbas* – people who come to pray and recite the Koran at weddings, funerals or during Ramadan, in expectation of a good meal – who get to eat it. It is the family's Friday meal where any vegetables left over from the week's provisions goes in, and also famously the food sent to the mosque by the pious to be distributed to the poor.

Couscous is associated with the indigenous Berbers who call it *kesksou*, a name said to be derived from the sound steam makes as it passes through the grain. No written reference to it was made until the thirteenth century – a time when the Berber Almohad dynasty ruled Andalusia and all of North Africa – when it featured prominently in Arabic culinary manuscripts of the Maghreb (North Africa) and Andalusia. The special type of durum wheat that is used originated in Ethiopia and was supposedly introduced into the region by the Arabs by the tenth century. But it is in the Berber lands, where steaming in a clay colander placed over a boiling pot was an age-old practice, that the special way of rolling the grain and then cooking it over a broth was developed.

Until not very long ago, every family bought its wheat at the market and took it to the local mill to be ground to the degree of fineness they preferred, then brought it home to be processed or 'rolled' by hand. This is traditionally done by the following method. A few handfuls of semolina (medium-ground durum wheat) are spread in a wide shallow wooden or clay dish. The semolina is sprinkled with a little cold salted water to moisten it and rolled with the open hand with a circular clockwise movement as it is gradually sprinkled with flour, until the granules are evenly coated with a fine film of flour to form very tiny balls. These are shaken through two or three sieves with different-sized holes (the first with larger holes) to sort them by size, and lastly through a very fine sieve to eliminate any excess flour. Larger granules are enlarged with more moistening and rolling in flour and are used as a type of pasta called *berkoukes* or *mhammas*. Without this coating of flour, the grain would cook into a stodgy porridge.

Large amounts of grain were prepared in advance, either to be stored or for special occasions such as a wedding or circumcision or a return from a pilgrimage to Mecca. Women from the family and neighbours assembled to work together. It took hours but it was a day of fun and rejoicing as they gossiped and laughed and sang. Before the rolled grain was stored, it was first steamed for about 20 minutes then dried for two days on sheets laid out on roof-tops. This ensured it would keep for a long time.

Nowadays, very few women roll their own grain, even in the country areas. The process has been industrialized and the vast majority now buy it ready-processed or in an instant pre-cooked variety which can be bought in three different grades: fine, medium and large. Those who insist on having the time-honoured home-made couscous for a special event call in professional artisans – Berber women or dadas (see p.24) – to the house to make it. Traditional purists find the pre-cooked instant variety unacceptable, even offensive. It does not have the special quality of the real thing made by hand, but I suspect they are also mourning the loss of an old culture and the rituals that accompanied it. Nevertheless, the pre-cooked instant couscous is used in many North African restaurants abroad and by busy North African families in France as well as in Morocco. It can be perfectly good if handled properly.

I visited a couscous-processing factory in Sfax during an international conference in 1993 which took us on a fabulous gastronomic tour of Tunisia. We were received with welcoming banners, and offered a tasting of dozens of couscous dishes, both savoury and sweet. Women in Berber dress gave demonstrations of the old ancestral ways of rolling couscous by hand and steaming it. When the owner of the factory showed us around the plant, I asked him what he advised was the best way to use his product since packets sold abroad gave different instructions. He said that, although steaming is a ritual and part of the culture of North Africa which the people are used to and hold on to, you can just as well add water and heat it through in the oven – even, he added very quietly, in a microwave, which many of the women now do.

The couscous we get in Britain is the pre-cooked instant variety. Our supermarkets sell the medium-sized granules that are best for ordinary couscous dishes, while the 'fine' variety called 'couscous *seffa*', used for stuffings and sweet couscous (see the

كسكسى
COUSCOUS
IUM • MITTELGROß
IO • MEDELGROV • متوسط

FERRERO

cous-ferrero.com   F.A.G

كسكسى
COUSCO
MOYEN • MEDIUM • MIT
MIDDELGROTE • MEDIO • MEDELC

PRÊT EN
5 min
READY IN

1kg e

FERRERO

www.couscous-ferrero.com

couscous
ZAKIA

كسكسي

MOYEN · MEDIUM · MITTELGROB
MIDDELGROTE · MEDIO · متوسط

EAG

POIDS NET
NET WEIGHT
NETTOGEWICHT
NETTO GEWICHT **1kg** e
PESO NETO
PESO NETTO

dessert section) can be found in specialist Moroccan and a few Middle Eastern stores. With care, it is possible, even with pre-cooked couscous, to prepare it so that it swells and becomes light, fluffy and airy, each grain soft and separate from its neighbour. Moroccans describe it as 'velvety'.

There are many regional and seasonal versions of couscous dishes. These can be very simple, with the couscous plus just one vegetable such as fresh peas, or quite grandiose, with stuffed pigeons sitting on a mountain of couscous mixed with almonds and raisins. Every family makes it in their own special way and it is always different every time they make it. It can, with experience, be the easiest thing to prepare in advance and to serve at a large dinner party. It can be spectacular and there is something about the dish that inspires conviviality. By tradition, couscous is a communal dish. The old traditional way was to eat it with one hand straight from the serving dish. Nowadays, couscous is eaten with a spoon – the meat is supposed to be so tender that you can pull it apart with your fingers and you don't need to cut it with a knife.

The traditional method of cooking couscous is by steaming it over a broth or over water in a *couscoussier* – a large round pot with a colander on top that holds the couscous. The grain needs to be steamed three times, and between each steaming it is taken out and moistened with cold water and rubbed so any lumps are removed. In all, the process takes about three-quarters of an hour.

Since all the couscous available in Britain is of the pre-cooked variety, it requires a different treatment. I use a very simple method (p.120), which cannot fail. However, even with this method of preparing pre-cooked couscous, there is an art in achieving light, airy, separate grains.

About Warka *or* Brick *for* Bstilla *and* Briwat

Large, ever-so-thin pancakes called *warka* are used to make large round pies called *bstilla* (or *pastilla*) and small ones called *briwat*. These are made in the shape of cigars, triangles, cornets and square parcels with a variety of fillings, and are deep-fried.

Making *warka* is a highly skilled operation and these days it is left to specialists. A dough is made with hard-wheat (or bread) flour, a pinch of salt and warm water and then kneaded for a long time as more water is worked in to obtain a soft, very moist, spongy elasticity. Then the dough is left to rest for an hour, covered with a film of warm water. Lumps the size of an egg are picked up with one hand and dabbed on to the oiled surface of a round tray placed bottom side up over a fire. As the dough touches the tray with repeated dabs, a thin, almost transparent, film of pastry is built up and gradually expanded into a round about 30 cm in diameter.

Nowadays, you can buy the vacuum-packed round pastry sheets in Moroccan stores as 'feuilles de brick'. *Brick* is the Tunisian name of the little fried pies. I buy these sheets from North African stores in Golborne Road, London W10, and they are in all French supermarkets. They freeze very well. I personally prefer to use filo instead, because I like baking rather than frying the pies, and the round sheets of brick are wonderfully crisp when they are deep-fried, but come out unpleasantly tough when baked.

I started using filo for Moroccan pies long ago but I always felt a little guilty about not using the real thing until a young Moroccan cook who had been sent to Disneyland in America to demonstrate Moroccan cooking at an international festival of tourism told me about her team's experience. They had not anticipated the extent of the demand for *briwat* and quickly ran out of pastry. A Lebanese contingent nearby lent the Moroccan cooks filo and they continued to make the pies with this pastry which turned out perfectly satisfactory.

About Spices and Aromatics

What is most surprising and fascinating to us is the way Moroccans mix savoury with sweet, and the way they mix a number of spices to achieve a very delicate, subtle flavour. There are no sweet-and-sour dishes, but sugar or honey can be part of savoury dishes such as meat stews and vegetable dishes. Dozens of aromatics are used and some are ubiquitous. Cumin, which is believed to stimulate the appetite, ginger, paprika and chilli are common in appetizers as well as in fish dishes. Saffron, ginger and cinnamon are the constant aromatics of sweet tagines. There are spice mixtures for minced meat, *kefta* (coriander seed, cumin, mace, allspice, paprika or chilli pepper) and mixtures for soup (cinnamon, caraway, cumin, ginger, pepper). *Ras el hanout* (meaning 'the head of the shop') is a legendary mixture of twenty-seven spices including the golden beetle that is the aphrodisiac, Spanish fly. Spice merchants have their own secret blends and now there are brands made by small local producers that you can buy in Europe.

The most prestigious and also ubiquitous spice used extensively in soups and tagines is saffron. In Morocco, it is cultivated in the region of Taliouine between Taroudant and Ouarzazate. Because it is expensive, many Moroccans use a low-grade adulterated powder that gives a yellow colour and has hardly any taste or aroma, but using the 'threads' or stigmas of the *Crocus sativus* or a very good-quality powder, makes all the difference to a dish. Turmeric is the poor man's saffron. You can smell it in the aroma of stews and soups sold by street vendors. It is yellow but the flavour is nothing like that of saffron.

When you cook a Moroccan dish, it is most important to achieve a delicate marriage of flavours and, with the sweet tagines especially, a balance between sweet and salty. Dishes with sugar and honey must have enough salt and also plenty of black pepper to mitigate the sweetness. They say you must 'weigh with your eye', but of course you must also taste and you must learn to trust your taste. Preserved lemon peel is used as an aromatic, and oils also contribute their flavour. Sophisticated cooks now commonly replace the traditional groundnut oil by extra virgin olive oil for cooking as well as for dressings. Argan oil (p.39), which has a distinctive nutty flavour, is also used as a dressing. Flower waters, made from the blossoms of bitter oranges and roses (see pp. 10 and 11) are used to perfume puddings and pastries. People make them at home. In the spring, mountains of the flowers are to be seen in huge floppy baskets in all the markets.

About Argan Oil

This is obtained from the nut in the yellow fruit of the argan tree, which grows exclusively in south-west Morocco. It has a distinctive nutty flavour and is used as a dressing. It does not keep very well.

Goats famously climb into the trees and jump from one branch to another, munching the argan fruit. The pulp is digested and the stone is expelled. The stones are then collected and cracked to release the nut from which the oil is made. The oil is believed locally to have aphrodisiac properties. It is also valued for its medicinal and cosmetic qualities. Women rub it on their faces and necks as a night lotion, and into their hair.

About Bread

In Moroccan society bread is considered almost sacred. It is a symbol of generosity and conviviality, of giving and taking. If a piece falls on the ground, someone is sure to pick it up, kiss it and place it somewhere high. When you see the extraordinary bread bins with cone-shaped hats made of wicker and brightly coloured leather or, more grandly, of copper or silver, you realize how favourably bread is held.

Hardly any dish is eaten without bread. It is used to mop up sauces and also to pick up morsels of food. Loaves are round and dense, made from wheat flour and semolina, and also from maize, barley and rye flours; sometimes they are embellished with seeds such as sesame and aniseed. Families used to take their wheat to be ground at the mill. They would make bread at home every morning with leaven they kept in a clay pot, and then send the loaves to the public oven with errand boys who carried them on trays balanced on their heads, a sight that can still be seen today. Every family makes a distinctive mark on their uncooked loaves so that when the baker puts them into the oven with his wooden oar, he knows whose they are, and can bake them as each family likes them – soft and white or crisp and brown. In the last twenty years, since people have had home ovens, the old public ovens have mostly closed down. They are now seen mainly in poorer neighbourhoods near the public baths, as the wood they burn also heats the water for the baths.

In courtyards of large town houses and in the countryside, rustic breads are baked in small outdoor conical clay ovens with a hole on top, called *tannours*. The dough is slapped on to the inside walls of the *tannour*. When it is cooked, it falls and continues to cook in the ashes. Flat breads, leavened or unleavened, are cooked on domed griddles and in clay tagines. In city souks you see vendors making small thick, spongy pancakes called *baghrir* and a kind of soft, greasy puff pastry called *trid* and *rghaif*.

About Drinks

Alcoholic drinks are forbidden by Islam, but Morocco is nevertheless a wine-producing country. Established since Roman times, wine-making was developed extensively by French colonizers, but production has shrunk since they left in 1956. Now it is still made for export, and tourists can find it locally. Their rosés and gris (light reds) go well with the spicy flavours of Moroccan food, as does the light beer. A spirit called *mahya*, made by Jews from figs or dates, is drunk as an aperitif or digestive on festive occasions. *Samet* is a drink made from a mix of fruits such as grapes, apples, pears, plums that are left to ferment together in an earthenware pot.

Non-alcoholic beverages are fresh fruit juices – orange, date, grape, apple and pomegranate – sometimes with a drop of orange blossom water, and also almond milk. Water (often from a well in the courtyard) is perfumed with orange blossom water or with the aroma of burning gum mastic (p.10). Infusions are made from orange blossom petals, verbena, marjoram, thyme and sage. The rural drink of welcome is milk served with dates. Milk with a touch of orange blossom and the slightly acid buttermilk called *lben* are drunk with certain couscous dishes.

The famous, very sweet mint tea is a symbol of hospitality: it is served as soon as guests arrive at a house, and at all times of the day. English traders introduced tea in the nineteenth century, and the drink, with added fresh mint, acquired a ceremonial ritual with its own rules. On grand occasions, a specialist is hired to prepare and pour the tea in front of the guests. It is served in ornate Victorian-style silver teapots (once upon a time they came from Manchester) on silver trays with tiny legs and poured from a great height into small ornamented coloured glasses.

The old-style Turkish coffee, scented with orange blossom water or gum mastic or spiced with cardamom, cinnamon, cloves or *ras el hanout*, has been generally replaced by espresso and is only rarely to be found.

PRODUCT C

SIOF   SIO

PRODUIT DU

F SI OF

F MORROCO

F SI OF

MAROC

About Olives

A recurring feature in many tagines is the use of olives in partnership with preserved lemon peel. Moroccan olives are among the best in the world. There are basically three varieties – green, violet and black – that reflect the stage of their ripeness (all olives start green and gradually turn violet and then black as they ripen). After they are picked, they are soaked in changes of water for days or weeks to get rid of their bitterness and mellow their flavour. The violet ones are cured in the juice of bitter oranges. Green olives cured in salt are also variously flavoured with herbs, garlic and chilli pepper. Black olives are salted and allowed to lose their juices and are then dried in the sun.

Use green or violet olives for your tagines. If you find them too salty, soak them in water for up to an hour.

About Preserved Lemons

Lemons pickled in salt lose their sharpness and acquire a distinct flavour. They are one of the most common ingredients in Moroccan cooking. They are sold loose in Moroccan markets where you see them, soft and oozing with juice, piled high on stalls beside mountains of different coloured olives. The two are often used together in dishes.

You can now find jars of these lemons in some supermarkets here but they are easy enough to make.

PRESERVED LEMONS
Laymoun Hamid M'rakade

Although preserved lemons can now be bought, it is worth making your own. They are not difficult to make, and they will taste better. They take about 4 weeks to mature to be ready to use and will keep for a year. Normally the peel alone is used and the pulp is thrown away, but some people like to use the pulp too. You can use small lemons with thin skins or ordinary lemons with thick ones, and they must be unwaxed. There are three common ways of making them.

LEMONS PRESERVED in
SALT and LEMON JUICE

In this method, which is considered the most prestigious and gives the best results, no water is used. The lemon juice, which is the pickling liquor, can be re-used for further batches.

> 4 lemons
> 4 tablespoons sea salt
> juice of 4 additional lemons, or more to taste

Wash and scrub the lemons. The classic Moroccan way is to cut each lemon in quarters but not right through, so that the pieces are still attached at the stem end, and to stuff each with a tablespoon of salt and squeeze it closed. Put them into a sterilized preserving jar, pressing them down so that they are squashed together, and close the jar.

Leave for 3–4 days by which time the lemons will have disgorged some of their juices and the skins will have softened a little. Open the jar and press the lemons down as much as you can, then add fresh lemon juice to cover them entirely.

Close the jar and leave in a cool place for at least a month. The longer they are left, the better the flavour. (If a piece of lemon is not covered, it develops a white mould which is harmless and just needs to be washed off.)

Before using, scoop out and discard the pulp and rinse the lemon peel under the tap to get rid of the salt.

LEMONS PRESERVED in BRINE

This is the same procedure as above, but instead of adding lemon juice, cover the lemons with brine made by adding 2 tablespoons of salt to warm (boiled) water. Lemons prepared this way take longer to mature. Some people pour a little oil on top as a protective film.

LEMONS BOILED in BRINE and PRESERVED IN OIL

I am especially fond of this quick, unorthodox method which gives delicious results in 4 days.

With a sharp knife, make 8 superficial, not deep, incisions into the skin from one end of the lemon to the other. Put the lemons into a large pan with salted water (4 tablespoons salt for 4 lemons) to cover. Put a smaller lid on top of them to keep them down since they float, and boil for about 25 minutes or until the peel is very soft.

When cool enough to handle, scoop out the flesh, pack the skins in a glass jar and cover with sunflower or light vegetable oil.

Starters and Kemia

A Moroccan meal begins with an assortment of cold appetizers called *kemia* served with bread. These are mostly vegetable salads, either raw or cooked, in which cumin, ginger and paprika – which are believed to whet the appetite – are ubiquitous aromatics and preserved lemon peel and olives are characteristic ingredients. The salads are usually left on the table to act as side dishes with the main course.

Among the hot dishes that you can serve as a first course are soups, grilled meats on skewers and pies.

SWEET TOMATO PURÉE
Matesha Masla

The honey sweetness of this speciality from Marrakesh is surprising and enchanting.
Serve it cold as an appetizer with bread, or hot to pour over meat or chicken, and
sprinkle, if you like, with chopped toasted almonds or sesame seeds.

SERVES 6

2 tablespoons extra virgin olive oil
1kg ripe tomatoes, peeled and chopped
salt
1 tablespoon sugar
$^1/_2$ teaspoon ground cinnamon
$^1/_2$ teaspoon black pepper
1 tablespoon clear honey

Heat the oil in a pan and add the tomatoes, a little salt, and the sugar. Cook for
45 minutes or until the liquid has gone and the purée is thick and jammy and almost
caramelized. It is vital to stir often so that it doesn't stick to the pan and burn. Add
the cinnamon, pepper and honey and a little salt to taste, and stir well. Cook for
a further minute or so.

BELL PEPPER PURÉE
Slada Felfla

This bright red creamy purée has an alluring mix of flavours. Serve it as a dip
or to accompany fish.

SERVES 6–8

6 red bell peppers
2 garlic cloves, crushed
4–5 tablespoons vinegar or the juice of 1$^1/_2$ lemons
pinch of ground chilli pepper
1 teaspoon ground cumin
4 tablespoons extra virgin olive oil
salt

2 tablespoons chopped flat-leaf parsley
2 tablespoons chopped coriander
peel of $^1/_2$ preserved lemon, chopped

Place the peppers on a sheet of foil on an oven tray under a pre-heated grill, 6–9cm from the grill. Turn them until their skins are black and blistered all over. Alternatively – and more easily – roast them in the hottest oven for about 30 minutes or until they are soft and their skins blistered and blackened, turning them once after 15 minutes.

To loosen the skins further, put them into a plastic freezer bag, twist it shut and leave for 10–15 minutes. Another old way that has the same effect is to put them into a pan with a tight-fitting lid for the same length of time. When the peppers are cool enough to handle, peel them and remove the stems and seeds.

Blend them to a purée in the food processor with the garlic, vinegar or lemon juice, chilli, cumin, oil and a little salt to taste.

Put the purée into a serving bowl and mix in the chopped parsley, coriander and preserved lemon peel.

COURGETTE PURÉE and
BABY PLUM TOMATOES
Slada Bil Gharaa Wal Tamatem

I like the contrasts of colour and texture in this little dish that can be served hot or cold.

SERVES 6

500g courgettes, cut into thick slices
4 tablespoons extra virgin olive oil
500g baby plum tomatoes, cut in half
6 garlic cloves, sliced
salt and black pepper
bunch of flat-leaf parsley or coriander, chopped

Boil the courgettes in salted water until very tender. Drain and chop them with a sharp knife in the colander or strainer, then mash them with a fork, letting their excess juices escape.

In a large frying pan, heat 2 tablespoons of the oil, then take it off the heat. Put in the tomatoes, cut side down, and the garlic. Cook over a medium–high heat until the tomatoes have softened and the garlic begins to colour. Turn over the tomatoes once, and season with salt and pepper.

Add the courgette purée to the pan with the tomatoes and stir in the remaining oil, a little salt and the parsley or coriander. Serve hot or cold.

MASHED AUBERGINE and TOMATO SALAD
Zaalouk

I love this favourite Moroccan salad. It is best made several hours in advance so that the flavours have time to penetrate.

SERVES 6

750g aubergines
juice of $1/2$–1 lemon
500g tomatoes, peeled and chopped
5 garlic cloves, chopped coarsely
salt
4 tablespoons argan (p.39) or extra virgin olive oil
$1/2$ teaspoon paprika
good pinch of ground chilli pepper, to taste
1 teaspoon ground cumin
bunch of flat-leaf parsley, chopped
bunch of coriander, chopped
To garnish: a handful of black olives

Prick the aubergines with a pointed knife to prevent them from bursting in the oven. Place them on a large piece of foil on a baking sheet and roast them in a hot oven pre-heated to 240°C/475°F/Gas 9 for about 45–55 minutes or until they feel very soft when you press them and the skins are wrinkled. When cool enough to handle, peel and drop them into a strainer or colander with small holes and press out as much of their juices as possible. Still in the colander, chop the flesh with a pointed knife, then mash it with a fork or wooden spoon, letting the juices escape through the holes.

Cook the tomatoes with the garlic and a little salt over a low heat for about 20 minutes or until reduced to a thick sauce, stirring occasionally. Mix with the mashed aubergines and the rest of the ingredients and add salt to taste.
To serve, spread flat on a plate and garnish with olives.

GRATED CUCUMBER
and MINT SALAD
Khiar Bil Na'na

This is a wonderfully refreshing salad. The tiny bit of orange blossom water (p.10) gives it a mysterious flavour. Try to get small cucumbers from Middle Eastern or Asian stores. They have a better taste and texture than the large ones found in our supermarkets.

SERVES 4

1 large cucumber or 3 small ones
3 tablespoons extra virgin olive oil
2 tablespoons lemon juice
1 teaspoon orange blossom water, or to taste
salt
leaves of 2 sprigs of mint, chopped

Peel and grate the cucumber or cucumbers. You can do this in a food processor. Drain off the juices in a colander then mix with the rest of the ingredients.

POTATO and OLIVE SALAD
Slada Batata Bil Zaytoun

Moroccan olives are among the best in the Mediterranean and they find their way into many salads. Look for good ones for this salad which is best made in advance so that the dressing and flavours are absorbed.

SERVES 4

500g new potatoes
3 tablespoons extra virgin olive oil
juice of $^1/_2$ lemon
$^1/_2$ teaspoon paprika
$^1/_2$ teaspoon ground cumin
pinch of chilli pepper
salt
bunch of flat-leaf parsley, chopped
$^1/_2$ large mild red or white onion, chopped finely
12 black olives

Peel the potatoes and boil them in salted water until tender. Drain them and cut them in half, or quarters if large, but leave them whole if small.

Prepare the dressing in the serving bowl. Mix the oil with the lemon juice, paprika, cumin, chilli pepper and salt.

While still warm, turn the potatoes in the dressing, add the parsley, onion and olives and mix gently.

PEAR and LEAF SALAD
Slada Bouawid

Use pears that are ripe but still firm (Comice is a good variety), and salad leaves such as chicory, curly endive, purslane, cress, rocket and lamb's lettuce. You can stick to one type only or use a mixture.

SERVES 4

juice of $^1/_2$ lemon
3 tablespoons extra virgin olive oil or a 50/50 mix with argan oil
salt and black pepper
2 pears
about 100g salad leaves

Prepare the dressing in a flat serving dish, mixing lemon juice, oil, salt and pepper. Peel the pears and cut them lengthways into 8 slices each, removing the cores. Turn the slices in the dressing, ensuring that the pear pieces are all well covered in order to avoid discolouration. Just before serving, toss the pear pieces with the salad leaves.

VARIATION

You can make this salad with figs, washed or peeled and cut into quarters.

CARROT SALAD with CUMIN and GARLIC
Jazar Bil Kamoun Wal Toum

Carrot salads are very common in Morocco. This one is sold by street vendors and is particularly delicious. Use older carrots which have a better taste than young ones.

SERVES 4–6

5 large carrots (about 600g)
4 tablespoons extra virgin olive oil
4 cloves garlic, crushed
1 teaspoon ground cumin
salt and black pepper
juice of 1/2 lemon

Peel or wash and scrape the carrots and trim off the tops and tails. Cut them in quarters lengthways, then cut each quarter into half to produce sticks. Boil in salted water for 10–15 minutes until tender but not too soft, then drain.

   In a large frying pan, heat the oil and put in the carrots, garlic, cumin, and some salt and pepper. Sauté on a medium–high heat, stirring and turning the carrots over, until the garlic just begins to colour. Sprinkle with lemon juice and serve cold.

CARROTS with GARLIC and MINT
Jazar Bil Na'na

These minty carrots are tasty and aromatic. Serve them hot or warm as an appetizer or to accompany grilled or roast meat or chicken.

SERVES 4

500g carrots
salt
2 garlic cloves, crushed
1 tablespoon crushed dried mint
2 tablespoons extra virgin olive oil

Peel or wash and scrape the carrots and trim off the tops and tails, then cut them into 1-cm slices. Put the carrots into a pan and barely cover with water. Add salt and simmer, covered, for 10 minutes or until almost tender. Then uncover to let the liquid reduce, and cook for about 10 minutes more.

Add the garlic, mint and oil, and more salt to taste if necessary, and cook for a further few minutes.

ORANGE, OLIVE and ONION SALAD
Slada Bortokal Bil Zaytoun

Bitter oranges – Seville oranges – are commonly used in Morocco, but this salad is also good with sweet ones. Argan oil (p.39) gives it a nutty flavour.

SERVES 6

4 oranges
16 black olives
1 large mild red onion, chopped finely
juice of $^1/_2$ –1 lemon
3 tablespoons argan or extra virgin olive oil
salt
$^1/_2$ teaspoon ground cumin
$^1/_2$ teaspoon paprika
pinch of ground chilli pepper
bunch of flat-leaf parsley, chopped

Peel the oranges, removing the pith. Cut them into thick slices and then into quarters with a fine serrated knife. Put them on to a flat serving plate with the olives and chopped onion on top.

Make a dressing with a mixture of lemon juice, argan or olive oil, salt, cumin, paprika and chilli pepper and pour over the salad. Sprinkle with the chopped parsley.

VARIATION
Instead of lemon juice, add a whole lemon, peeled, pith removed and cut into slices then into small pieces.

ROASTED TOMATOES
Tamatem Halwa

These tomates confites have a deliciously intense flavour. Serve them hot or cold as an appetizer or with grilled meat or fish. Considering their versatility and their great use in Moroccan cuisine, it is extraordinary that tomatoes were adopted by Morocco as late as 1910. It is best to use plum tomatoes. Although they take a long time to cook, you can cook them in advance, even days in advance, as they keep well in the refrigerator.

SERVES 6–8
12 ripe but firm tomatoes
olive oil
3 tablespoons sugar
salt and black pepper

Cut the tomatoes in half lengthways. Brush an oven dish or baking sheet (or a piece of foil) with oil and place the tomatoes on it, cut side up. Sprinkle each with sugar, salt and pepper and cook in an oven pre-heated to 140°C/275°F/Gas 1 for 3$^1/_2$–4 hours until shrivelled and shrunken. Serve them, cut side up, on a flat serving plate.

ROAST PEPPER, TOMATO and APPLE SALAD
Slada Felfla Bil Tamatem Wal Tofah

Peppers and tomatoes are often partnered around the Mediterranean but the surprise of finding sweet apples and chilli peppers makes this a very special first course to serve with bread. The peppers can also be fried with the onion but I like to roast them.

SERVES 6

3 fleshy red bell peppers
1 large onion, sliced
3–4 tablespoons extra virgin olive oil
4 garlic cloves, chopped
500g tomatoes, peeled and chopped
1 or 2 chilli peppers, left whole
salt and black pepper
2 sweet apples (such as Golden Delicious)

Place the peppers on a sheet of foil on an oven tray under a pre-heated grill, 6–9cm from the grill. Turn them until their skins are black and blistered all over. Alternatively – and more easily – roast them in the hottest oven for about 30 minutes or until they are soft and their skins blistered and blackened, turning them once after 15 minutes.

To loosen the skins further, put them in to a plastic freezer bag, twist it shut and leave for 10–15 minutes. Another old way that has the same effect is to put them into a pan with a tight-fitting lid for the same length of time. When the peppers are cool enough to handle, peel them and remove the stems and seeds. Now cut them into ribbons from the stem end.

In a wide pan, fry the onion in 2 tablespoons of oil over a medium heat, stirring often until lightly coloured. Add the garlic and stir until it just begins to colour, then add the tomatoes and chilli peppers. Season with salt and pepper and cook gently for about 15–20 minutes.

Leaving the peel on, quarter and core the apples. Stir the red pepper ribbons into the onion mixture, then put in the apple quarters, cut side down. Cook gently until the apples are tender, adding a little water if the pan becomes too dry. Turn the apples skin side down towards the end. Serve cold, dribbling over the remaining oil.

ROAST PEPPERS and CHICKPEAS with FRESH GOAT'S CHEESE
Felfla Wal Hummas Wa Jban

A mild and soft fresh goat's cheese, jban, is one of the rare cheeses produced in Morocco. If you are not keen on raw garlic, you can leave that out.

SERVES 4–6

4 fleshy red bell peppers

1 x 400g tin of chickpeas

4 tablespoons extra virgin olive oil

juice of 1 lemon

salt and black pepper

3 garlic cloves, crushed

3 sprigs of oregano, chopped, or 1 tablespoon dried

300g fresh goat's cheese

Place the peppers on a sheet of foil on an oven tray under a pre-heated grill, 6–9cm from the grill. Turn them until their skins are black and blistered all over. Alternatively – and more easily – roast them in the hottest oven for about 30 minutes or until they are soft and their skins blistered and blackened, turning them once after 15 minutes.

To loosen the skins further, put them into a plastic freezer bag, twist it shut and leave for 10–15 minutes. Another old way that has the same effect is to put them into a pan with a tight-fitting lid for the same length of time. When the peppers are cool enough to handle, peel them and remove the stems and seeds. Now cut them into thin ribbons from the stem end.

Drain the chickpeas. Dress them with a mixture of 3 tablespoons of oil, the lemon juice, salt and pepper, 2 crushed garlic cloves, and about one-third of the oregano; mix well, then gently mix with the peppers.

Mash the goat's cheese with the remaining garlic clove, the last tablespoon of oil and the remaining oregano, and shape it into a mound on a serving plate. Arrange the peppers and chickpeas in a ring around it.

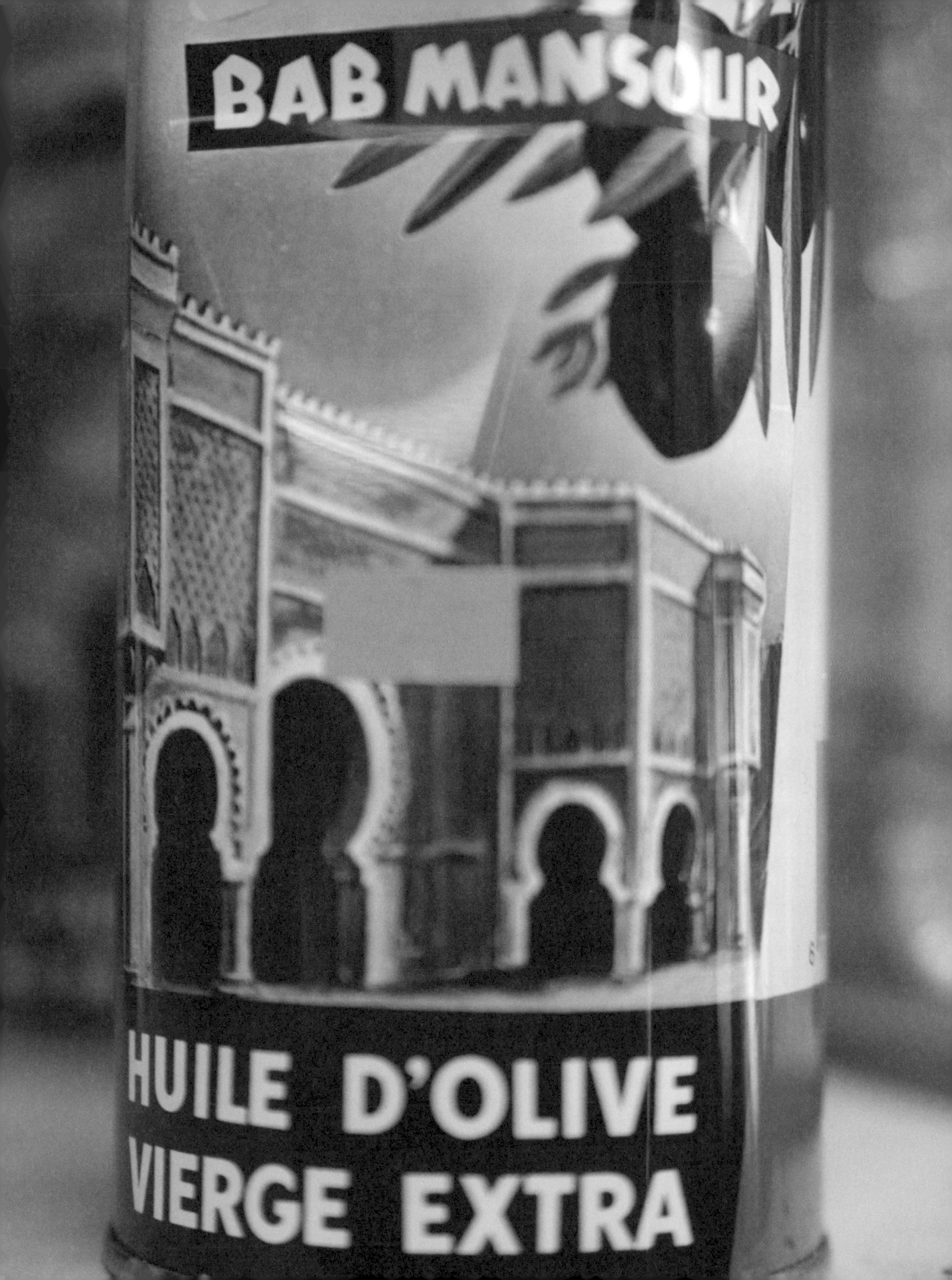
BAB MANSOUR
HUILE D'OLIVE
VIERGE EXTRA

SPINACH SALAD with PRESERVED LEMON and OLIVES
Salkh Bil Hamid Wal Zaytoun

Preserved lemons bring one of the defining flavours to Moroccan salads and are often used together with olives. Cook the spinach in two batches if your saucepan is not large enough for the bulky spinach leaves. Keep back 4–5 whole olives as a garnish.

SERVES 4–6

1kg spinach

3 garlic cloves, chopped

3–4 tablespoons extra virgin olive oil or argan oil (p.39)

peel of $^1/_2$ preserved lemon, chopped (p.46)

75g violet olives, chopped

salt and black pepper

Wash the spinach and remove the stems only if they are thick and hard. Put the leaves into a large pan. Cover with a lid and set over a low heat until the leaves crumple into a soft mass. They steam in the water that clings to them in 1–2 minutes. Drain well.

Heat the garlic in 1 tablespoon of oil in a large pan until the aroma rises. Add the preserved lemon peel, the chopped olives and the cooked spinach. Season with salt and pepper, mix well and cook over high heat for a moment or two.

Stir in the remaining oil and serve cold, garnished with the whole olives.

ARTICHOKE and BROAD BEAN SALAD with PRESERVED LEMON
Slada L'Korni Wal Ful

I use the frozen artichoke bottoms obtainable from Middle Eastern and Asian grocers who also sometimes sell frozen skinned broad beans. Some supermarkets sell freshly shelled broad beans. You do not need to remove the skins if the broad beans are young. If you wish to use fresh artichokes, see p.12.

SERVES 4

2 tablespoons extra virgin olive oil

1 teaspoon ground cumin

$^1/_2$ teaspoon ground ginger (optional)

3–4 garlic cloves, crushed

200g artichoke bottoms, defrosted

200g broad beans (shelled weight)

salt

peel of $^1/_2$ preserved lemon (p.46)

To garnish: 8 green olives (optional)

In a pan, stir the oil with the cumin, ginger (if using) and garlic, then put in the quartered or halved artichoke bottoms and the broad beans. Cook over a low heat for a moment, stirring, until the aroma of the garlic rises.

  Almost cover with about 250ml water, and add salt. Simmer, covered for the first 5 minutes, then uncovered for 10–15 minutes until the beans are very tender, and the sauce is reduced. Add the preserved lemon, cut into thin slices, towards the end.

  Serve warm, garnished, if you like, with a few olives.

SWEET POTATO SALAD
Slada Batata Halwa

Sweet potatoes are very popular in Morocco. In this recipe, their sweet delicate flavour marries well with the mixture of aromatics.

SERVES 4

1 large onion, chopped coarsely

5 tablespoons extra virgin olive oil

500g orange-fleshed sweet potatoes, peeled

$^1/_2$ teaspoon ground ginger

$^1/_2$ teaspoon ground cumin

$^1/_2$ teaspoon paprika

salt

6 or 7 green olives

peel of $^1/_2$ preserved lemon, chopped (p.46) (optional)

juice of $^1/_2$ lemon

2 tablespoons chopped flat-leaf parsley

Fry the onion in 2 tablespoons of the oil until golden. Cut the sweet potatoes into pieces (about 2.5 cm cubes), add to the pan and barely cover with water. Add ginger, cumin, paprika, a little salt and 2 more tablespoons of oil. Cook until the potato pieces are tender, and the liquid reduced to a sauce, turning the potatoes over once, and keeping watch so that they do not suddenly fall apart.

Serve at room temperature, mixed with the olives and preserved lemon peel, if using, and sprinkled with lemon juice, the remaining olive oil and the chopped parsley.

POTATOES with CELERY and FENNEL
Batata Bil Bisbas

This herby vegetable dish is as good hot as it is cold. The potatoes can be peeled or not, as you wish.

SERVES 4

4–5 tablespoons extra virgin olive oil

400g new potatoes

3 sticks celery

2 fennel bulbs

2 garlic cloves, crushed

salt and black pepper

4 sprigs of mint, chopped coarsely

4 sprigs of basil, chopped coarsely

juice of $^1/_2$–1 lemon

Put 2 tablespoons of the oil and the potatoes into a large pan. If large, cut them in half or in quarters. Cut the celery into 2cm pieces, quarter the fennel bulbs then cut each quarter in half. Place the celery and fennel on top of the potatoes. Add the garlic, salt and pepper and enough water to almost cover the green vegetables. Bring to the boil and simmer, covered, for about 15 minutes.

Stir in the mint and basil and cook, uncovered to reduce the liquid, for about 10 minutes or until the vegetables are very tender.

Serve sprinkled with lemon juice and the remaining oil.

VARIATION

Add the peel of $^1/_2$ preserved lemon (p.46) and about 12 green olives at the same time as the herbs.

TOMATOES STUFFED with ROAST PEPPERS, TUNA, CAPERS and OLIVES
Tamatem Ma'Amrine

The tomatoes can be served hot or cold. I prefer them cold. For vegetarians, they make an elegant main dish accompanied by a potato or carrot salad. Use large or beef tomatoes.

SERVES 6

4 red bell peppers
salt
3 tablespoons extra virgin olive oil
1 x 200g tin of tuna, flaked
2 tablespoons capers
4 tablespoons chopped black olives
peel of $^1/_2$ preserved lemon, chopped (p.46) (optional)
2 tablespoons chopped flat-leaf parsley
6 large tomatoes

Place the peppers on a sheet of foil on an oven tray under a pre-heated grill, 6–9cm from the grill. Turn them until their skins are black and blistered all over. Alternatively – and more easily – roast them in the hottest oven for about 30 minutes or until they are soft and their skins blistered and blackened, turning them once after 15 minutes.

To loosen the skins further, put them into a plastic freezer bag, twist it shut and leave for 10–15 minutes. Another old way that has the same effect is to put them into a pan with a tight-fitting lid for the same length of time.

When the peppers are cool enough to handle, peel them and remove the stems and seeds. Then cut them into strips about 2cm wide. Mix with the rest of the ingredients except the tomatoes.

Cut a small circle around the stalk of each tomato and cut out a cap. Remove the centre and seeds with a pointed teaspoon. Fill the cavities with the roast pepper mixture and replace the caps. Arrange in a shallow baking dish and bake in an oven pre-heated to 180°C/350°F/Gas 4 for 20–30 minutes, or until the tomatoes are a little soft. Keep a watch, however, that they do not fall apart.

FISH CAKES
Kefta Bil Hout

These fish cakes can be served as a first course with grated cucumber or salad leaves. They also make good finger-food for a party. Use cod, haddock or other firm white fish.

MAKES 15 SMALL FISH CAKES

500g fish fillets, skinned
$1^{1}/_{2}$ teaspoons ground cumin
good pinch of chilli pepper
salt
3 garlic cloves, crushed
1 egg, beaten lightly
peel of $^{1}/_{2}$ –1 preserved lemon, chopped finely (p.46) (optional)
handful of chopped flat-leaf parsley or coriander, or a mix of both
about 5 tablespoons flour
olive oil for deep-frying
To garnish: 1 lemon, cut into wedges

Cut the fish fillets into pieces and put them into a food processor with the rest of the ingredients except the flour. Process for about 5 seconds only, until the ingredients are finely chopped and well mixed. It is important not to let it turn into a paste.

Sprinkle the flour on to a plate. Wet your hands, take a lump of the fish mixture the size of a small egg, roll it into a ball, and flatten it. Do the same with the rest of the mixture, then turn the fish cakes in the flour to cover them all over.

Shallow-fry the cakes in hot oil until browned, turning them over once. Lift them out and drain on kitchen paper. Serve hot or cold, accompanied by lemon wedges.

VARIATION

You can use the same fish mixture as above to make balls rather than cakes. These are very good poached in a tomato sauce. For the sauce, fry 4–5 finely chopped garlic cloves in 2 tablespoons olive oil for a moment or two, add 1kg peeled and chopped tomatoes, 1–2 teaspoons sugar, salt and a pinch of chilli pepper, and cook for 10 minutes. Roll the fish mixture into balls, drop them into the sauce and simmer for 5 minutes.

LITTLE PIES with FRESH GOAT'S CHEESE and OLIVES
Briwat Bil Jban

Use a soft, fresh-tasting, mild goat's cheese for these little pies. Use the filo in sheets that measure 30cm x 18cm which you can find fresh in some supermarkets or use the large sheets measuring 48cm x 30cm, and cut them in half. See the note on filo on p.15.

You can freeze these pies and you can put them straight from the freezer into the oven without thawing, but they will need a little more cooking time. They make elegant and tasty party fare.

MAKES 20 TRIANGLES

300g fresh goat's cheese
1 egg, beaten lightly
14 black olives, stoned and chopped
10 large or 20 small sheets of filo (see above)
75g butter, melted

First prepare the filling by mixing the goat's cheese with the beaten egg and olives. Take out the sheets of filo from their wrapper only when you are ready to use them since they dry out quickly, and cover them with cling film when you are not using them.

Keeping the first sheet of filo on the pile, brush it lightly with melted butter. Fold it lengthways to produce a strip about 8.5cm wide. Brush the top of the strip lightly with melted butter. Take a heaped teaspoon of filling. Place it at one end of the strip, about 3 cm from the edge, and fold the end over the filling. Now pick up a corner and fold diagonally making a triangle. Continue to fold, trapping the filling, until the whole strip has been folded into a triangular parcel, making sure that you close any holes as you fold so that the filling does not ooze out.

Place the little parcels close to each other on a greased baking tray. Brush the tops with melted butter, and bake in an oven pre-heated to 180°C/350°F/Gas 4 for 30 minutes or until crisp and golden.

Serve the pies hot or warm. You can make them in advance and warm them up.

MEAT CIGARS
Briwat Bil Kefta

In Morocco, these meat cigars are made with warka (see p.37) and deep-fried, but it is not only much easier to use filo and to bake them, the result is also very good. See the note on filo on p.15. I used sheets measuring about 48cm x 30cm. This is very good finger food to serve at a party.

MAKES ABOUT 60 CIGARS

1 medium onion, chopped finely

4 tablespoons vegetable oil

750g minced beef or lamb

2 teaspoons ground cinnamon

1/2 teaspoon ground ginger

salt

black pepper or good pinch of ground chilli pepper

bunch of flat-leaf parsley, chopped

bunch of coriander, chopped

5 eggs, lightly beaten
500g large sheets of filo
175g butter, melted, or about 150ml vegetable oil

First prepare the filling. In a large frying pan, soften the onion in the oil. Add the meat, spices, salt and pepper or chilli pepper, and cook, crushing the meat with a fork and turning it over, for about 10 minutes until it changes colour. Then stir in the parsley, coriander and the beaten eggs, and cook gently for a moment or two, stirring all the time, until the eggs set to a creamy consistency. Let the filling cool. Taste and add more spices and pepper if you like.

With large scissors, cut all the sheets of filo together, without separating them, into 3 strips of about 15 cm x 30cm, and put the 3 piles together in one pile so that they do not dry out. Brush the top one very lightly with melted butter or oil.

Put a tablespoon of filling in a line along one of the short ends, about 2cm from the three edges. Roll up like a cigar, folding in the long sides at half way so that the filling does not fall out, then continue to roll, letting the sides unfold so that the cigars appear open.

Place the rolls side by side on a greased baking tray, brush the tops with melted butter and bake in an oven pre-heated to 180°C/350°F/Gas 4 for 30 minutes or until golden.

Serve them hot. You can make them in advance and warm them up.

VARIATIONS
◈ Before serving, dust the rolls first with icing sugar and then with cinnamon.
◆ These rolls are very nice deep-fried, so if you want to fry a few for an instant snack, do so in medium-hot vegetable oil, turning them over once, until browned, and drain on kitchen paper.

CHICKEN and ONION CIGARS
Briwat Bil Djaj

The rolls are delicious if made with the chicken and onion filling on p.76. Prepare in the same way as the meat cigars above and bake for 30 minutes in an oven pre-heated to 180°C/350°F/Gas 4. Serve hot, dusted with icing sugar and then with cinnamon.

POTATO and TOMATO CAKE
Almokhtalitat Bil Tamatem Wal Batata

This thick omelette can be made in advance. Served hot or cold, and cut into big or small wedges, it makes a substantial first course or vegetarian main dish.

SERVES 4–6

500g floury potatoes, peeled
1 large onion, chopped
2 tablespoons extra virgin olive oil
2 garlic cloves, chopped finely
300g tomatoes, peeled and chopped
salt and black pepper
1 teaspoon sugar
$^{1}/_{2}$ chilli pepper, chopped finely (optional)
4 eggs
bunch of flat-leaf parsley, chopped
1 tablespoon butter

Boil the potatoes in salted water until tender, then drain and mash them. In a wide frying pan, fry the onion in the oil until golden, stirring occasionally. Stir in the garlic and fry briefly without letting it colour. Add the tomatoes, season with salt, pepper and sugar, add the chilli pepper, if using, and cook the mixture over a high heat until it is reduced to a thick, jammy sauce; stir every so often.

Beat the eggs lightly, then beat them into the mashed potatoes. Add this to the tomato sauce and mix vigorously. Stir in the parsley and adjust the seasoning.

Heat the butter in a large frying pan, preferably non-stick. When it sizzles, pour in the omelette mixture. Cook over a low heat until the bottom sets (about 10 minutes), then cook the top under a pre-heated grill until it is firm and lightly browned.

Serve hot or cold, turned out and cut into wedges.

CHICKEN and ONION PIE
Bstilla Bil Djaj

This is a 'poor man's' version of the famous pigeon pie called bstilla (or pastilla) which is such a favourite at weddings and festive occasions, and which Moroccans say was brought back by the Moors from Andalusia. I have to admit that this pie, which comes from Fez, is very much more to my taste than the grander version that contains lots of eggs. Don't be put off by what might seem a difficult recipe; it is truly scrumptious and you must try it.

In Morocco, the pie is made with trid, an oily puff pastry made by pulling an elastic dough until it is paper-thin and layering it. Since trid is not available in this country, use filo which is a perfect substitute. It comes in various commercial sizes. It is best to use the large-size sheets which are available in frozen packs from Middle Eastern and other specialist stores. The sheets I use for this pie (from a popular brand) measure about 48cm x 30cm. If you can only find smaller sheets, such as the ones measuring 30cm x 18cm available in supermarkets, you can have more of them overlapping. Wrap any sheets that are left over in cling film and keep in the refrigerator for future use.

SERVES 4–6

2 large onions, sliced (about 500g)

3 tablespoons sunflower oil

50g blanched almonds

$^1/_2$ teaspoon ground ginger

$1^1/_2$ teaspoons ground cinnamon

300g chicken thigh fillets, skinned

salt and black pepper

large bunch of coriander, chopped (about 100g)

7 large sheets of filo (about 200g)

about 75g melted butter

1 egg yolk

To decorate: icing sugar and ground cinnamon

Put the onions into a wide saucepan with $2^1/_2$ tablespoons of the oil and cook over a low heat with the lid on, stirring occasionally, for up to 30 minutes until they are very soft and just beginning to colour.

Fry the almonds in the remaining drop of oil, stirring and turning them over, until lightly golden. Drain on kitchen paper and chop them coarsely.

When the onions are cooked, stir in the ginger and cinnamon, then put in the chicken cut into bite-size pieces, and season with salt and pepper. Cook, uncovered, stirring occasionally, for about 15–20 minutes, until the onions are pale gold. If by this time there is still some liquid left (which would make the pastry soggy), remove the chicken pieces and continue to cook the onion until the liquid has evaporated and you can see the oil sizzling. Now return the chicken, add the coriander and mix very well.

Open out the sheets of filo when you are ready to use them and leave them in a pile so they don't dry out. Fit the first sheet in a greased round baking pan about 24cm in diameter and brush it entirely with melted butter, pressing the filo into the corners with the brush and letting the longer edges hang over the sides. Repeat with 4 sheets, brushing each with melted butter first, including the ends that overhang the sides at different points (again, to prevent them from drying out).

Spread the chicken and onion mixture evenly in the hollow, then bring the overlapping filo up over the filling to cover it. Sprinkle all over with the chopped almonds.

Lay another sheet of filo over the top, brush it with melted butter, then lay the final sheet on top of that. Do not brush the last sheet with melted butter. Cut the longer overhanging ends of the sheets in a curve, leaving a wide margin round the pan. Now tuck these edges into the sides of the pan around the pie.

Brush the top with egg yolk mixed with a drop of water. Bake the pie in an oven pre-heated to 180°C/350°F/Gas 4, for 30–40 minutes until it is puffed up, crisp and golden. Now put the pie on the bottom surface of the oven for about 15 minutes which will help to brown the bottom.

Serve the pie hot, dusting the top with icing sugar and then making a geometric pattern in the white icing sugar with the golden-brown cinnamon.

VARIATION

For a version which comes from Tetouan, add the juice of $^1/_2$ lemon and the chopped peel of $^1/_2$ preserved lemon (p.46) to the filling. In this case, do not sprinkle the top of the pie with sugar or cinnamon.

CHICKPEA and LENTIL SOUP
Harira

Harira is the generic term for a soup full of pulses – chickpeas, lentils or beans – with little meat, few vegetables and plenty of herbs and spices. Every day during the holy month of Ramadan, when Muslims fast between sunrise and sunset, the smell of this soup permeates the streets as every household prepares its own version to be eaten when the sound of the cannon signals the breaking of the fast.

While ingredients and spices vary, a particular feature is the way the soup is given what is described in Morocco as a 'velvety' touch by stirring in a sourdough batter or simply flour mixed with water. In the cities in Morocco, it serves as a one-dish evening meal, and in rural areas, it is also eaten as breakfast before peasants go out to work in the fields. During Ramadan, it is served with lemon quarters and accompanied by dates and honeyed pastries.

The soup can be made a long time in advance, but if you are adding the tiny bird's-tongue pasta – douida in Morocco (you find it in Middle Eastern stores), orzo in Italian stores (or you can use vermicelli) – these should be added only 10–15 minutes before you are ready to serve otherwise they will get bloated and mushy. I have given measurements for a large quantity because it is a rich, substantial soup that you might like to serve as a one-dish meal at a party. The best cuts of meat to use are shoulder or neck fillet.

SERVES 10

2 marrow bones, washed (optional)
500g lamb or beef
2 large onions, chopped coarsely
200g chickpeas, soaked overnight
150g large brown lentils, rinsed
500g ripe tomatoes, peeled and chopped
4 celery stalks, diced
1 tablespoon tomato paste
1 teaspoon black pepper
1 teaspoon ground ginger
2 cinnamon sticks
$1/2$ teaspoon saffron threads or powder or 1 teaspoon turmeric
salt
5 tablespoons plain flour

150g bird's-tongue pasta or vermicelli (optional)
juice of 1 lemon
100g coriander, chopped
large bunch of flat-leaf parsley, chopped
To serve with: 3 lemons, cut into quarters; dates (optional)

If using marrow bones, blanch them in boiling water for a few minutes then throw out the water. Put the bones into a large pan with the meat, cut into 1cm pieces, the onions and drained chickpeas. Cover with about 3 litres water and bring to the boil. Remove the scum and simmer, covered, for 1 hour.

Remove the bones (if using), scoop out the soft marrow with a knife and drop it back into the soup.

Add the drained lentils, tomatoes and celery (include some leaves), the tomato paste, pepper, ginger, cinnamon and saffron or turmeric. Simmer for a further 15 minutes, adding more water if necessary as the level drops, and salt when the lentils begin to soften.

In the meantime, put the flour into a small pan and gradually add 500ml cold water, a little at a time, beating vigorously with a wooden spoon to blend well and to avoid lumps. Put over a medium heat and stir constantly until the mixture thickens, then simmer for 10 minutes. Pour this batter into the soup, stirring vigorously, and cook for a few minutes until the soup acquires a light creamy texture.

If you are using the tiny pasta or vermicelli (crush them with your hand into small pieces), add this to the soup 10 or so minutes from the end, adding the lemon juice, chopped coriander and parsley at the same time.

Serve with lemon wedges and if you like, also dates.

VARIATION

Instead of meat, you can use 500g chicken fillets, preferably thighs, and crumble in 3 chicken stock cubes.

CREAM *of* DRIED BROAD BEAN SOUP
Bessara

Bessara is the name of the soup as well as a creamy paste, made in the same way but with less water (see variation). You can buy the split and skinless dried broad beans in Asian and Middle Eastern stores. They look creamy-white without their dried brown skins.

SERVES 4

250g split skinless dried broad beans, soaked overnight
3 whole garlic cloves
2 chicken stock cubes
1 teaspoon ground cumin
1 teaspoon paprika
good pinch of ground chilli pepper
salt
To serve with: extra virgin olive oil; 2 lemons, cut into quarters

Rinse and drain the soaked beans and put them into a pan with the garlic and 1^1/$_2$ litres water. Simmer, covered, for about 1 hour. Crumble in the stock cubes and simmer for another 30 minutes, until the beans fall apart.

Still in the pot, mash the beans with a potato masher and then add the cumin, paprika and chilli pepper and, if necessary, a little salt, bearing in mind the saltiness of the stock cubes. Stir thoroughly and cook for a few minutes more. For a thicker soup, cook uncovered for a while longer.

When serving, pass round the oil for people to dribble on to their soup, and the lemon quarters for them to squeeze over.

VARIATION
Make a broad bean purée, using half the quantity of water. Serve it with little bowls of ground cumin, paprika, ground chilli pepper, lemon juice and extra virgin olive oil for people to sprinkle on their purée as they wish. Serve it with bread to dip in.

COUSCOUS

ZAKIA

FIN - FINE - FIJN

هذا الكسكسي مصنوع من سميد
القمح القمح كما في العادة
القديمة

PRODUCT OF FRANCE

INGREDIENTS : Semoule de blé dur
Durum wheat semolina
INGREDIENTEN : Harde tarwe griesmeel

Main Courses

The most common and most typical of the Moroccan main dishes, apart from couscous, is a braise or stew of chicken or meat called a tagine which takes its name from the clay pot in which it is cooked. In Morocco, these tagines are served with bread, never with couscous. In the West, however, with the increasing popularity of Moroccan dishes, the grain is sometimes served as an accompaniment. In North African restaurants in Paris, it is not uncommon to accompany tagines with a separate dish of the fine-ground couscous called *seffa* (see p.36), which comes decorated with lines of cinnamon and a few almonds or raisins. Many tagines differ only by one or two main ingredients, such as the vegetable or the fruit, and often chicken and meat are interchangeable in the same recipe. Do try the different versions because each is special and unique.

Tagines that marry meat or chicken with fruit, and are delicately flavoured with saffron, ginger and cinnamon and sometimes also honey, are celebratory dishes cooked on festive and special occasions. Many of these sweet tagines originate in Fez, the oldest imperial city in Morocco that was founded by Idriss I who came from Baghdad with his Arab entourage in the eighth century. Fez kept its ties with Baghdad over many centuries and, in later times, the city became the refuge of Jews and Muslims chased from Andalusia. Its cooking is a fusion of culinary memories of the court of Haroun al Rashid and those of Muslim Spain. Fez is now a city of artisans – dyers, tanners, weavers, potters, silversmiths – crowded in a labyrinth of narrow streets in the medina. Most of the grand old families have left for Rabat and Casablanca, but the city is still the intellectual, artistic and religious capital of Morocco, and it boasts the most refined and exquisite cuisine.

The long, slow cooking in a clay tagine produces meat so tender that you can pull it off the bone with your fingers. A good alternative to a tagine is a lidded, heavy-bottomed casserole or stainless steel pan. The meat most commonly used for tagines is boned shoulder of lamb. You may use other cuts of lamb such as the neck fillet, shank or the leg. Veal or beef, which now sometimes replaces lamb in Morocco, may also be used. The liquid in a tagine must be almost completely reduced at the end, producing a rich, thick and unctuous sauce. It is best to start with only a little water and to add more, if necessary, as you go along. If you have too much liquid at the end, you should lift out the meat and reduce the sauce over a high heat.

ROAST COD with POTATOES and TOMATOES
Hout Bi Bata Wa Tamatem

The marinade and sauce called chermoula that gives the distinctive flavour to this dish is used in most Moroccan fish dishes, whether fried, steamed or cooked in a tagine. Every town, every family, has its own special combination of ingredients. Bream, haddock and turbot can also be used.

SERVES 6

6 cod fillets (each weighing 200–225g), skin left on
salt
1kg new potatoes
500g tomatoes, peeled
extra virgin olive oil

FOR THE CHERMOULA MARINADE AND SAUCE
large bunch of coriander (about 75g), chopped
4 garlic cloves, crushed
1 teaspoon ground cumin
1 teaspoon ground paprika
$^{1}/_{2}$ teaspoon ground chilli pepper
6 tablespoons extra virgin olive oil
juice of 1 lemon or 3 tablespoons white wine vinegar

Sprinkle the fish with salt. Mix all the *chermoula* ingredients in a dish, and marinate the fish in half the quantity for about 30 minutes.

Peel the potatoes if you wish and cut into slices about 7mm thick, and the tomatoes into slices 1cm thick. Brush the bottom of a baking dish with oil, put in the potatoes and tomatoes, and dribble a little oil on top. Sprinkle with salt, then turn the vegetables so they are well seasoned and lightly coated all over with oil. Put the dish in a very hot oven pre-heated to 240°C/475°F/Gas 9 for 50 minutes, or until the potatoes are tender. During the cooking, turn them over once so that the top ones bathe in the juice released by the tomatoes.

Take the potatoes and tomatoes out of the oven, place the fish fillets on top, skin side up, and return to the oven. Bake for 10–12 minutes or until the fish is cooked through – it will be when the flesh flakes when you cut into the thickest part.

Just before serving, pour the remaining *chermoula* over the fish, letting it dribble on to the vegetables.

DEEP-FRIED BREAM with CHERMOULA SAUCE
Hout Maqli Bil Chermoula

This is good hot or cold and can be made well in advance. The best fish to use are bream, cod, haddock or turbot.

SERVES 4

4 bream fillets (each weighing 200–225g), skin left on
1 teaspoon ground cumin
salt
juice of 1 lemon
handful of coriander, chopped
1–4 garlic cloves, crushed
$1/2$ chilli pepper, seeded and finely chopped (optional)
4 tablespoons extra virgin olive oil
flour
olive oil for frying

Rub the fish with a mixture of cumin and salt.

Prepare a sauce by mixing the lemon juice with the chopped coriander, garlic (I like the larger amount but you may prefer to use only one clove), the chilli pepper, if using, a little salt and the oil.

Dredge the fish fillets in flour, turning to cover them lightly all over. Deep-fry briefly in sizzling oil until golden, turning the pieces over once. Test the fish by cutting into one piece with a pointed knife. When the flesh begins to flake, lift out and drain on kitchen paper.

Serve hot with the lemon and coriander sauce poured over. If serving cold, turn the fish in the sauce and leave to marinate, covered, in the refrigerator for an hour or longer.

ROAST SEA BASS with HERBS and ONION CONFIT
Hout Bil Bassal M'Zgueldi

Other large white fish such as sea bream and turbot can be cooked in this way. When you buy the fish, ask the fishmonger to scale and clean it but to leave the head on.

SERVES 4

500g onions, sliced
4 tablespoons extra virgin olive oil
pinch of saffron threads
1 tablespoon clear honey
salt and plenty of black pepper
1 large sea bass (weighing about 1.5–2kg)
handful of chopped flat-leaf parsley
handful of chopped coriander
4 garlic cloves, crushed
juice of 1 lemon
To serve with: 1 lemon, cut into quarters

In a covered pan, cook the onions in 2 tablespoons of the oil over a very low heat, for about 30 minutes, stirring occasionally, until they are very soft and lightly coloured. Stir in the saffron and honey, and season with salt and pepper. Cook, uncovered, for another 10 minutes or until most of the liquid has evaporated, then spread over the bottom of an oven-proof dish.

Slash the fish in a few places across the thickest part to ensure that it cooks evenly. Rub the fish with salt and the remaining oil, then stuff with a mixture of the parsley, coriander, garlic, lemon juice and a little salt and pepper.

Place the stuffed fish on the bed of onions and roast in an oven pre-heated to 190°C/375°F/Gas 5 for about 25 minutes or until the flesh flakes away from the bone when you cut into the thickest part with the point of a knife. Serve with the lemon quarters.

TUNA with RED BELL PEPPER SAUCE
Hout Bil Felfla

Tuna steaks are best seared quickly, leaving the flesh still pink and almost raw inside. The sauce is also good with other grilled or pan-fried fish.

SERVES 4

3 tablespoons olive oil
4 thick tuna steaks
salt
small bunch of flat-leaf parsley, chopped

FOR THE SAUCE

4 fleshy red bell peppers
2 garlic cloves, unskinned
3 tablespoons red or white wine vinegar
3 tablespoons extra virgin olive oil

Prepare the sauce first. Place the peppers and garlic on a sheet of foil on an oven tray under a pre-heated grill, 6–9cm from the grill. Turn the peppers until their skins are black and blistered all over. Remove the garlic when it feels soft. Alternatively – and more easily – roast both the peppers and garlic in the hottest oven for about 30 minutes or until the peppers are soft and their skins blistered and blackened, turning them once after 15 minutes. Take out the garlic when it feels soft.

To loosen their skins further, put the peppers into a freezer bag, twist it shut and leave for 10–15 minutes. When the peppers are cool enough to handle, peel them and remove the stems and seeds. Peel the roasted garlic cloves.

Blend the roasted peppers and garlic in a food processor with the rest of the sauce ingredients.

Heat the oil in a large, preferably non-stick, frying pan. Put in the tuna slices and cook over a high heat for less than 1 minute on each side, sprinkling lightly with salt. The time depends on the thickness of the piece. Cut into a steak with a pointed knife to test it; it should be soft and still pink inside.

Serve the tuna steaks on top of the sauce, sprinkled with the chopped parsley.

PRAWNS in SPICY TOMATO SAUCE
Kimroun Bi Tamatem

These prawns are deliciously rich in flavour and are good hot or cold. Serve them with
mashed potato (p.174) or with a little couscous (p.120) moistened with olive oil.

Use raw king prawns: they are grey and turn pink when they are cooked. Some
supermarkets sell them fresh and ready-peeled. You can also buy them frozen with their
heads off from some fishmongers. The weight of these packs is inclusive of a thick ice
glaze which means that you need double the weight – i.e. for 500g peeled prawns
(about 25), you need a 1 kg pack.

SERVES 6

500g raw king prawns, peeled, or 1kg pack frozen prawns
1 medium onion, chopped
2 tablespoons extra virgin olive oil
3 garlic cloves, chopped finely
400g tomatoes, peeled and chopped
^{1}/2 teaspoon ground ginger
pinch of saffron threads (optional)
pinch of chilli pepper
salt
bunch of flat-leaf parsley, chopped
bunch of coriander, chopped

If using frozen prawns, defrost them thoroughly. Pull the legs off the prawns, then
peel off the shells, and pull off the tails (they are usually sold headless). If you see
a dark thread along the back, make a fine slit with a pointed knife and pull it out.

In a large frying pan, fry the onion in the oil, stirring, until it begins to colour.
Add the garlic and cook until it just begins to colour. Then add the tomatoes,
ginger, saffron (if using), chilli pepper and some salt and cook for about 20 minutes
until the sauce is reduced.

Now put in the prawns and cook them for 3–5 minutes, until they turn pink,
turning them over once. Stir in the coriander and parsley at the end.

SKATE with PRESERVED LEMON and GREEN OLIVES
Hout Bil Laymoun M'Rakade Wal Zeytoun

All kinds of white fish fillets can be cooked in this way but I am particularly fond of skate 'wings' with these flavours. The flesh is fine and delicate and easily parts from the layer of soft cartilaginous 'ribs'. Small skate wings can be sautéed but the thicker, more prized wings of the larger fish must be poached (see variations).

SERVES 4

4 tablespoons extra virgin olive oil
4 small skate wings, skinned (weighing about 1 kg)
salt
juice of 1 lemon
peel of 1 preserved lemon, chopped (p.46)
8–12 large green olives, stoned and chopped
2 tablespoons chopped parsley or coriander
To serve with: 1 lemon, cut into quarters

Heat the oil in a non-stick frying pan and put in the skate wings. Sprinkle lightly with salt and cook over a low heat for 4 minutes, then turn over, add the lemon juice, and cook for a further 4 minutes or until the flesh begins to come away from the long soft bones. The time depends on the thickness of the wings.

Add the preserved lemon peel and green olives, parsley or coriander and let them heat through in the oil and juices. Serve with the lemon wedges.

VARIATIONS

◆ For a spicy version using small wings, stir into the oil just before you put in the fish, 2 crushed garlic cloves, a pinch of ground ginger, a pinch of ground cumin and a pinch of ground chilli pepper.

◇ Instead of olives you can add 1–2 tablespoons of capers.

◆ If using larger wings, buy 4 thick middle strips weighing about 250g each (they are sold skinned) rather than side wedge pieces. Poach them in salted water, just below simmering point, for 15–20 minutes, then drain thoroughly. Heat the oil and lemon juice with the preserved lemon peel, olives and herbs and pour over the fish.

TAGINE of CHICKEN with PRESERVED LEMONS and OLIVES
Tagine Djaj Bi Zaytoun Wal Hamid

This is the best-known Moroccan chicken dish. It was the only one, apart from appetizers, served during an evening of Arab poetry and story-telling, accompanied by musicians, that I attended in a Paris restaurant. The olives do not have to be stoned. If you find them too salty, soak them in 2 changes of water for up to an hour.

SERVES 4

3 tablespoons extra virgin olive oil

2 onions, grated or chopped very finely

2–3 garlic cloves, crushed

$1/2$ teaspoon crushed saffron threads or saffron powder

$1/4$ –$1/2$ teaspoon ground ginger

1 chicken, jointed

salt and black pepper

juice of $1/2$ lemon

2 tablespoons chopped coriander

2 tablespoons chopped parsley

peel of 1 large or 2 small preserved lemons (p.46)

12–16 green or violet olives (see above)

In a wide casserole or heavy-bottomed pan that can hold all the chicken pieces in one layer, heat the oil and put in the onions. Sauté, stirring over low heat, until they soften, then stir in the garlic, saffron and ginger.

Put in the chicken pieces, season with salt and pepper, and pour in about 300ml water. Simmer, covered, turning the pieces over a few times and adding a little more water if it becomes too dry. Lift out the breasts after about 20 minutes and put them to one side. Continue to cook the remaining pieces for another 25 minutes or so, after which time return the breasts to the pan.

Stir into the sauce the lemon juice, the chopped coriander and parsley, the preserved lemon peel cut into quarters or strips, and the olives. Simmer, uncovered, for 5–10 minutes, until the reduced sauce is thick and unctuous. If there is too much liquid, lift out the chicken pieces and keep them on one side while you reduce the sauce further, then return the chicken to the pan and heat through.

Present the chicken on a serving dish with the olives and lemon peel on top of the meat.

TAGINE *of* CHICKEN *with* ARTICHOKE BOTTOMS, PRESERVED LEMONS *and* OLIVES
Djaj Bi Korni

This is marvellous! I use frozen artichoke bottoms that come from Egypt and are available here in Middle Eastern and Asian stores. You get about 9 in a 400g pack and that is enough for 4.

Follow the recipe for Tagine of Chicken with Preserved Lemons and Olives. Ten minutes before the end, when you put in the coriander and parsley, lemon peel and olives, lift the chicken pieces and put the artichoke bottoms in the sauce beneath them. Add a little water if necessary, and cook about 10 minutes or until the artichokes are tender.

CHICKEN with CARAMELIZED BABY ONIONS and HONEY
Djaj Bil Assal

This is one of the classics of Moroccan cooking and this version, with shallots or baby onions, is sensational. The art is to reduce the sauce at the end until it is rich and caramelized. It is important to taste in order to get the right balance between sweet and savoury.

SERVES 4

500g shallots or baby onions
1 onion, chopped
4 tablespoons sunflower oil
good pinch of saffron threads
1 teaspoon ground ginger
1 teaspoon ground cinnamon
1 chicken, jointed
salt and black pepper
1–1$^{1}/_{2}$ tablespoons clear honey
To garnish: 100g blanched almonds or a handful of
   sesame seeds (optional)

To peel the shallots or baby onions, blanch them in boiling water for 5 minutes and when cool enough to handle, peel off the skins and trim the root ends.

Soften the chopped onion in the oil over a medium heat in a heavy-bottomed pan or casserole dish large enough to hold the chicken pieces in one layer. Stir in the saffron, ginger and cinnamon, then put in the chicken. Season with salt and pepper, and turn to brown lightly all over.

Add about 250ml water and cook, covered, over a low heat, turning the pieces over, for 15 minutes or until the chicken breasts are done. Lift out the breasts and put them on one side. Add the shallots or baby onions and continue to cook, covered, for about 25 minutes, or until the remaining chicken pieces are very tender. During the cooking, turn the chicken pieces and stir the onions occasionally; add a little water if necessary.

Lift out the chicken pieces, and set to one side. Stir the honey into the pan. Check the seasoning. You need quite a bit of pepper to mitigate the sweetness. Cook, uncovered, until all the water has evaporated, and the onions are brown and caramelized, and so soft that you could crush them, as they say in Morocco, 'with your tongue'.

Return the chicken pieces to the pan, spoon the onions on top of them and heat through. A few minutes should be enough. Serve, if you wish, sprinkled either with blanched almonds fried in a drop of oil until they are lightly golden, or with toasted sesame seeds.

CHICKEN with CARAMELIZED BABY ONIONS and PEARS
Djad Bil Bouawid

This is one of my favourites. You will be surprised just how good it is. Follow the recipe above for Chicken with Caramelized Baby Onions and Honey. Choose firm pears; if the fruit is too soft, they tend to collapse during the cooking. Comice and Conference are good varieties.

Cook the chicken as above. Quarter and core 4 small or 2 large pears but do not peel them. Over a medium heat, sauté the pieces in a large frying pan in about 40g unsalted butter and 1 tablespoon sunflower oil until they are soft and lightly coloured.

When serving, present them on top of the chicken pieces or beside them.

CHICKEN with CARAMELIZED BABY ONIONS and QUINCES
Djaj Bil Sfargal

I love quinces and used to make this dish whenever I could find them. However, they are now available from Middle Eastern stores for much of the year since they are imported from several countries, in particular Iran, Turkey and Cyprus, where their seasons vary. Follow the recipe above for Chicken with Caramelized Baby Onions and Honey.

Start with the quinces as they take a long time to cook. Wash and scrub 2 quinces, then boil them whole for about 1 hour or until they feel soft. The time varies greatly depending on their size and degree of ripeness, so watch them and don't let them fall apart. Drain them, and when the chicken is nearly ready, cut them into quarters and cut away the cores, but do not peel them. Then cut each quarter in half so you end up with fat slices.

Fry the slices in shallow sunflower or vegetable oil until they are brown on the cut sides. This gives them a delicious caramelized taste. Lift them out and drain on kitchen paper. Serve the chicken surrounded by the quince slices.

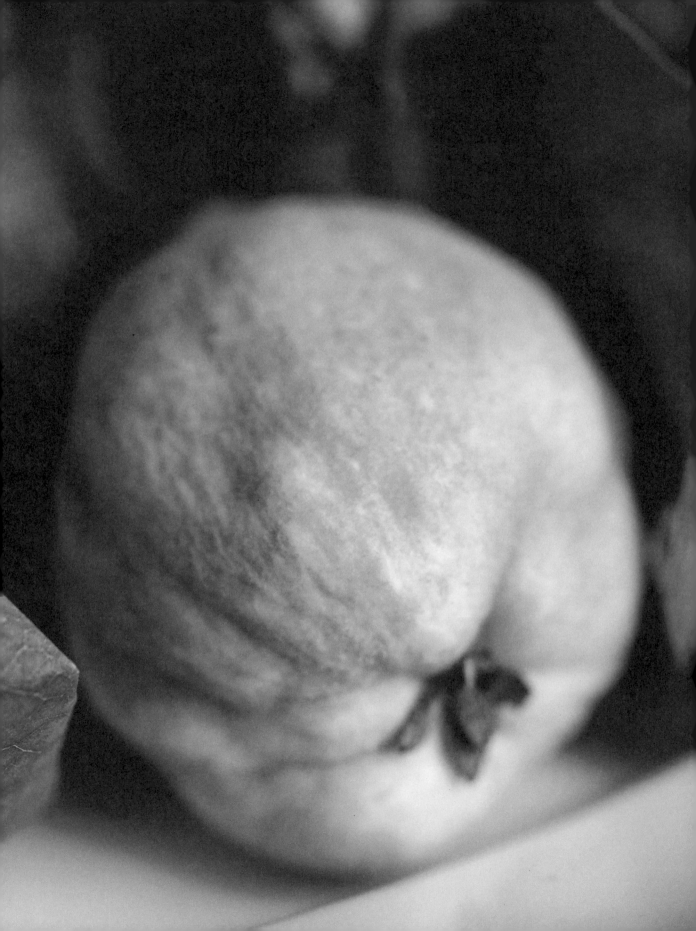

CHICKEN with CHESTNUTS
Djaj Bil Kastal

There are some excellent varieties of vacuum-packed or frozen chestnuts now available, making this dish very easy.

SERVES 4

25g butter
1 tablespoon sunflower oil
2 large onions, sliced
1 teaspoon ground ginger
good pinch of saffron threads
1 teaspoon ground cinnamon
1 chicken, jointed
salt and black pepper
1–1$^{1}/_{2}$ tablespoons clear honey
500g chestnuts, vacuum-packed, or frozen and defrosted

Heat the butter and oil in a large pan. Put in the onions, cover, and let them soften slowly over a medium heat, stirring from time to time. When they begin to colour, stir in the ginger, saffron and cinnamon. Put in the chicken pieces, season with salt and pepper, and turn to brown them lightly all over.

Add 250ml water and cook, covered, turning the chicken pieces over at least once. Lift out the breasts when they are done, after about 15–20 minutes, and put them on one side. Lift out the remaining chicken pieces about 25 minutes later, when they are very tender.

Let the onions reduce to a rich brown sauce. Stir in the honey (I use only 1 tablespoon) and taste to make sure you have enough salt to balance the sweetness and enough pepper to mitigate it.

Put in the chestnuts and simmer for 5–10 minutes or until they are tender, adding a little water, if necessary. Return the chicken pieces to the pan and simmer for a few minutes until the chestnuts are soft and the chicken has absorbed the honeyed flavours.

CHICKEN with DATES
Djaj Bil Tmar

Morocco is a country of dates and there are several varieties. Use 125g dates of a soft, moist variety such as the Tunisian Deglet Nour or Californian ones that you can find in supermarkets. Remove the stones, replacing each one with a blanched almond.

Follow the recipe on p.99 for Chicken with Chestnuts until the sauce has reduced, but omit the honey. At this point, add the dates instead of the chestnuts. Cook for 2–5 minutes, turning them over once, and taking care that the dates do not fall apart. Put the chicken pieces back into the sauce under the dates, and heat through.

CHICKEN with FRESH FIGS
and WALNUTS
Djaj Bil Karmous Wal Joz

Follow the recipe on p.99 for Chicken with Chestnuts until the sauce has reduced and has become caramelized. At this point, add 50g walnut halves and 4–8 fresh figs (4 black ones or 8 little green ones), peeled or simply washed, and cut in half. Cook them for 2–5 minutes, turning them over once. Take care that the figs do not fall apart. Put the chicken pieces back into the sauce under the figs, and cook for a few minutes more until the chicken is heated through and has absorbed the honey flavours.

Another appealing way with the figs is to slash their stalk ends, making a cross. Sprinkle inside with a little lemon juice and a little caster sugar, and put them under the grill for a few minutes to barely caramelize. Then serve them as a garnish on top of the chicken pieces.

ROAST DUCK with APRICOTS
Bata Bil Meshmesh

I have used the ingredients of a chicken tagine as an accompaniment to duck, which is not a Moroccan bird, because the combination of fatty duck with sharp apricots is great.

SERVES 4

1 duck (weighing about 2.25kg)
salt and black pepper
1 teaspoon ground ginger
3 tablespoons sunflower oil
500g baby onions or shallots
1/2 teaspoon ground cinnamon
35g butter
600g fresh apricots
juice of 1/2 lemon
3 tablespoons clear honey

Sprinkle the duck with salt, pepper and 1/2 teaspoon of the ginger, then rub with 1 tablespoon of the oil. Prick the skin with a fork or pointed knife in several places so that the melting fat can ooze out. Put the duck, breast-side down, on a rack in a baking dish or roasting pan in an oven pre-heated to 200°C/400°F/Gas 6.

Cook for 1 hour, then pour off the fat and turn over the duck. Return to the oven and cook for another hour or until the juices run clear, not pink, when you cut into the inside leg with a pointed knife. The skin should be crisp and brown and the flesh still soft and juicy.

Blanch the onions or shallots in boiling water for 5 minutes and when cool enough to handle, peel off the skins and trim the roots. Sauté them in the remaining 2 tablespoons oil for about 15 minutes, covered, over a low heat until softened; shake the pan occasionally so the onions brown all over. Stir the remaining ginger and the cinnamon into the pan, add the butter and put in the apricots. Cook, covered, over a low heat, until the apricots begin to collapse. Add the lemon juice and honey and cook, stirring, for about 15 minutes until jammy. Serve the duck accompanied by the apricot and onion relish.

ROAST CHICKEN with COUSCOUS, RAISIN and ALMOND STUFFING
Djaj M'Ammar Bil Kesksou

The couscous stuffing is the traditional one used for all birds, especially Mediterranean pigeons (the French pigeonneaux) and chickens. A generous amount of stuffing is made, enough to fill the chicken and to have some on the side, but it makes more sense not actually to bother stuffing the chicken. It is best to use the fine-ground couscous called seffa (p.36) but you can use the ordinary medium one.

SERVES 4

1 large chicken (about 1.5kg)
$1^1/_2$ tablespoons extra virgin olive oil
juice of $^1/_2$ lemon
$^1/_2$ teaspoon ground ginger
$^1/_2$ teaspoon ground cinnamon
salt and black pepper
2 tablespoons clear honey

FOR THE STUFFING
250g fine couscous
300ml water
salt
1 tablespoon caster sugar
2 tablespoons sunflower oil
1 teaspoon ground cinnamon
1 tablespoon orange blossom water (p.10)
2 tablespoons raisins, soaked in water for 10 minutes
100g blanched almonds
50g butter

Rub the chicken with a mixture of olive oil, lemon juice, ginger, cinnamon, salt and pepper. Put it breast-side down – so that the fat runs down and prevents the breasts from drying out – in a roasting dish and pour about 4–5 tablespoons water into the dish.

Cook in an oven pre-heated to 200°/400°/Gas 6 for 40 minutes per kg. Turn the chicken breast-side up after about 50 minutes, brush it with the honey and continue to cook until it is well done and brown. Test that it is ready by cutting into a thigh with a pointed knife. The juices should run clear, not pink. You will find that most of the honey will have slid down the chicken to mix with the juices and make a delicious honey sauce.

For the stuffing, put the couscous into a baking dish and moisten with 300ml warm water mixed with $^1/_2$ teaspoon salt. Stir vigorously so that it is evenly absorbed. After about 10 minutes, rub the couscous between your hands to air it and break up any lumps. Stir in the sugar, $1^1/_2$ tablespoons oil, the cinnamon, orange blossom water and drained raisins. Fry the almonds in the remaining oil until lightly coloured, coarsely chop them, and mix them into the stuffing. The butter will be stirred in later, before serving.

Put the couscous stuffing into the oven with the chicken 20–30 minutes before you are ready to serve. Stir in the butter, cut into small pieces, and fluff up the couscous with a fork. Taste, since you might like to add a little salt.

Carve the chicken and serve with the sauce poured over, accompanied by the stuffing.

MEDITERRANEAN PIGEONS or POUSSINS STUFFED with COUSCOUS
L'Hamam M'Ammar Bil Kesksou

Because they are small birds, with one per person, it is worth stuffing them. A few butchers sell the special baby Mediterranean pigeons or pigeonneaux. Otherwise, buy the smallest poussins possible. Our native pigeons are a different type altogether, and should not be used for this dish.

Make the same couscous stuffing as in the recipe on p.104 for Roast Chicken with Couscous, Raisin and Almond Stuffing. Fill each pigeon or poussin with about 3 tablespoons of stuffing – they should not be too tightly filled or the stuffing may burst out – and use toothpicks to secure the openings.

Rub the birds with double the quantities of oil, lemon juice, ground ginger, ground cinnamon, salt and pepper as given on p.104. Roast them in an oven pre-heated to 200°C/400°F/Gas 6, breast-side down for the first half hour, then turn them breast-side up, and brush them with 3–4 tablespoons honey. Return the birds to the oven for a further 30 minutes (it takes longer to cook them than usual because they are stuffed).

Heat through the remaining stuffing for 20–30 minutes in the same oven and serve alongside the pigeons.

MEDITERRANEAN PIGEONS or POUSSINS STUFFED with DATE and ALMOND PASTE
L'Hmam Bel Tamr Wal Loz

This is great and also easy to make. Use a moist variety of dates such as the Deglet Nour of Tunisia. A few butchers sell the special baby Mediterranean pigeons or pigeonneaux. Otherwise get small poussins or squabs.

SERVES 4

4 small Mediterranean pigeons or poussins
4 tablespoons extra virgin olive oil
juice of 1 lemon
salt
$^1/_2$ teaspoon ground ginger
1 tablespoon clear honey

FOR THE STUFFING
100g blanched almonds
150g dates, pitted
2 tablespoons butter

For the stuffing, grind the almonds in the food processor. Add the dates and the butter and blend to a paste. Stuff the birds with this and close the openings with toothpicks.

Rub the birds with a mixture of the oil, lemon juice and salt, and place them breast-side down in a baking dish. Roast them in an oven pre-heated to 200°C/400°F/Gas 6. The time depends on their size. I used 350g poussins (not very small) and it took as long as $1^1/_2$ hours. The reason they take so long is because they are stuffed. Small Mediterranean pigeons would take less time. Turn them over after $1^1/_4$ hours when their backs are brown and brush their breasts with a mix of ginger and honey. Put them back into the oven until the juices run clear when the inside leg is cut with a pointed knife.

Serve hot.

TAGINE of KNUCKLE of VEAL with ARTICHOKES and PEAS
Tagine Bil Korni Wal Jelban

Ask your butcher to saw the knuckle of veal into rounds, retaining the marrow in the centre of the bone (as for Italian osso buco). You can buy very good frozen artichokes which come from Egypt from Middle Eastern stores: they come in packets weighing 400g and containing about 9 small artichoke bottoms. If you want to use fresh artichoke hearts or bottoms, see p.14.

Use young fresh peas or frozen petits pois.

SERVES 4

50g butter or 3 tablespoons sunflower oil
1 onion, chopped
2 garlic cloves, crushed or chopped finely
$^1/_2$ teaspoon ground ginger
$^1/_2$ teaspoon saffron threads
4 thick rounds cut from the knuckle of veal
salt and black pepper
1 x 400g packet frozen artichoke bottoms, defrosted
juice of $^1/_2$ lemon
peel of $^1/_2$–1 preserved lemon (p.46) (optional)
400g fresh young peas (shelled weight), or frozen, defrosted
bunch of coriander, chopped
8 green olives (optional)

Heat the butter or oil in a wide pan or casserole. Put in the onion, garlic, ginger and saffron, and the meat. Cook over a low heat for about 5 minutes, turning over the meat.

Cover with water, season with salt and pepper, and simmer, with the lid on, for $1^1/_2$–2 hours, or until the meat is so tender it almost comes away from the bone. If necessary, add water to keep the meat covered and stir occasionally to make sure it does not stick to the bottom of the pan. Remove the lid towards the end to reduce the sauce.

Add the artichoke bottoms, cut in half or quartered, the lemon juice and preserved lemon peel cut into strips (if using), and cook for 5 minutes. Then add the peas and coriander, and the olives (if using). Cook for 5 minutes, or until the vegetables are tender. The sauce should be reduced and thick.

TAGINE of KNUCKLE of VEAL with FENNEL
Tagine Bil Bisbas

Bulb fennel has an attractive, intense aniseed flavour. Follow the recipe on p.108 for Tagine of Knuckle of Veal but, instead of artichokes and peas, use 4 medium-sized fennel bulbs. Trim the base, cut away the hard ends of the round stalks and remove the outer layer if it is stringy or bruised. Cut in half or quarters, lengthways. Add to the meat and cook for 30 minutes or until very soft.

TAGINE of KNUCKLE of VEAL with AUBERGINES
Tagine Bil Brania

For this tagine, follow the recipe on p.108 for Tagine of Knuckle of Veal with Artichokes And Peas, but instead of adding the artichokes and peas at the end, serve the meat with a purée of mashed aubergines poured over it.

Roast 1kg aubergines in the hottest oven, peel, chop and mash them as described on p.14. Heat 2 tablespoons extra virgin olive oil in a frying pan with 4 crushed cloves of garlic. When the aroma rises, add the aubergine purée with a squeeze of lemon and cook for 1–2 minutes. Pour over the meat and heat through just before serving.

You can also add tinned chickpeas – a 400g tin drained of their water – to the meat towards the end of the cooking.

LAMB TAGINE with POTATOES and PEAS
Tagine Bil Batata Wal Jelban

The best lamb to use for this tagine is either boned shoulder or neck fillet. Trim away some of the excess fat before cooking. Some supermarkets sell fresh shelled peas which are young and sweet, but frozen petits pois will also do very well. If the olives are very salty, soak them in water for up to an hour.

SERVES 6

3 tablespoons extra virgin olive oil

1 onion, chopped

2 garlic cloves, crushed

1 teaspoon ground ginger

$1/2$ teaspoon saffron threads

1.5 kg lamb, cut into 6–8 pieces

salt and black pepper

1kg new potatoes, peeled

500g fresh young peas (shelled weight) or frozen, defrosted

peel of $1-1^1/2$ preserved lemon (p.46) (optional)

16 or more green olives

2 tablespoons chopped coriander

2 tablespoons chopped flat-leaf parsley

Heat the oil in a wide pan or casserole. Put in the onion, garlic, ginger and saffron, and the meat. Cook over a low heat for about 5 minutes, turning the meat. Cover with water, season with salt and pepper and cook, covered, over a low heat, for $1-1^1/2$ hours or until the meat is very tender, turning the pieces over once in a while.

Add the potatoes, cutting any large ones in half. Top up the water if necessary and cook for 20 minutes or until the potatoes are tender. Then add the peas, preserved lemon peel cut into thin strips (if using), olives, coriander and parsley, and cook, uncovered, for a further 5 minutes, or until the peas are tender and the sauce reduced and thick.

VARIATION

Young broad beans can be used instead of peas but they will need to be cooked for at least 10 minutes.

TAGINE *of* LAMB *with* CARAMELIZED BABY ONIONS *and* PEARS
Tagine Bil Bouawid

This is a recipe that is similar to the chicken tagine on p.97, but the result is quite different. The sweetness of the pears goes surprisingly well with the lamb. Choose firm pears; if the fruit is too soft, they tend to collapse during the cooking. Comice and Conference are good varieties. Use a boned shoulder of lamb or neck fillets, and trim only some – not all – of the fat.

SERVES 6–8

1.5 kg boned shoulder of lamb
5 tablespoons sunflower or vegetable oil
1 onion, chopped
salt and plenty of black pepper
$^1/_2$ teaspoon ground ginger
$^1/_2$ teaspoon ground cinnamon
$^1/_2$ teaspoon saffron threads
500g baby onions or shallots, peeled
3 large pears
40g butter

Cut the meat into 6–8 pieces, and put it into a wide pan with 2 tablespoons of the oil over a medium heat; turn to brown the pieces all over. Add the chopped onion and barely cover with water. Stir in salt and pepper, the ginger, cinnamon and saffron, and simmer, covered, over a low heat for $1^1/_2$ hours, turning the pieces over a few times.

To peel the onions or shallots, blanch them in boiling water for 5 minutes and when cool enough to handle, peel off the skins and trim the roots. Sauté them in a frying pan in 2 tablespoons of the oil over a low heat for 5–10 minutes, shaking the pan, until the onions have slightly coloured. Then add them to the meat and cook for a further 30 minutes, until the meat is very tender and the baby onions are so soft that, as they say in Morocco, 'you can crush them with your tongue'. Towards the end of the cooking time, cook uncovered to reduce the sauce. There should only be a small amount of liquid remaining.

Wash the pears. Quarter and core them but do not peel them. Sauté them in a large frying pan in a mixture of butter and the remaining tablespoon of oil over a medium heat until their cut sides are slightly brown and caramelized. If they have not softened right through (that depends on their size and degree of ripeness), put them into the pan over the meat, skin side up, and continue to cook, covered, until they are very tender. This could take 15 minutes, but you must watch them as they can quickly fall apart.

VARIATIONS

◇ Stir in 1–1^{1}/$_{2}$ tablespoons of clear honey when you put in the pears and adjust the seasoning so that there is enough salt and plenty of pepper to mitigate the sweetness.

◆ Add 100g blanched almonds to the meat at the start. They will soften during the cooking.

◇ Instead of pears, sharp green apples like Granny Smiths may be used.

◆ Use veal instead of lamb.

TAGINE *of* LAMB *with* CARAMELIZED BABY ONIONS *and* QUINCES
Tagine Bil Sfargal

Follow the recipe on p.111 for Tagine of Lamb with Caramelized Baby Onions and Pears but instead of the pears, use 3 quinces weighing about 1kg. You can now find quinces in many Middle Eastern and Asian stores and they are available for much of the year since they are imported from various countries such as Iran, Turkey and Cyprus which have different seasons.

Wash and scrub the quinces. Boil them whole for about 1 hour or until they feel soft. The time varies greatly depending on their size and degree of ripeness, so watch them and do not let them fall apart. Drain them, and when cool enough to handle, cut them into quarters, cut away the cores but do not peel them.

In a large frying pan, sauté the quarters in a little sunflower oil until the cut sides are brown. This gives them a delicious caramelized flavour. Alternatively, for a honeyed version, sauté the quinces in a mixture of 40g unsalted butter, 1 tablespoon sunflower oil and $1^1/2$ tablespoons clear honey. You may also add 100g walnut halves which gives a wonderful contrast of texture.

Put the quinces – caramelized or honeyed – into the pan with the meat, skin side down, and cook until they are soft but, again, watch them so that they do not fall apart. If there is not enough room, lift out the meat, and put in the fruits, returning the meat to heat through before serving. Serve hot, with the quinces, skin side up, on top of the meat.

TAGINE *of* LAMB *with* APRICOTS
Tagine Bil Mashmash

The combination of lamb and apricots has become popular here, and with good reason – they go beautifully together. Follow the recipe on p.111 for Tagine of Lamb with Caramelized Baby Onions and Pears until the meat is very tender and the sauce reduced. Instead of the onions and pears, stone 1kg fresh apricots, add them to the meat and cook for minutes only until they soften.

Another particularly splendid version (my favourite – which you must try) is with dried apricots. Soak 500g dried apricots in water for an hour or longer, drain and cook for about 1 hour in water to cover (you will need to keep adding water) until they are very soft. Then let the liquid reduce to practically nothing. Add 1–2 tablespoons of clear honey and 50g unsalted butter, and cook, stirring, until the apricots begin to turn brown and caramelize. Spoon them on top of the meat when serving. Sprinkle the dish, if you like, with 50g blanched almonds fried in 1 tablespoon sunflower oil.

TAGINE *of* LAMB *with* DATES *and* ALMONDS
Tagine Bil Tmar Wal Loz

In an Arab culture born in the desert, dates have something of a sacred character. Considered the 'bread of the desert', they symbolize hospitality and are much loved and prestigious. You would find this dish at wedding parties. Some people find it too sweet so you might prefer it, as I do, without the optional honey. The dates give it a slightly sticky texture. Use the semi-dried moist varieties from California or the Deglet Noor dates from Tunisia.

SERVES 6–8

1.5 kg boned shoulder or neck fillet of lamb
50g butter or 4 tablespoons sunflower oil
2 onions, chopped, finely
$^1/_2$ teaspoon saffron threads
$^1/_2$ teaspoon ground ginger
salt and plenty of black pepper

1 cinnamon stick
1–2 tablespoons clear honey (optional)
1 teaspoon ground cinnamon
300g dates, pitted
To garnish: 100g blanched almonds; 3 tablespoons
sesame seeds (optional)

Trim any excess fat from the lamb and cut into 6–8 pieces. Heat the butter or 3 tablespoons of the oil in a large pan, put in the meat and brown it lightly all over. Take out the meat, put in the onions and cook, stirring, until they begin to colour. Stir in the saffron and ginger and return the meat to the pan. Add salt and pepper and put in the cinnamon stick. Cover with water and simmer, covered, for 2 hours or until the meat is very tender, turning the pieces occasionally.

Take out two pieces of meat in order to make room in the pan, stir in the honey, if using, and the ground cinnamon and more pepper (it needs plenty to counterbalance the sweetness). Move the meat around so the honey and cinnamon is spread around and then return the two pieces. Cook until the sauce is reduced, turning the meat over as you do so. Add the dates and cook for 5–10 minutes more.

Fry the almonds in the remaining tablespoon of oil until lightly golden. Leave whole or chop coarsely, and sprinkle over the meat when serving, adding lightly toasted sesame seeds if you like.

VARIATION
Stuff the pitted dates with walnut halves. In this case, omit the almonds and sesame seeds.

TAGINE *of* LAMB *with* PRUNES *and* ALMONDS
Tagine Bil Barkok Wal Loz

This is the best-known fruit tagine outside Morocco. Restaurants in Paris accompany it with couscous seffa made with fine-ground couscous (p.36) with plenty of butter, one bowl of boiled chickpeas and another of stewed raisins. The best prunes to use are the moist Californian ones which are already pitted.

SERVES 6–8

1.5 kg boned shoulder, or neck fillet of lamb
4 tablespoons sunflower oil
1 large onion, chopped finely or grated
2 garlic cloves, chopped
1 teaspoon ground ginger
$1/2$ teaspoon saffron threads
salt and plenty of black pepper
2 teaspoons ground cinnamon
350g prunes (see above)
To garnish: 100g blanched almonds; 3 tablespoons sesame seeds (optional)

Trim any excess fat from the lamb and cut it into 6 or 8 pieces. Put the meat into a pan with 3 tablespoons of the oil, the onion, garlic, ginger, saffron, salt, pepper and 1 teaspoon of the cinnamon. Cover with water and simmer gently, with the lid on, for $1^1/2$–2 hours until the meat is very tender, adding water to keep it covered.

Add the prunes and the remaining cinnamon. Stir well, adjust the seasoning and simmer, uncovered, for 30 minutes more until the sauce is reduced and thickened.

Fry the almonds in the remaining oil until they are lightly coloured, and sprinkle these over the meat before serving. If you wish, you can also garnish with lightly toasted sesame seeds.

VARIATIONS
◆ Put the almonds in with the meat from the start of the cooking. They will become soft.
◇ Add 1–2 tablespoons clear honey at the same time as the prunes.

TAGINE of LAMB with CHESTNUTS
Tagine Bil Kastal

Follow the recipe on p.116 for Tagine of Lamb with Prunes and Almonds until the meat is very tender and the liquid reduced to a thick sauce. But instead of prunes, add 400g frozen (and defrosted) or vacuum-packed peeled chestnuts and cook for 10 minutes or until the chestnuts are soft and heated through. You could add 1 tablespoon clear honey with the chestnuts, in which case, adjust the seasoning; you will need quite a bit of pepper to mitigate the sweetness. The sauce should be reduced and creamy. In this version, leave out the almonds and sesame seeds.

ROAST SHOULDER of LAMB with COUSCOUS and DATE STUFFING
Dala M'Aamra Bi Kesksou Wa Tmar

This is sumptuous and extremely easy. The meat is cooked very slowly for a long time until it is meltingly tender and you can pull the meat off with your fingers. The stuffing is sweet with dates and raisins, and crunchy with almonds. (In Morocco, they add sugar or honey but that makes it too sweet for me.) The couscous needs plenty of butter as there is no sauce, but you can substitute oil if you prefer. Try to get the fine-ground variety of couscous called seffa (p.36) For the dates, use the Tunisian Deglet Nour or Californian varieties that you can find in supermarkets.

A shoulder of spring lamb is always fat but most of the fat melts away during the long cooking. If it appears too fatty, as might be the case with an older lamb, carefully remove some of the fat before cooking. Alternatively, you may use leg of lamb instead of shoulder.

SERVES 4–5

1 shoulder of lamb (weighing about 1.5–2kg)
salt and black pepper
250g fine or medium couscous
1 tablespoon orange blossom water (p.10)
1 teaspoon ground cinnamon
2 tablespoons sunflower or vegetable oil
150g dates, stoned and cut into small pieces
50g raisins
100g blanched almonds, chopped coarsely
65g butter, cut into small pieces
To garnish: 8 dates and 8 blanched almonds

Put the joint, skin side up, in a baking dish or roasting pan, sprinkle with salt and pepper, and roast in an oven pre-heated to 240°C/475°F/Gas 9 for 15 minutes. Then lower the heat to 180°C/350°F/Gas 4 and cook for 3 hours until the skin is crisp and brown and the meat is juicy and meltingly tender. Pour off the fat after about 2 hours.

For the stuffing, put the couscous into another baking dish, and add the same volume of warm water – about 300ml – mixed with a little salt, the orange blossom water and cinnamon. Stir well so that the water is absorbed evenly. After about

10 minutes, add the oil, and rub the grain between your hands to air it and break up any lumps. Mix in the remaining ingredients, apart from the butter, cover with foil, and put into the oven with the lamb for the last 20 minutes or until it is steaming hot. Before serving, stir in the butter so that it melts in and is absorbed evenly. With a fork, fluff up the couscous stuffing, breaking up any lumps. Add a little salt to taste, if necessary.

For the garnish, remove the stone from each date and replace with the blanched almonds. Serve the meat with the couscous stuffing decorated with these dates.

PREPARING COUSCOUS

This is an easy, foolproof method of preparing the pre-cooked couscous available in this country (*see* p.36). I make it straight into the round clay dish in which it will be served with its broth and other accompaniments. In Morocco, 500g serves 4 people but by our standards in Britain, it is enough for 6. If you are cooking for 8 or 10 people, it is worth making 1kg if only because a mountain of couscous looks good.

You need the same volume of salted water as couscous. The volume of ordinary medium couscous and of the fine-ground *seffa* couscous is 600ml. The volume of barley couscous is 500ml.

Put 500g couscous into an oven dish. Gradually add 600ml (or 500ml if using barley couscous) warm salted water, made with $^{1}/_{2}$–1 teaspoon salt, stirring vigorously so that it is absorbed evenly. Leave to swell for about 10 minutes, then mix in 2 tablespoons oil and rub the couscous between your hands above the bowl to air it and break up any lumps. That is the important part.

Put the dish into an oven pre-heated to 200°C/400°F/Gas 6 and heat through for 20 minutes or until it is steaming hot (it takes longer for 1kg couscous). Before serving, work in 40g butter cut into small pieces, or 2 tablespoons oil, and fluff it up again, breaking up any lumps.

COUSCOUS with SPRING VEGETABLES
Keksou L'Hodra

This aromatic herby couscous with green young tender vegetables makes a lovely main dish. Vegetarians will love it. Use fresh young broad beans and peas (some supermarkets sell them already shelled) or frozen petits pois and if you can, artichoke bottoms.

Try it with barley couscous which is now available in a pre-cooked form in Moroccan stores and in a few specialist stores in London. It is sold as Sakssou Al Belboula. It was the first grain used to make couscous by the Berbers, before they used wheat, and it is still very popular, especially in south Morocco. It has a distinctive flavour and texture. Prepare it in the same way as ordinary (wheat) couscous as described in the basic recipe on p.120. The only difference is that it absorbs less water (see method below).

SERVES 6
- 500g barley or ordinary couscous
- 1/2–1 teaspoon salt
- 6 tablespoons mild extra virgin olive oil
- 1 litre stock made with 2 vegetable or chicken stock cubes
- 400g young broad beans (shelled weight), or frozen, defrosted
- 250g spring onions, trimmed and sliced
- 400g frozen artichoke bottoms or baby artichokes, quartered (optional)
- salt and black pepper
- 400g young peas (shelled weight), or frozen petits pois, defrosted
- large handful of chopped flat-leaf parsley
- large handful of chopped coriander
- handful of chopped mint

Following the basic recipe for making couscous on p.120, put the couscous into a wide ovenproof dish, add the warm water mixed with a little salt gradually – 500ml of water if using barley couscous or 600ml if using the ordinary couscous – stirring so that it gets absorbed evenly. After about 10 minutes, when the couscous has become plump and almost tender, add 3 tablespoons olive oil and rub the couscous between your hands to air it and break up any lumps. This can be done in advance and then heated through for 20–30 minutes before serving in an oven pre-heated to 200°C/400°F/Gas 6 until it is steaming hot.

For the broth, bring the stock to boiling point, then add the broad beans, spring onions and artichokes and cook for 10 minutes or until tender. Season with salt and pepper, taking into consideration the saltiness of the stock cubes. Add the peas, and cook for 2 minutes or until they are just tender. Stir in the herbs just before you are ready to serve.

Before serving, fluff up the couscous with a fork, breaking up any lumps in it, and stir in the remaining olive oil. Arrange the vegetables on top and pass the broth around in a bowl for everyone to help themselves.

VARIATION

You may like to melt in 50g of butter at the end and omit the olive oil.

COUSCOUS with LAMB, ONIONS and RAISINS
Kesksou Tfaya

The special feature of this dish is the exquisite mix of caramelized onions, honey and raisins called tfaya which is served as a topping to the long-cooked, deliciously tender meat.

SERVES 4–6

1kg lamb, boned shoulder or leg

1.25kg onions

salt and black pepper

$^1/_2$ –1 teaspoon ground ginger

$2^1/_2$ teaspoons ground cinnamon

4 cloves

$^1/_2$ teaspoon saffron threads or powder

40g butter

1 tablespoon extra virgin olive oil

2 tablespoons clear honey

150g raisins, soaked in water for 20 minutes

200g blanched almonds

500g couscous

600ml warm water

$^1/_2$–1 teaspoon salt

3 tablespoons sunflower or vegetable oil

50g butter

Prepare the couscous in a large round ovenproof dish as described on p.120, leaving the final heating in the oven to be done 20–30 minutes before serving.

Prepare the meat broth in a large pan. Put in the meat, with about 250g of the onions, chopped, and cover with 1.75 litres water. Bring to the boil and remove the scum. Add salt and pepper, ginger, 1 teaspoon cinnamon and the cloves. Simmer for 1$^1/_2$ hours. At this point, add the saffron and more water if necessary, and simmer for another 30 minutes or until the meat is so tender you can pull it apart with your fingers.

At the same time, prepare the honeyed onion *tfaya*. Cut the remaining onions in half and slice them. Put them into a pan with 250ml water. Put the lid on and cook over a low heat for about 30 minutes until the onions are very soft. Remove the lid and cook further until the liquid has evaporated. Add the butter and oil and cook until the onions are golden. Stir in the honey and the remaining 1$^1/_2$ teaspoons cinnamon, the drained raisins and a pinch of salt. Continue cooking for another 10 minutes or until the onions caramelize and become brown.

Fry the almonds in a drop of oil until golden, turning them over, then drain on kitchen paper and coarsely chop about half of them.

About 20–30 minutes before the end of the cooking time, put the couscous into the oven, pre-heated to 200°C/400°F/Gas 6, and heat through until it is steaming hot, fluffing it with a fork after about 10 minutes. Before serving, fork the butter, cut into small pieces, into the couscous and again fluff up the couscous as it melts in.

To serve, moisten the couscous with a ladle of broth and mix in the chopped almonds. Leave it in the baking dish, or turn it on to a large round platter; shape it into a mound, and make a wide shallow hollow in the centre. Put the meat into the hollow, cover with the onion and raisin *tfaya*, and sprinkle with the remaining whole fried almonds. Serve the broth separately.

'BURIED in VERMICELLI'
Shaariya Medfouna

This speciality of Fez – shaariya medfouna which means 'buried in vermicelli'–
is a fabulous surprise dish, a chicken tagine hidden under a mountain of vermicelli.
It is a grand festive dish, a kind of trompe-l'œil as the vermicelli is decorated like a
sweet dessert couscous (p.135), with alternating lines of icing sugar, cinnamon and
chopped fried almonds. It sounds complex but it is really worth making for a large
party. You can leave out the icing sugar if you think your guests are likely to prefer
it without, and instead pass the sugar round in a little bowl for those who would like
to try. The vermicelli is traditionally steamed like couscous but it is easier to boil it.
It is more practical to cook the chickens in 2 large pans and to divide the ingredients
for the stew between them.

    In Morocco they also cook pigeons and lamb in the same way.

SERVES 10

2 large chickens

4 large onions, chopped coarsely

2 teaspoons ground cinnamon

1 teaspoon ground ginger

1 teaspoon saffron threads or powder

salt and black pepper

120g butter

1 tablespoon clear honey

2 teaspoons orange blossom water (p.10) (optional)

large handful of chopped flat-leaf parsley

large handful of chopped coriander

200g blanched almonds

1^1/$_2$ tablespoons sunflower or vegetable oil

1kg vermicelli nests

To decorate: 2 teaspoons ground cinnamon; icing sugar (optional)

Use two pans and into each put 1 chicken. To each pan, pour in 500ml water,
bring to the boil and remove the scum. Add 2 of the chopped onions, 1 teaspoon
cinnamon, ^{1}/$_2$ teaspoon ginger, and ^{1}/$_2$ teaspoon saffron. Add salt and pepper and
simmer, covered, for about 1 hour. Turn the chickens occasionally so they are
well cooked all over.

Lift out the chickens and when cool enough to handle, remove the skin and bones and cut the meat into medium-sized pieces.

Pour the chicken stock with the onions into one pan only and reduce by boiling it down until a thick sauce results. Stir in 50g of the butter, the honey and orange blossom water (if using) and cook a few minutes more. Taste, and add extra salt and pepper if necessary.

Add the herbs and return the chicken pieces to the sauce. All this can be done in advance and reheated when you are about to serve.

Fry the almonds in the oil until lightly browned, then drain on kitchen paper. Crush them with a pestle and mortar or coarsely chop them.

Just before serving, break the vermicelli into small pieces by crushing the nests in your hands. Cook in rapidly boiling salted water for 5 minutes, until *al dente*, stirring vigorously at the start so that the threads do not stick together in lumps. Drain very quickly and then pour it back into the pan. Stir in the remaining butter, cut into small pieces, and some salt.

Put the chicken with its sauce into a very large deep round serving dish. Cover with a mountain of vermicelli, and decorate this with lines of cinnamon, icing sugar (if using) and chopped almonds emanating from the centre like rays.

VARIATION

For 'buried in couscous' (couscous *medfoun*), the fine-ground couscous, *seffa*, is used instead of vermicelli. Prepare 1kg as described on p.120, and heat it through in the oven. Cover the chicken with a mountain of couscous. As above, make a design by sprinkling thin lines of cinnamon and icing sugar, fanning down like rays from the top, and decorate the bottom of the mound with whole or chopped toasted almonds or walnut halves, and raisins or dates.

Desserts

Morocco is a fruit lovers' paradise. In *riads*, traditional Arab houses with interior gardens, there are always fruit trees, and their scents permeate the air. It is from the Persians and their notion that paradise was an orchard that the Arabs adopted and passed on their love of fruit. Bowls of dried fruit and nuts are ready in every home to greet visitors – sometimes the hostess will fill a date or a fig with an almond or a walnut and hand it to you. And the usual way to end a meal is with fruit. For guests, it is served either simply cut up on a plate or as a fruit salad.

Pastries are for special occasions, or for visitors when they drop in. They are filled with almonds, pistachios or walnuts and with dates and usually soaked in sugar or honey syrup

FRUIT SALAD with HONEY and ORANGE BLOSSOM WATER
Slada Bil Fawakih

For this delicately scented fruit salad, have a mix of fruit chosen from three or four of the following: peaches, nectarines, apricots, bananas, plums, grapes, apples, pears, strawberries, mangoes, melon, pineapple, dates, pomegranate seeds.

SERVES 4

juice of 1 large orange
2 tablespoons clear honey
1 teaspoon orange blossom water (p.10)
750g mixed fruit
To garnish: a few mint leaves

Mix the orange juice, honey and orange blossom water straight into a serving bowl. Wash or peel the fruits, core or remove stones, and drop them into the bowl as you cut them up into pieces so that they do not have time to discolour.

Leave in a cool place for an hour or longer before serving, garnished with the mint leaves.

ORANGE SALAD
Slada Bil Bortokal

This is the most common Moroccan dessert, but it is always appealing and perfect to serve after a rich meal.

SERVES 4

6 large oranges
1 tablespoon orange blossom water (p.10)
2 tablespoons icing sugar (optional)
To decorate: 1 teaspoon ground cinnamon

Peel the oranges, taking care to remove all the white pith. Cut into slices, remove any pips, and arrange in circles on a serving plate. Sprinkle with orange blossom water and icing sugar, if using.

Just before serving, decorate with lines of ground cinnamon.

VARIATIONS
◆ Sprinkle with 50g walnuts, coarsely chopped, and 8 dates, coarsely chopped.
◇ Replace 3 of the oranges with blood oranges.

CANDIED ORANGE SLICES
Mrabbet Bortokal

These orange slices can be served with coffee or tea, or as an improvised sweet at the end of a meal, accompanied by clotted or thick double cream. They keep for weeks in the refrigerator so you can bring them out on different occasions. Choose oranges with thick skins, which must be unwaxed.

10 SERVINGS   1kg oranges, unwaxed

400g sugar

Wash the oranges and cut them in thin slices, removing any pips.

Sprinkle the bottom of a large heavy-bottomed pan with a little of the sugar. Arrange some of the orange slices on top so that they overlap slightly and sprinkle generously with more sugar. Make layers of orange slices, each sprinkled with sugar and finishing with sugar.

Pour cold water over the slices so that they are only just covered. Cut a circle of foil or waxed paper and press it on top of the oranges to avoid evaporation. Cook over a low heat for about 2 hours until the orange slices are very soft and the white pith is translucent. The syrup should have the consistency of liquid honey when cool. Test a little on a plate. If it is too thick and sticky, add a little water and bring to the boil again.

SWEET COUSCOUS
Kesksou Seffa

A sweet couscous made with the fine-ground couscous called seffa is served hot, accompanied by a drink of cold buttermilk or milk perfumed with a drop of orange blossom water (p.10) served in little glasses. The couscous needs quite a bit of butter (unsalted) because there is no broth. See the suggestions below for extra garnishes.

SERVES 6–8

500g fine-ground couscous (*seffa*)
600ml warm water
$1/2$–1 teaspoon salt
2 tablespoons sunflower or vegetable oil
100g or more unsalted butter
2 tablespoons caster sugar
To decorate: icing sugar and ground cinnamon
To serve with: icing sugar, ground cinnamon and honey

Prepare the couscous as described on p.120. Before serving, cut the butter into small pieces and work it and the caster sugar into the hot couscous, fluffing up the grain with a fork and breaking up any lumps.

Shape the couscous into a cone in a round flat dish. Dust the pointed top with icing sugar and draw lines, fanning down the sides, with icing sugar and cinnamon. Decorate further with one or two of the fruit and nut garnishes listed below.

Serve in bowls and pass round bowls of honey, sugar and cinnamon, and more of the fruit and nuts, for people to help themselves as they wish.

EXTRA GARNISHES TO CHOOSE FROM

Arrange dessert raisins such as Muscatels or Smyrna sultanas with blanched almonds (toasted or fried in a drop of oil until lightly golden), or dates and walnut halves, around the bottom of the cone or between the lines of icing sugar and cinnamon. (The same nuts, coarsely chopped, and small raisins can be mixed with the couscous before it is shaped into a cone.) Sweet grapes or shiny pink pomegranate seeds are an alternative garnish to sprinkle over the mound of couscous.

ALMOND 'SNAKE'
M'Hencha

This splendid Moroccan pastry filled with a ground almond paste is a very long coil, hence the name m'hencha, meaning snake. It is stunning to look at and exquisite to eat. In Morocco, it is made with the pastry called warka or brick (p.37) but that turns out tough if it is baked and not deep-fried. It is better to use filo pastry. I give very large quantities because it is the kind of thing to make for a great festive occasion, but of course you can make it smaller and reduce the quantities accordingly. The finished 'snake' will be about 35cm in diameter. If your oven is not large enough to take it, you can make two small ones. You need large filo sheets measuring about 48cm x 30cm (and if the filo is frozen, you will need to allow 3 hours for it to defrost; see p.15).

SERVES 30 – 40

FOR THE FILLING
1.5kg ground almonds
1kg caster sugar
2 tablespoons ground cinnamon
200–250ml orange blossom water (p.10)
a few drops almond essence (optional)

FOR THE PASTRY
500g sheets of filo
125g unsalted butter, melted
2 egg yolks for glazing
To decorate: icing sugar, 1 tablespoon ground cinnamon

Mix all the filling ingredients together and work them into a paste with your hands. Take the sheets of filo out of the packet only when you are ready to use them and keep them in a pile (so they do not dry out) with one of the longer sides facing you. Lightly brush the top sheet with melted butter. Take lumps of the almond paste and roll into 'fingers' about 2cm thick. On the top sheet, place the 'fingers' end-to-end in a line all along the long edge nearest to you, about 2cm from the edge, to make one long rod of paste. Roll the sheet of filo up over the filling into a long, thin roll, tucking the ends in to stop the filling oozing out.

Lift up the roll carefully with both hands and place it in the middle of a sheet of foil on the largest possible baking sheet or oven tray. Very gently curve the roll into a tight coil. To do so without tearing the filo, you have to crease the pastry first like an accordion by pushing the ends of the rolls gently towards the centre with both hands.

Do the same with the other sheets until all the filling is used up, rolling them up with the filling inside, and placing one end to the open end of the coil, making it look like a coiled snake.

Brush the top of the pastry with the egg yolks mixed with 2 teaspoons of water and bake in an oven pre-heated to 170°C/325°/Gas 3 for 30–40 minutes until crisp and lightly browned.

Let the pastry cool before you slide it, with its sheet of foil, on to a very large serving platter or tray.

Serve cold, sprinkled with plenty of icing sugar and with lines of cinnamon drawn on like the spokes of a wheel. Cut the pastry as you would a cake, in wedges of varying size. It is very rich and some will only want a small piece.

VARIATION

For a pistachio *m'hencha*, use ground pistachios instead of almonds and rose water instead of orange blossom water. Although less common, this too is fabulous!

ALMOND MACAROONS

These are good to serve with coffee or tea.

MAKES ABOUT 20 MACAROONS

400g ground almonds
150g caster sugar
grated zest of 1 lemon, unwaxed
2–3 drops almond essence
1 large egg white
icing sugar

Put all the ingredients except the icing sugar in a food processor and blend into a soft, malleable paste.

Put some icing sugar on a small plate. Rub your hands with oil so that the almond paste does not stick to your hands. Take lumps of the paste the size of a large walnut and roll into balls. Now press one side of each ball into the icing sugar, flattening it a little, and place it on a buttered oven sheet. Bake in an oven pre-heated to 200°C/400°F/Gas 6 for 15 minutes.

Let the macaroons cool before lifting them off the sheet. They will be lightly coloured and crackled and soft inside.

DATES STUFFED *with* ALMOND *or* PISTACHIO PASTE
Tmar Bi Loz

In Morocco, this is the most popular sweetmeat. The almond stuffing is coloured green to give the semblance of pistachios which are considered more prestigious. Use the slightly moist dates such as the Tunisian Delget Nour or Californian varieties.

200g ground almonds or pistachios
100g caster sugar
2–3 tablespoons rose water (p.11) or orange blossom water (p.10)
500g dates

Mix the ground almonds or pistachios with the sugar, and add just enough rose or orange blossom water to bind them into a firm paste. Put less than you seem to require, since once you start kneading with your hands, the oil from the almonds will act as an extra bind. Alternatively, you can start with blanched almonds or pistachios and blend all the ingredients except the dates to a paste in a food processor.

Make a slit on one side of each date with a pointed knife and pull out the stone. Take a small lump of almond or pistachio paste, pull the date open wide, press the paste into the opening, and close the date over it only slightly so that the filling is revealed generously.

ALMOND PASTRIES in HONEY SYRUP
Briwat Bi Loz

These exquisite pastries called 'the bride's fingers' feature in medieval Arab manuscripts found in Baghdad, fried and sprinkled with syrup and chopped pistachios. In Morocco, they are made with the thin pastry called warka or brick (p.37) and deep-fried. I prefer to make them with filo and then bake them. For a large-sized version of the pastries, I use a supermarket brand where the sheets are about 30cm x 18cm.

I especially recommend you try the dainty little 'bride's fingers' (see the variation). I make them for parties and I keep some in a biscuit tin to serve with coffee. They are great favourites in our family; my mother always made them and now my children make them, too.

MAKES ABOUT 14 PASTRIES

250g clear honey

100ml water

200g ground almonds

100g caster sugar

1 teaspoon ground cinnamon (optional)

2 tablespoons orange blossom water (p.10)

14 sheets of filo

65g unsalted butter, melted

Make the syrup by bringing the honey and water to the boil in a pan, and simmering it for a minute or so. Then let it cool.

Mix the ground almonds with the sugar, cinnamon and orange blossom water. Open the packet of filo only when you are ready to make the pastries (see p.15). Keep them in a pile so that they do not dry out. Lightly brush the top one with melted butter.

Put a line of about 2–2$^1/2$ tablespoons of the almond mixture at one of the short ends of the rectangle, ending about 2cm from the short and long edges. Roll up loosely into a fat cigar shape. Turn the ends in about one-third of the way along to trap the filling, then continue to roll with the ends open. Continue with the remaining sheets of filo.

Place the pastries on a baking sheet, brush them with melted butter and bake them in an oven pre-heated to 150°C/300°/Gas 2 for 30 minutes, or until lightly golden and crisp.

Turn each pastry, while still warm, very quickly in the syrup and arrange on a dish. Serve cold with the remaining syrup poured all over.

VARIATIONS

◈ Instead of the honey syrup, make a sugar syrup by simmering 250ml water with 400g sugar and 1 tablespoon lemon juice for about 5–8 minutes until it is thick enough to coat the back of a spoon, and adding 1 tablespoon orange blossom water towards the end.

◆ Instead of rolling the pastries in syrup, sprinkle them with icing sugar. These keep very well for days in an airtight biscuit tin.

◇ For the dainty little 'bride's fingers', cut sheets of filo into narrow strips – they can measure from 9–12cm wide and be about 30cm long. You can use larger sheets cut into 3 or 4 strips. Use 1 heaped tablespoon of the filling for each roll. It makes about 28.

WALNUT PASTRIES in HONEY SYRUP
Briwat Bi Joz

Follow the recipe on p.140 for Almond Pastries in Honey Syrup but use the
following filling.

Coarsely grind 200g shelled walnuts in a food processor. Add 75g sugar and
the zest (finely grated peel) of 1 unwaxed orange, and mix well.

Add $1^1/_2$ tablespoons orange blossom water (p.10) to the syrup.

DATE ROLLS in HONEY SYRUP
Briwat Bi Tmar

Follow the recipe p.140 for Almond Pastries in Honey Syrup but use the
following filling.

Use a moist variety of dates such as the Tunisian Deglet Nour or the Californian
varieties. You will need about 700g once they have been stoned. Blend them in a food
processor, adding a little water, if necessary, by the tablespoon, to achieve a soft paste.

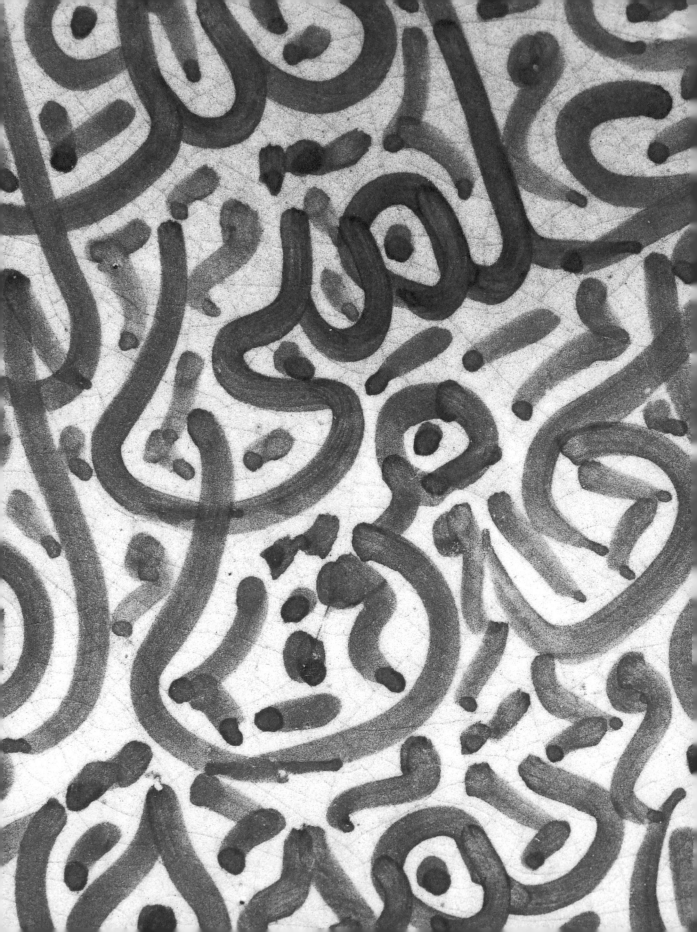

Turkey

A sophisticated aristocratic cuisine developed in Constantinople – now Istanbul – when it was, for more than 400 years, the glittering capital city of the Ottoman Empire that spread over most of the Middle East, the Balkans, and parts of North Africa, southern Russia and the Caucasus. That cuisine came to be considered on a par with those of France and China. While many of the more elaborate dishes have disappeared, what you find in homes in Istanbul today and on the standard menus of Turkish restaurants, are simplified adapted versions of that high style.

In Anatolia, which covers much of the landmass of modern Turkey, the cooking reflects the changing geography, climate and local produce, as well as the diversity of cultures. Regional cuisines were hardly known outside their localities until the arrival, in the last couple of decades, of millions of migrants from rural and eastern Turkey in the big cities. You can now find regional dishes in restaurants that have opened in the last fifteen years and you can catch a whiff of the cooking in the blocks of tall buildings that have mushroomed around the city. That cooking is for the most part spicy, hot and garlicky. It is not popular with the worldly 'Stambouli' bourgeoisie who see themselves as Europeans with a taste for pure, mild and delicate flavours. For them, the strongly flavoured food represents the 'Arab' and 'Oriental' tastes of the provincials who have swamped their once cosmopolitan sophisticated city and changed its image in a way they do not like. Istanbul, this dream of the Orient with her cupolas and minarets, hamams (old-style bath houses) and bazaars, is torn between town and country, East and West, tradition and modernization, but remains attached to her past and her culinary memories and legacies.

Specialities of Istanbul – kebabs and pilafs, filo pies, yoghurt and cucumber salads, aubergine purées and stuffed vegetables, milk puddings and nutty, syrupy pastries – are common in all the main cities of the countries that were part of the Ottoman Empire. When I lived in Egypt – it was the time of King Farouk and I was there for the revolution in 1953 – the royal family was an Ottoman Albanian dynasty and the aristocracy was Turkish, as was the haute cuisine. The country was annexed to the Ottoman Empire in 1517, and stayed under Turkish rule until 1805 when Mohammed Ali became its Governor and established a dynasty that owed only nominal allegiance to the Sultan of Turkey. The food served in the Egyptian palaces was no different to that served to the Ottoman sultans, and the Palace cooks were brought over from Constantinople. When Turkey became a republic in 1923, many members of the old Ottoman aristocracy moved to Egypt. In 1995, at the celebration launch of the Royal Club Mohamed-Aly in Cairo, the buffet was prepared by cooks from Istanbul. I have the menu – and most of the dishes listed on it are in this book.

The Story Behind the Cooking

The area that is Anatolia today was successively colonized by the Greeks and Persians and by Alexander the Great before it came under Roman rule. Emperor Constantine established the then Greek city of Byzantium as the new second capital of the Roman Empire in AD 330 and it was renamed Constantinople after him. When the Empire split into eastern and western sections in AD 395, Constantinople became the capital of the Eastern Roman Empire.

The Turks came on the scene many centuries later. They were nomadic people from the steppelands of Central Asia on the edge of China who migrated west with their flocks. They started to convert to Islam in the eighth century. As slave soldiers in the armies of the caliphs of Baghdad, they were formidable warriors who, by the eleventh century, came to form a number of small local dynasties of their own in territories they captured from the Byzantines as well as in parts of the disintegrating Arab Empire. One of the most important dynasties, the Seljuks, seized Isfahan in Persia in 1051, and in the twelfth century established a sultanate which controlled most of Anatolia from its capital, Konya.

Konya became a brilliant centre of culture that attracted scholars, poets, artists and mystics from all over the Islamic world. It was the home of the great Sufi mystic and poet Jalal al-Din Rumi known as Mevlana (the Master). The highly sophisticated culture that developed, including cooking traditions, was influenced by Persia. By the thirteenth century, following the onslaught of Mongol invasion, the great Seljuk dynasty had ended but its cultural influence continued by means of the establishment of principalities by lesser Seljuk clans throughout Anatolia. Part of their legacy is seen in the many traces of old Persian styles in the Turkish kitchen today, and in Konya in particular.

Another nomadic Turkish branch, the Osmanlis, or Ottomans, who were also warriors, captured Constantinople in 1453 and went on to establish the most powerful Muslim empire ever. The original Ottoman diet consisted mainly of the nomadic staples, yoghurt and meat, and the pasta they adopted from the Chinese and Mongols whom they had been fighting for centuries. Shish kebabs are said to have originated on the battlefield when their invading armies camped outdoors in tents. The sultans came to place great importance on their kitchens. When Sultan Mehmet II conquered Constantinople in 1453 and made it his imperial capital, he built the Topkapi Palace with a giant four-domed kitchen. A century later, Sultan Süleyman the Magnificent added a new kitchen building with six domes, and ten

further sections were added by Sultan Selim II in the sixteenth century. By the following century, on festive occasions, as many as 10,000 people, including the sultan, his harem and eunuchs, palace workers, vizirs (ministers), Janissarary Corps, the military élite, members of the divan (cabinet), and foreign ambassadors and their retinues, were fed from the kitchens in which 1,370 cooks worked.

An extraordinary number and variety of dishes were developed in the court kitchens and the palaces of the aristocracy. Some originated in the cultures – Persian, Arab, Syrian – that had been absorbed into the Islamic world; some were adopted from the Byzantine Empire. Others arose as a result of the unique cosmopolitan character of the early Empire and its ruling class whose members entered as the sultan's slaves and remained part of the Ottoman Slave Household. The profession of public slaves was all-important and glorious. Most were Christians, or the children of Christians, who were converted to Islam. Some were captured in battle or were bought in markets. Many were plucked from Caucasian highlands, from Russian forests and Eurasian steppelands; others came from western Europe including some given as gifts by Venetian traders. Some were sold by their parents. Wrenched from all family ties and roots, public slaves were expected to serve more loyally. The more able recruits became courtiers. The royal family, the sultan's wives, palace and government officers, Grand Vizirs, the standing army – all were Household slaves or their descendants.

In this unique cosmopolitan society, where products arrived from the far corners of the Empire, and Palace cooks learned their trade as slave page-boys in the palace cooking school, a wide variety of foods of various origins entered the culinary pool. Cooking was considered one of the most important of the arts. Poets, physicians and princes all wrote recipes, sang songs and recited poems about food. The importance of food was especially evident in the famous Janissary corps, the Imperial guard. The Janissaries received their daily food rations direct from the Palace, and their insignia, a pot and spoon, indicated a standard of living higher than that of other troops. The titles of the officers were drawn from the camp kitchen, from 'First Maker of Soup' to 'First Cook' and 'First Carrier of Water', and the massive cauldron in which they cooked became an icon symbolizing their privileged relationship with the sultan. They overturned it to signal dissatisfaction and rebellion. This could happen, for instance, at payment day ceremonies.

The kitchen also had an important place in the communal life of the Turkish Sufi brotherhoods, the *tarikat*, which ran hospices and soup kitchens, and who were very influential. The Mevlana order of Whirling Dervishes in Konya, followers of the mystical philosopher and poet Jalal al-Din Rumi and his descendants, famously elevated food to a particularly high position. Rumi, whose interest in food is legendary, wrote poems celebrating food. He associated it with spirituality and equated cooking with man's path to spiritual knowledge. The order's kitchen served as a place of initiation and training. Many Palace cooks were Sufis who cooked instinctively 'by feel' and taste while at the same time observing a strict discipline and organization.

Until the early seventeenth century the Palace table or *sofra* was characterized by the quantity and variety of dishes. European ambassadors and foreign visitors marvelled at their number – up to 300, I have heard – that arrived one after the other at banquets in their honour. By the mid-nineteenth century, when Ottoman cuisine reached its pinnacle, foreign guests extolled its exquisiteness and refinement in their letters and diaries. It was a time of western influence when the Turkish élites became fascinated by French cuisine and assimilated French ways as well as the ingredients from the New World that had arrived in western Europe long before.

The Professional Cooks from Bolu

In the latter part of the Empire, Palace cooks were recruited in the *vilayet* (region) of Bolu near Lake Abant. According to legend, the nobles were so pleased with the young men who cooked their meat for them in the open after they had spent the day hunting in the mountain forests of the Black Sea region that they brought them back to the city. It soon became the tradition that all the young men from Bolu went to serve at the Palace and in the homes of the nobility in Constantinople, leaving the women to till the fields and raise the children. At the age of twelve or thirteen, boys were sent to work in the kitchens near their fathers, uncles and male cousins. They would go back to the village to marry, only to leave their wives and return to their kitchens. This is how the closed society of chefs that still exists today was formed.

In her family chronicle *Three Centuries* (1963), the Turkish writer Emine Foat Tugay wrote about that old generation of cooks who came from Bolu: 'Turkish cooking of the past ranked among the great cuisines of the world. Much of it has disappeared

together with the excellent chefs, who had learnt their trade as apprentices in konaks (grand old-style mansions) and palaces . . . They gradually worked their way up under the master chef from scullery-boy or apprentice to become third, second, and finally first assistant cook. After ten or twelve years the chef would declare his first assistant capable of working on his own account. The old chefs almost always brought their complete staffs with them when they were appointed and took them away with them when they left.'

When Turkey became a modern secular republic under President Mustafa Kemal Atatürk in 1923, the huge kitchen staff at the Palace lost their jobs. The cooks who worked for the Turkish aristocracy that now moved to Egypt went with their employers. Others opened kebab houses and eateries, offering so-called *saray* (Palace) cooking in Istanbul and other Turkish cities, while still others became makers of specialities such as pickles or puddings.

The Turkish Restaurant and
Specialist Food Producers

The earliest Turkish word for restaurant, *lokanta*, comes from the Italian, meaning inn. Today, while a lokanta offers modest homely food in a cafeteria-style environment for workers and shoppers at lunchtime, a *restoran* is more upmarket and can be very grand. The oldest eating-and-drinking places are the *meyhane*, the old-style taverns or drinking houses of Istanbul situated near the markets in the old neighbourhoods which were once the preserve of Greek, Armenian and Jewish minorities, such as Pera (now known as Beyoglu), Galata, Kumpkapi and Balat. A large number opened in the mid-nineteenth century following a policy of westernization and modernization in the Empire. They were formerly owned and run by Christians and some still are. When the secular state was founded, Muslims too were allowed to run them. *Meyhanes* offer large selections of *meze* – hot and cold appetizers or hors d'œuvre – to accompany *raki*, the anis-flavoured spirit, beer and wine, while itinerant singers and musicians croon nostalgic love songs and play classic Turkish and Gipsy music and arabesks around the tables.

Meze are also a feature of the kebabcis that specialize in grilled meats, and of the fish restaurants along the Bosphorous that have recently become very popular. There is a whole parade of fish restaurants in Ortakoy, the former Jewish quarter in Istanbul where I found my grandmother Eugénie's old home. Many regional restaurants have opened in Istanbul in the last few years, while those in Gaziantep in the south of the country which offer dishes similar to those from neighbouring Syria, have been particularly appreciated. Recently, for the first time, a restaurant opened offering Kurdish specialities. I was taken there by Kurdish friends who could hardly contain their joy.

The high degree of specialization in the food trade is a legacy of the organization in the Ottoman Palace kitchens where cooks were entrusted with one type of food only, such as soups or kebabs or jams. Now pidecis specialize in *lahmacun*, a Turkish type of meat pizza; *börekçis* specialize in all kinds of pies; *işkembecis* are tripe soup eateries; muhallebicis offer a variety of milk puddings, and baklavacis sell baklavas and other pastries. There are also those who specialize in producing cured meats and sausages, cured fish, cheese, pickles and jams to sell in the bazaars and streets. To protect their trade in the new Republic, food makers formed craft guilds that are still important today. But because young men are now not so keen to work as hard as their fathers and are leaving the family business to work in other professions, the food trades are no longer jealously guarded and many outsiders have been allowed to join.

As I mentioned earlier, until a few decades ago most professional cooks came from Bolu and many still do, especially from the towns of Gerede and of Mengen where a catering school was opened in 1985. The prestige with which cooks are still regarded in Turkey today has never been equalled anywhere in the Middle East or North Africa. The strict hierarchy that reigns in restaurant kitchens, denoted by different shapes and sizes of cooks' hats, is also a legacy from Palace days. And women still never enter a professional kitchen – unless they own the restaurant.

Since the late eighties, a new modern restaurant trade has developed with the growth of tourism. International hotel chains were the first to open grand restaurants offering local cuisine of a high standard. I was there when the Holiday Inn in Istanbul asked my friend, the food writer Nevin Halici, to teach their highly trained local kitchen staff regional dishes in which they had previously had little interest.

In the early 1990s, a renaissance of 'Ottoman Cuisine' began to take place. The first to give new life to the old dishes was the young chef Vedat Basaran who introduced an Ottoman menu at the Tura Restaurant in the Çiragan Palace – the sumptuous palace in Istanbul to which the sultans moved from Topkapi in the nineteenth century – renovated by the Kempinski Hotel chain. The idea was quickly copied by other hotel chains. Travel agents began offering 'Ottoman gourmet tours'; companies sponsored the publication of illustrated coffee-table books featuring translations of nineteenth-century recipes. Vedat Basaran next opened the Feriye Lokantasi in a renovated pavilion in the palatial precinct of the Çiragan Palace. His dishes are Ottoman in the broad sense: they include seventeenth-century recipes from countries that were part of the Ottoman Empire, such as Syria and Egypt, and are inspired by recipes from his huge collection of old cookery books and from manuscripts found in the Palace archives. But he interprets them in a modern way. I think his food is exquisite – I experienced a magical evening there.

Istanbul

The Istanbul skyline with its domes and minarets, the call of the *muezzin*, the smells at the bazaar conjure up memories of my childhood in Egypt with a thrilling feeling of exaltation. The city also brings back my maternal grandmother Eugénie's stories of her life in that city. Recently I found hundreds of letters written by her father in an archive in Paris. My great-grandfather, Joseph Alphandary, was a headmaster at the Alliance Israëlite Française, an organization that brought French education to Jewish children in Arab and Ottoman countries. He taught in schools in Salonica, Haifa, Tanta in Egypt, and in Istanbul where he was born. His beautifully written letters to the president of the organization in Paris are necessarily official yet also personal. Those from Istanbul bring the city's past alive for me in an incredibly vivid way. In a little synagogue near the mosque in Ortaköy by the Bosphorous, I found him in a group photograph. As I wandered around Istanbul, I very much felt his presence.

In the markets you are aware, by the way shoppers behave, that you are in a country where people love food. The labyrinth-like spice market with the vaulted roof is called Misir Çarşisi, which means Egyptian Bazaar, because the spices once arrived via Egypt. Amid the carpet shops, jewellers and leather goods sellers, food vendors display their wares. Giant chunks of white cheese sit by piles of olives and cured fish. Lamb sausages hang over jumbled mountains of thinly sliced spiced beef. Syrupy pastries filled with nuts are arranged beside creamy white milk puddings. Spice merchants, *baharatci*, sell every kind of aromatic as well as dried fruit and nuts, grains and dried vegetables such as baby okra, little red chillies, and hollowed aubergines that look like leather bells.

Regional Cooking

In the late 1970s, I was invited by Gulsen Kahraman, the then director of the Turkish Tourist Office in London, to travel through Turkey. Having asked me where I wanted to go, who I wanted to meet and what I wanted to see and eat, she arranged the most extraordinary trip. One of my stops was Konya where the local Cultural Association ran the Mevlana festivals of Whirling Dervishes, troubadour, folk music and poetry festivals, rose festivals, horse racing, racing pigeon competitions, javelin throwing and Koran reading competitions. They also organized national food symposiums and cookery competitions for the surrounding villages and I suggested to the Halici family, who were behind all these activities, that they should put on an international food event.

Enthusiastically, they asked for a list of people who might like to attend such an event and the following year found many of us at their international congress. It was organized by Feyzi Halici, a poet and one-time senator, and his sister Nevin who had made a study of Turkish regional cooking by going from village to village and knocking on doors. We travelled around the country with them and tasted all kinds of foods, some unknown even to the Turkish gastronomes travelling with us. We heard scholarly lectures ranging from the history of Turkish food to nutrition, visited Palace kitchens and food bazaars, and went to see artisans at work. In one town, we visited a factory where the workers brought dishes they had cooked at home, producing a great banquet for us. We were invited into people's homes and one family cooked several lambs for us in a pit. We ate in their garden, sitting on cushions around low tables consisting of large trays set on small wooden trestles.

In Turkey, entertaining guests is a central part of social customs. Sharing food is a strict rule of almost religious importance; indeed, it is a command of the Prophet. Sayings such as 'guests are the blessing of the house' and 'eat together since communal meals are blessed' attest to this. For outsiders like us, their hospitality was an overwhelming experience.

Biennial congresses followed until they stopped due to lack of funds. A good deal of what I know about Turkish food I owe to Nevin Halici, who has accompanied me on many research trips, and to one of her friends, the much-loved gastronome Tuğrul Şavkay who sadly died in 2003, far too young.

About Alcoholic Drinks

Alcoholic drinks are prohibited by Islam, but Turkey is a secular state and tolerant about alcoholic prohibition. *Raki*, a powerful spirit made from the distilled fermented juice of white grapes flavoured with aniseed, is the national drink for all but the very religious. It is drunk neat or with iced water which turns it milky-white, with or without ice. It is produced by the state, as are many of the local wines. The government also encourages a privately owned quality wine trade. *Boza* is a rich thick drink made from fermented millet. It is of ancient nomadic origin and has a very distinctive flavour.

One of my most amusing and exciting memories of Turkey is the inaugural evening to celebrate the formation of the Turkish wine-lovers' branch of the Chevaliers du Tastevin. I happened to be in Istanbul and my friend the late Tuğrul Şavkay invited me to the ceremony and dinner. The venue was the grand ballroom of a yet to be opened five-star hotel. An enormous banqueting table was set in the middle of the empty ballroom. With Ottoman lavishness, course upon course of modern nouvelle cuisine-style Turkish delicacies were served, accompanied by a succession of local and foreign wines, while toasts were proposed in an atmosphere of convivial jollity. The scene was enchantingly fairy-like, with an added cloak and dagger feel. The event had been secretly arranged to foil Islamic fundamentalists (there were whispers of a possible bomb). Velvet cloaks, hats, gold chains and a great sword had been promised by the Chevaliers' Californian branch which was renovating its wardrobes. The regalia arrived an hour late, which created some anxiety. In due course, however, the women were seated in rows to watch the 'knighting by the sword' of their dressed-up men while classical music created an elevated feeling of ceremony. As each man knelt on a velvet cushion to be knighted, the women giggled helplessly.

About Tea, Coffee and Other Beverages

Coffee made with pulverized grounds and sugar in a *cezve* (a small pot with a wide base, narrower neck and long handle) and served in tiny cups has an important place in Turkish cultural identity. It is a symbol of hospitality and is highly esteemed, but in the last twenty-five years its consumption has waned in favour of tea, and it is reserved now for drinking after main meals and for special occasions.

Tea became the favoured all-day beverage at a time of economic crisis because it was cheaper than coffee, and it has remained so. It is served in tulip-shaped glasses without milk and with lumps of sugar. Herbal infusions such as sage, thyme, mint and melissa (lemon balm) as well as apple tea and cinnamon tea are also popular. Salep is a hot drink of milk thickened with the ground root of an orchid flavoured with rose water and served with a sprinkling of cinnamon and ground pistachios. In winter, it is sold by street vendors.

In summer, fresh fruit juices – in particular cherry, apricot and orange – are fashionable. A wonderfully refreshing and very popular drink that is served at meal times is *ayran*: this is yoghurt beaten with the same amount of water or soda water and just a touch of salt. In Islamic culture, water has symbolic importance. It is seen as a divine gift, a purifier, and saintly. Spring water is much appreciated: people pride themselves in recognizing where it comes from, and it is sometimes served with a slice of lemon or perfumed with rose petals.

Starters and Meze

In Turkey, *meze* – hot and cold appetizers or hors d'œuvre – are traditionally served with *raki* to counteract the effect of the strong spirit while delighting the palate. Palace cooks are said to have been familiar with at least two hundred different types. The *meyhanes*, the old-style taverns where women were rarely seen until recently, and the little fish restaurants by the sea, have made of them a speciality. In the past, when families entertained at home, *meze* were served before the meal at a separate 'raki table' where men alone gathered. Now, although *raki* is still considered a virile drink, women have joined the men at the *raki* table and enjoy the *meze* with them.

A well-chosen selection makes a great start to a meal but they should not fill you up. They should be light and tasty, varied and colourful. Serve them with pitta bread (*pide* in Turkey) or with Turkish breads you find in Middle Eastern stores: there are crusty white loaves, very large spongy flat breads like the Italian *focaccia*, very thin ones called *lavaş*, and bread rings covered with sesame seeds called *simit*.

The salads and vegetable dishes in this chapter can also be served to accompany main dishes. Also included are dishes, such as soups and pies, a cold pilaf, and pastas, which make good first courses in their own right as opposed to being part of a *meze*. In Turkey, meals at home often begin with soup, which is regarded as a symbol of happiness. Seasonal vegetables cooked in olive oil, served as a first course or on their own after the main meat dish, are an important feature of traditional home cooking.

Yoghurt in Turkey is the best in the world – the one made with buffalo's milk is sensational – and they use it lavishly in so many of their dishes that it is ubiquitous.

AUBERGINE PURÉE with YOGHURT
Yoğurtlu Patlican Salatasi

Turks claim to have a hundred ways of preparing aubergines. For them, it is the king and queen of vagetables. Yoghurt softens the flavours and adds to the creamy texture of this refreshing purée.

SERVES 6–8

2–3 aubergines (weighing about 750g)
juice of $^1/_2$–1 lemon
2 tablespoons extra virgin olive oil
250g strained Greek Style yoghurt
2–3 cloves garlic, crushed (optional)
salt
To garnish: 1–2 tablespoons finely chopped flat-leaf
parsley or mint (optional)

Prick the aubergines with a pointed knife to prevent them from bursting. Turn them under the grill until the skins are blackened and they feel very soft when you press them. Alternatively, place them on a large piece of foil on a baking sheet and roast them in a hot oven pre-heated to 240°C/475°F/Gas 9 for about 45–60 minutes or until they feel very soft and the skins are wrinkled. When cool enough to handle, peel and drop them into a strainer or colander with small holes. Press out as much of the water and juices as possible. Still in the colander, chop the flesh with a pointed knife, then mash it with a fork or wooden spoon, letting the juices escape through the holes.

Beat in the lemon juice, oil and yoghurt, the garlic (if using) and a little salt. Serve garnished, if you like, with parsley or mint.

TARAMA

Grey mullet roe was originally used in Turkey for this famous dip (known here under the Greek name taramasalata) but smoked cod's roe has now generally replaced it.

SERVES 6–8
1 slice of white bread, crusts removed
200g smoked cod's roe
juice of 1 lemon
3 tablespoons sunflower oil
2 tablespoons extra virgin olive oil

Soak the bread in water. Skin the smoked cod's roe and blend in a food processor. Add the bread, squeezed dry, the lemon juice, sunflower oil and olive oil and blend to a creamy consistency that should still be a little rough, adding 1–2 tablespoons of water if necessary. Serve it with pitta bread.

CUCUMBER and YOGHURT SALAD
Cacik

This salad is popular throughout the Middle East. Unless it is to be eaten as soon as it is made, it is best to salt the cucumber and let the juices drain before mixing with the yoghurt; otherwise it gets very watery. If possible, use the small cucumbers sold in Middle Eastern and Asian stores – they have a finer flavour than the large ones. Cacik is served as part of a meze and also as a side dish – to be eaten with spoons from little individual side bowls – to accompany pies, meat dishes and rice. It even makes a lovely cold summer soup. Use natural (full-fat) yoghurt.

SERVES 4–6
4 small cucumbers or 1 large one
500g natural (full-fat) yoghurt
2 garlic cloves, crushed (optional)
2 sprigs of finely chopped mint or dill or 2 teaspoons
  crushed dried mint

Peel and dice or grate the cucumber or cucumbers, or cut them in half lengthways, then into half-moon slices. Unless the salad is to be served immediately, sprinkle with salt and leave for ¹/₂–1 hour in a colander for the juices to drain.

Beat the yoghurt in a serving bowl with the crushed garlic (if using) mint or dill and fold in the cucumber. Add a little salt, taking into account the saltiness of the cucumber if you have salted it, although most of the salt will have gone with the drained juices.

COURGETTE FRITTERS
Kabak Mücveri

Fried onions, feta cheese and herbs lift what is otherwise a bland vegetable. These little fritters can be served hot or cold. They can be made in advance and reheated.

SERVES 4

1 large onion, chopped coarsely
3 tablespoons sunflower oil
500g courgettes, chopped finely
3 eggs
3 tablespoons plain flour
black pepper
2–3 sprigs of mint, chopped
2–3 sprigs of dill, chopped
200g feta cheese, mashed with a fork
oil for frying

Fry the onion in 3 tablespoons oil over a medium heat until it is soft and lightly coloured. Add the courgettes, and sauté, stirring, until they too are soft.

In a bowl, beat the eggs with the flour until well blended. Add pepper (there is no need for salt because the feta cheese is very salty) and the herbs, and mix well. Fold the mashed feta into the eggs, together with the cooked onions and courgettes.

Film the bottom of a preferably non-stick frying pan with oil and pour in the mixture by the half-ladle (or 2 tablespoons) to make a few fritters at a time. Turn each over once, and cook until both sides are browned a little. Drain on kitchen paper.

PEPPERY BULGUR SALAD
Kisir

Kisir is a salad from Gaziantep. You need the fine-ground (not medium) bulgur which you can find in Middle Eastern stores. Chilli peppers gives it a thrilling zing but you can leave them out. Serve it with little lettuce leaves that can be used as scoops.

SERVES 6

200g fine-ground bulgur
125ml boiling water
1 tablespoon tomato paste
juice of $1^1/_2$ lemons
5 tablespoons extra virgin olive oil
$^1/_2$–1 fresh red or green chilli pepper, chopped finely
salt
5–7 spring onions
300g tomatoes, diced
bunch of flat-leaf parsley (about 50g), chopped
bunch of mint (about 25g), chopped
To serve with: 2 baby Cos or Little Gem lettuces

Put the bulgur into a bowl, pour the boiling water over it, stir and leave for 15–20 minutes until the grain is tender. Don't be tempted to add more water since the juice from the lemons and tomatoes will soften it further.

Add the tomato paste, lemon juice and oil, the chilli, and some salt, and mix thoroughly. Trim the green tops off the spring onions, then slice them finely. Add them and the diced tomatoes to the bulgur mixture, together with the parsley and mint and mix well.

Serve with the small lettuce leaves stuck around the edges of the salad. Another way is to roll the bulgur mixture into balls the size of a small egg and to place each one in the hollow of a lettuce leaf.

VARIATION
Add 1–2 tablespoons of pomegranate molasses (p.10) to the dressing. This gives the grain a sweet-and-sour flavour.

ROASTED VEGETABLES with YOGHURT and FRESH TOMATO SAUCE

A very traditional meze is fried aubergines served with yoghurt and tomato sauce. I like to do the same with a mix of roasted vegetables, and I serve them either hot or cold. It is the kind of thing you can do easily in large quantities for a party. It can be done a day in advance, cooking the vegetables in batches if necessary, and reheating them, if you wish, on the day. The yoghurt should be at room temperature. The tomato sauce has a sweet-and-sour flavour and is served cold.

SERVES 6

2 medium aubergines
3 plump bell peppers
3 fat courgettes
4 medium onions, red or white
extra virgin olive oil
salt
500g natural (full-fat) yoghurt
2 teaspoons crushed dried mint
1–2 garlic cloves, crushed (optional)

FOR THE TOMATO SAUCE
3 garlic cloves, chopped
1–2 tablespoons extra virgin olive oil
750g tomatoes, peeled and chopped
1 tablespoon sugar
salt
good pinch of ground chilli pepper or flakes
2 tablespoons wine vinegar

Make the tomato sauce first: heat the chopped garlic in the oil for a few seconds only, stirring, until the aroma rises. Add the tomatoes, sugar, salt and chilli pepper, and cook, stirring occasionally, for about 20 minutes until reduced and thick. Add the vinegar towards the end.

Cut the aubergines in half lengthways, then into 1.5cm thick slices; cut the peppers in half through the stem end, de-seed them, and cut them in half again, lengthways; cut the courgettes into 1.5cm slices crossways and cut the onions into quarters.

Each type of vegetable should be placed on separate pieces of foil on baking trays since they take different times to cook. Sprinkle the vegetable pieces generously with oil and a little salt and turn them around with your hand so that they are lightly oiled all over.

Roast them in the hottest pre-heated oven for about 25 minutes or until the vegetables are tender and lightly browned, taking each type of vegetable out as they are done.

Serve the roasted vegetables hot or cold. They should be placed on a large serving dish and passed around with a bowl of yoghurt into which you have beaten a little salt, dried mint and, if you like, crushed garlic, and a bowl of the tomato sauce.

LEEKS with EGG and LEMON SAUCE
Terbiyeli Pirasa

An egg and lemon sauce is one of Turkey's culinary signature tunes. A touch of sugar gives it a slight sweet-and-sour taste. I like making the dish, which can be served hot or cold, with baby leeks, but larger ones can be used instead.

SERVES 4–6   600g baby leeks
2 egg yolks
juice of 1^1/$_2$ lemons
1 teaspoon sugar
salt

Wash the leeks in running water, making sure you remove any earth trapped between the leaves. Trim the root ends and the tough tops of the green leaves.

Boil the leeks in salted water until tender, then drain, reserving 250ml of the cooking water. Pour this cooking water back into the pan and bring to the boil.

In a small bowl, beat the egg yolks and lemon juice with the sugar. Pour in a little of the hot cooking water and beat well, then pour the egg and lemon mixture into the pan, beating vigorously, for seconds only until the sauce thickens slightly. Be careful not to let it boil or it will curdle. Add a little salt, if necessary, to taste.

Serve the leeks hot or cold with the sauce poured over.

CELERIAC with EGG and LEMON SAUCE
Terbiyeli Kereviz

Celeriac is a popular winter vegetable in Turkey. The creamy sauce with a gentle sweet-and-sour flavour enhances its delicate flavour. It is as good cold as it is hot.

SERVES 4

1 celeriac (weighing about 1kg)
juice of 1 lemon
salt
1 teaspoon sugar
2 egg yolks

Cut away the knobbly skin of the celeriac, and cut the flesh into 2cm cubes. (It is a very hard root and you need a big strong knife and to use quite a bit of force.)

Put the celeriac cubes into a pan and barely cover with water. Add the juice of 1/2 lemon, some salt and the sugar, and simmer, covered, for 15–20 minutes or until just tender.

Just before serving, beat the egg yolks with the remaining lemon juice in a little bowl. Beat in 2–3 tablespoons of the cooking water then pour the egg and lemon mixture into the pan, stirring vigorously. Heat through, stirring constantly, but do not let it boil or the egg will curdle.

Serve hot or cold with the sauce poured on top.

AUBERGINE SLICES *with*
WALNUTS *and* GARLIC
Cevizli Patlican

This strongly flavoured version of a very common meze originates in Georgia where walnut trees abound. There is plenty of garlic, but it is not overpowering because it is fried. The aubergine slices can be deep-fried but I prefer them roasted in the oven. They should be served cold, and they can be made in advance.

SERVES 6

1kg aubergines
extra virgin olive oil
2–3 tablespoons wine vinegar
salt
6–7 cloves garlic, crushed
60g walnuts
handful of chopped flat-leaf parsley

Wash the aubergines and cut them lengthways into slices about 1.5cm thick. Place them on a well-oiled piece of foil on an oven tray and brush them generously with oil on both sides. Cook in an oven pre-heated to 240°C/475°F/Gas 9 for about 20 minutes or until lightly browned and soft, turning them over once.

Arrange them on flat serving plates, then brush with vinegar and sprinkle lightly with salt.

Soften the garlic in 1 tablespoon of oil over a medium heat until the aroma rises but do not let it colour. Finely chop the walnuts in a food processor and mix with the chopped parsley in a bowl. Add the garlic with another tablespoon of oil and a sprinkling of salt, mix well and spread this paste on the aubergine slices.

ROASTED AUBERGINES
and PEPPERS with YOGHURT
and PINE NUTS

This is one of my favourites. It makes a good first course as well as a vegetarian main dish. The vegetables can be served hot or cold and the yoghurt should be at room temperature. I mix the two kinds of yoghurt – natural (full-fat) and strained Greek Style – to get a thick creamy texture that still pours well.

SERVES 6

4 small aubergines (weighing about 1kg)
3 large red bell peppers
1 tablespoon lemon juice
4 tablespoons extra virgin olive oil
salt and black pepper
125g natural (full-fat) yoghurt
125g strained Greek Style yoghurt
2 garlic cloves, crushed
50g pine nuts

Prick the aubergines with a pointed knife to prevent them exploding in the oven. Place them and the peppers on a large piece of foil on a baking sheet and roast in an oven pre-heated to 220°C/425°F/Gas 7 for about 45–60 minutes, until the aubergines feel soft when you press them. Turn the peppers one half turn after 25 minutes, and take them out before the aubergines when they are soft and their skins are blackened in places.

As the peppers come out of the oven, drop them into a plastic freezer bag and twist to seal it closed. When cool enough to handle, peel them, remove the stems and seeds, and cut them in half or into 4 long strips.

Peel the aubergines into a colander when they are cool enough to handle. Press the flesh gently to let their juices run out. Cut each into 4 pieces and turn them in a little lemon juice to prevent them discolouring.

Put the aubergines and peppers on one side of a shallow serving plate. Dress with 3 tablespoons of the oil, salt and pepper and mix gently. Mix the two types of yoghurt together, beat in the garlic and some salt, and pour on to the other side of the plate.

Just before serving, fry the pine nuts in the remaining oil, stirring, until very lightly browned, and sprinkle over the yoghurt. Pass the dish round for people to help themselves.

AUBERGINES STUFFED with ONIONS and TOMATOES
Imam Bayildi

Imam Bayildi is one of the most famous Turkish dishes. Conflicting stories are told about the origin of its name, which means 'the Imam fainted'. Some say it came about when an Imam (Muslim priest) fainted with pleasure when it was served to him by his wife. Others believe that the Imam fainted when he heard how much of his expensive olive oil had gone into its making. It is best cooked in a saucepan but you may find it easier in the oven. Serve it cold.

Small, elongated aubergines – at most 14cm long, each weighing about 125g, are best for this dish. You will find them in Asian and Middle Eastern stores.

SERVES 6

6 aubergines (see above)
250ml good-quality tomato juice
1 teaspoon sugar, or more to taste
salt
juice of 1 lemon
150ml extra virgin olive oil

FOR THE FILLING
$1^1/_2$ large onions, sliced thinly
2–3 tablespoons extra virgin olive oil
5 garlic cloves, chopped
4 tomatoes, peeled and chopped
large bunch of flat-leaf parsley, chopped
salt

Make the filling first. Soften the sliced onions gently in the oil, but do not let them colour. Add the chopped garlic and stir for a moment or two until the aroma rises. Remove the pan from the heat and stir in the tomatoes and the parsley. Season to taste with salt, and mix well.

Trim the caps from the ends of the aubergines (you may leave the stalks on). Peel off 1cm wide strips of skin lengthways, leaving alternate strips of peel and bare flesh. Make a deep cut on one side of each aubergine lengthways, from one end to the other, but not right through, in order to make a 'pocket'.

Stuff the 'pocket' of each aubergine with the filling and place them tightly side by side, with the opening face up, in a wide shallow pan. Mix the tomato juice with a little sugar, salt and the lemon juice and pour this and the oil over the aubergines. Cover the pan and simmer gently for about 45 minutes or until the aubergines are soft and the liquid much reduced.

Alternatively, you can cook the aubergines in the oven. Arrange them, cut side up, in a baking dish, with the rest of the ingredients poured over. Cover with foil and cook in the oven preheated to 200°C/400°F/Gas 6 for 1 hour or until soft. Allow to cool before arranging on a serving dish.

AUBERGINE PILAF
Patlicanli Pilav

This is a cold pilaf to serve as a first course. It has an exciting combination of ingredients and flavours, while a mix of cinnamon and allspice lend a beautiful light-brown colour.

SERVES 4
500g aubergines
salt
90ml extra virgin olive oil
1 medium onion, chopped
3 tablespoons pine nuts
200g long-grain rice
2 medium tomatoes, peeled and chopped
$1^1/2$ teaspoons sugar
2 tablespoons currants or small black raisins
salt and black pepper
1 teaspoon ground cinnamon
$1/2$ teaspoon ground allspice
4 tablespoons chopped dill

Peel the aubergines and cut them into 2.5 cm cubes. Place them on a sheet of foil on a baking tray. Sprinkle with salt and pour over enough oil so that when the aubergine pieces are turned, they are well covered with oil. Pre-heat the oven to the highest temperature and put the aubergines in for 25 minutes, or until they are soft and lightly browned.

Fry the onion in 2 tablespoons of the oil until it is soft and golden. Add the pine nuts and when they begin to colour, add the rice and stir until it is well coated with oil. Add the tomatoes and the sugar and simmer for 5 minutes.

Add the currants or raisins and 350ml water. Season with salt, pepper, cinnamon and allspice and stir gently. Cook, covered, over a low heat until the liquid is absorbed and the rice is tender. (Some brands that claim not to be parboiled or pre-cooked now take as little as 8–10 minutes, so read the information on the packet.) Remove the lid towards the end of cooking if it is too moist.

Stir in 4–5 tablespoons of oil and the dill. Very gently fold in the aubergines and serve cold.

MASHED POTATOES with OLIVE OIL, SPRING ONIONS and PARSLEY
Patates Salatasi

This is as good hot as it is cold and can be served as part of a meze or as a side dish.

SERVES 6

750g mashing potatoes
6 tablespoons extra virgin olive oil
salt and pepper
about 6 spring onions, chopped
handful of chopped flat-leafed parsley

Peel and boil the potatoes in salted water until soft. Drain, keeping about ¹/₂ cup of the cooking water.

Mash the potatoes and beat in the oil. Add salt and pepper to taste and a little of the cooking water – enough to make a soft, slightly moist texture. Then stir in the spring onions and the parsley.

BEETROOT with YOGHURT
Pancar Salatasi

Beetroot may be boiled or roasted but I think roasting, which takes much longer, gives them a deliciously intense flavour. It is best to buy small ones because they take less time to cook. Or, of course, you can buy them already cooked.

SERVES 6–8

1kg beetroot
2 garlic cloves, chopped (optional)
500g strained Greek Style yoghurt
2 tablespoons lemon juice
6 tablespoons extra virgin olive
salt
handful of chopped mint or flat-leaf parsley

Cut the stems and leaves about 2cm above the beetroot. To boil them, cook them in plenty of boiling salted water until tender – small ones will take about 30 minutes, larger ones about $1^1/2$ hours. To roast them, put them on a sheet of foil on a baking sheet, cover them with foil, and roast in an oven pre-heated to 200°C/400°F/Gas 6 for 2–3 hours, depending on their size, until one feels tender when cut right through with a knife. You could cut them in half (lay them cut side down) and reduce the cooking time considerably.

When cool enough to handle, peel and cut the beetroot into 1cm rounds or half-moon slices. Wear rubber gloves to avoid staining your hands.

Beat the chopped garlic (if using) into the yoghurt and spread the mixture on a serving plate. Arrange the beetroot slices on top. Beat the lemon juice with the oil and a little salt, stir in the mint or parsley, and spoon over the beetroot slices.

VARIATION
A Lebanese version uses $1^1/2$ tablespoons *tahina* (*see* p.11) beaten into the yoghurt.

VINE LEAVES STUFFED with RICE, RAISINS and PINE NUTS
Zeytinyağli Yaprak Dolmasi

Stuffed vine leaves were served at the court of King Khusrow II in Persia in the early seventh century. Their popularity spread through the Muslim world when the caliphs of Baghdad adopted Persian cooking traditions, while the Ottomans introduced them throughout their Empire. There are numerous versions of this delicacy today which is popular in every country throughout the Middle East. The following, with raisins and pine nuts, is a Turkish version. It is served cold.

Short-grain or risotto rice is used because the grains stick together. Vine leaves can be bought preserved in brine and vacuum-packed, but if you can get hold of young fresh tender ones, do use them. They freeze well raw, wrapped in foil.

SERVES 8 OR MORE

250g vine leaves
2 large onions, chopped finely
150ml extra virgin olive oil
2 tablespoons pine nuts
$^{1}/_{2}$ tablespoon tomato paste
200g short-grain or risotto rice
2 tablespoons currants or tiny black raisins
salt and black pepper
1 teaspoon ground allspice
handful of chopped mint
handful of chopped dill
2 tomatoes, sliced
1 teaspoon sugar
juice of 1 lemon, or to taste

If using vine leaves preserved in brine, remove the salt by putting them into a bowl and pouring boiling water over them. Make sure that the water penetrates well between the layers. Leave them to soak for 20 minutes, then rinse in fresh cold water and drain. If using fresh leaves, plunge a few at a time in boiling water for a couple of seconds only, until they become limp, then lift them out. Cut off the stalks.

For the filling, fry the onions in 3 tablespoons of the oil until soft. Add the pine nuts and stir until they are golden. Stir in the tomato paste, then add all the remaining ingredients down to and including the chopped dill. Mix well.

On a plate, place the first leaf, vein side up, with the stem end facing you. Put one heaped teaspoonful of filling in the centre of the leaf near the stem end. Fold that end up over the filling, then fold both sides towards the middle and roll up like a small cigar. Squeeze the filled roll lightly in the palm of your hand. Fill the rest of the leaves in the same way. This process will become very easy after you have rolled a few.

Line the bottom of a large heavy-bottomed pan with tomato slices and any left-over, torn or imperfect vine leaves, then pack the stuffed vine leaves tightly on top.

Mix the remaining oil with 150ml water, add the sugar and lemon juice, and pour over the stuffed leaves. Put a small plate on top of the leaves to prevent them from unrolling, cover the pan, and simmer very gently for about 1 hour, until the rolls are thoroughly cooked, adding more water occasionally, a coffee cupful at a time, as the liquid in the pan becomes absorbed. Let the stuffed vine leaves cool in the pan before turning them out.

BELL PEPPERS STUFFED *with* RICE, RAISINS *and* PINE NUTS
Zeytinyağli Biber Dolmasi

This is the classic Turkish rice filling for vegetables to be served cold. Choose plump bell peppers that can stand on their base. I prefer to use red peppers because they are sweeter and for the colour, but in Turkey green ones are more often used.

SERVES 6

1 large onion, chopped finely

6 tablespoons extra virgin olive oil

250g short-grain or risotto rice

salt and pepper

1–2 teaspoons sugar

3 tablespoons pine nuts

3 tablespoons currants or tiny black raisins

1 large tomato, peeled and chopped

1 teaspoon ground cinnamon

$1/2$ teaspoon ground allspice

handful of chopped mint

handful of chopped dill

handful of chopped flat-leaf parsley
juice of 1 lemon
6 medium green or red bell peppers
To serve with: 250g natural (full-fat) yoghurt mixed with 1 garlic clove, crushed (optional)

For the filling, fry the onion in 3 tablespoons of the oil until soft. Add the rice and stir until thoroughly coated and translucent. Pour in 450ml water and add salt, pepper and sugar. Stir well and cook for 15 minutes or until the water has been absorbed but the rice is still a little underdone. Stir in the pine nuts, currants or raisins, the tomato, cinnamon and allspice, mint, dill and parsley and the lemon juice, as well as the rest of the oil.

Retaining the stalk, cut a circle around the stalk end of the peppers and set on one side to use as caps. Remove the cores and seeds with a spoon and fill the peppers with the rice mixture. Replace the caps.

Arrange the peppers side by side in a shallow baking dish, pour about 1cm water into the bottom, and bake in an oven pre-heated to 190°C/375°F/Gas 5 for 45–55 minutes or until the peppers are tender. Be careful that they do not fall apart.

Serve cold, accompanied, if you like, by a bowl of beaten yoghurt, with or without crushed garlic.

TOMATOES STUFFED with RICE, RAISINS and PINE NUTS
Zeytinyağli Domates Dolmasi

Use the same filling as above for 6 firm large tomatoes (beef tomatoes are best) or 12 medium ones. Cut a small circle around the stalk and cut out a cap from each tomato. Remove and discard the centre and seeds with a pointed teaspoon. Fill with the rice stuffing given in Bell Peppers Stuffed with Rice, Raisins and Pine Nuts on p.179 and replace the caps.

Arrange the tomatoes in a shallow baking dish and bake in an oven pre-heated to 180°C/350°F/Gas 4 for 20–30 minutes, until the tomatoes are soft. Watch them carefully, and remove them if they start to fall apart.

Serve cold, accompanied by yoghurt flavoured, if you like, with the crushed garlic.

BAKED PASTA with CHEESE
Peynirli Erişte

A pasta like tagliatelle called erişte is a traditional Turkish food that is still made by hand in rural areas. This recipe, with feta cheese, eggs and milk is easy-to-make comfort food. It can be served as a first or main course and can be made in advance and heated through before serving.

SERVES 4

500ml milk
4 eggs
200g feta cheese, mashed with a fork
salt
300g dry tagliatelle nests

Bring the milk to the boil. Lightly beat the eggs in a bowl, then beat in the milk. Add the mashed feta to the milk and eggs with some salt (it still needs some despite the saltiness of the cheese).

Crush the tagliatelle nests into small pieces with your hands. Throw them into plenty of boiling salted water and cook until *al dente*, about 5–8 minutes. Drain and turn into a greased baking dish. Pour the milk, egg and cheese mixture over the pasta and mix well.

Bake in an oven pre-heated to 180°C/350°F/Gas 4 for 45–60 minutes, until the creamy mixture has set.

VARIATION
Another, quicker, dish is the same pasta tossed with melting butter, topped with plenty of crumbled feta cheese and a generous amount of chopped parsley.

ARTICHOKES STEWED in OIL
with PEAS and CARROTS
Zeytinyağli Enginar

This classic Turkish combination is gently flavoured with dill, lemon, garlic and a tiny bit of sugar. It looks wonderful on the serving dish.

I use the frozen artichoke bottoms from Egypt which I get in Middle Eastern stores and fresh young peas that I am lucky enough to find already podded from my supermarket; however, frozen petits pois will do very well. If you want to use fresh artichokes, see p.14 on how to prepare them.

SERVES 6

250g carrots, peeled and diced
2 garlic cloves, chopped
4 tablespoons extra virgin olive oil
1 x 400g packet artichoke bottoms, defrosted
salt and pepper
200g young peas (shelled weight) or frozen petits pois, defrosted
juice of 1 lemon, or to taste
1 teaspoon sugar
2–3 tablespoons chopped dill

Put the diced carrots into a wide pan – wide enough, if possible, to hold the artichoke bottoms in one layer – with the chopped garlic, 3 tablespoons of the oil and about 400ml cold water. Bring to the boil and simmer for 5 minutes.

Put in the artichoke bottoms, season with salt and pepper and simmer for 7–10 minutes until they are just tender, turning them over once. Then add the peas, lemon juice, sugar and dill, and cook for 2–5 minutes more (less if they are petits pois), until the peas are cooked.

Place the artichoke bottoms on a serving plate, and spoon some of the carrots and peas into each. Pour the remaining reduced sauce round them. Serve cold with a dribble of the remaining oil over the top.

VARIATIONS

⊙ Instead of peas use broad beans. Although it depends on how young they are, they usually need cooking a little longer, so put them in at the same time as the artichokes.

⊙ To add body to the sauce, put a diced potato in 5 minutes before the carrots. It will fall apart by the end of the cooking and thicken the sauce.

LAYERED CHEESE PIE
Peynirli Börek

This pie, made with filo pastry, can be served hot as a first course, a tea-time savoury or as a snack. Milk sprinkled between the sheets gives it a lovely soft, moist texture. The most common cheese used in these pies is beyaz peynir or 'white cheese' which is salty and much like feta cheese. Another cheese called lor is like our cottage cheese. I like to use a mixture of the two.

SERVES ABOUT 8

> 200g feta cheese, mashed with a fork
> 250g cottage cheese
> 2 eggs, lightly beaten
> black pepper
> large bunch of parsley (50–75g), chopped
> 100g butter
> 400g large sheets of filo (48 x 30cm)
> 120ml milk
> 1 egg yolk

For the filling, mix the mashed feta, cottage cheese and the eggs thoroughly until well blended. Add pepper and stir in the herbs.

Use a large rectangular or round pie dish, a little smaller than the sheets of filo, and brush it with melted butter or oil. Place half the packet of filo (about 7 sheets), one on top of the other, at the bottom of the dish, brushing each sheet with melted butter or oil and sprinkling each with about a tablespoon of milk. Let the sheets hang over the sides of the dish and press them into the corners with the pastry brush. If you are using a round dish, place the sheets so that the corners hang over in different places around the edge.

Spread the filling evenly on top. Then cover with the remaining sheets, brushing each, including the top one, with melted butter, and sprinkling all except the last two with a tablespoon of milk.

With a sharp pointed knife trim the filo around the edges, and score the top into 16 squares or diamonds with parallel lines, cutting only down to the filling, not right through to the bottom. Brush the top with egg yolk mixed with a drop of water.

Bake in an oven pre-heated to 180°C/350°F/Gas 4 for 30–45 minutes or until crisp and golden. Serve hot, cutting along the scored lines, this time right through to the bottom.

CREAMY FILO SPINACH PIE
Ispanakli Tepsi Böreği

This wonderful creamy pie is somewhere between a savoury flan and a spinach lasagne. The filo turns into a soft, very thin pasta, so don't expect it to be crisp and papery. It sounds complicated but it is quite easy and really worth the labour; in fact, I find it therapeutic. I am sure you will be delighted by the result. It can be made in advance and reheated. The pie is excellent when cut up into small pieces and served at a party.

Use a packet of filo containing large size sheets. (I used a 400g packet of sheets measuring 48cm x 30cm – minus 2 sheets.) The large sheets are usually sold frozen and you need to defrost them for at least 3 hours before using (see p.15 for information about filo). The Turkish kaşar, a sharp hard cheese, can be found in Turkish stores but mature Cheddar is equally good for the dish. From supermarkets, you can now buy packets of young spinach leaves, washed and ready to use, but you can use not-so-young spinach and remove any thick stems.

SERVES 8

500g young spinach leaves
200g feta cheese, mashed with a fork
4 eggs
75g butter
500ml milk
350g large sheets of filo
200g Turkish kaşar cheese or mature Cheddar, grated

To make the filling, wash the spinach, removing stems only if they are thick and tough. Put them to steam in a large pan with 4–5 tablespoons water over a medium heat, with the lid on. Within a very few minutes, they will have crumpled into a soft mass, so keep your eye on them. Strain well, then, when cool enough to handle, squeeze them dry, pressing all the water out with your hands. Still using your hands, mix the spinach into the mashed feta.

Beat the eggs with a fork in a large bowl. Heat the butter in a pan. When it has melted, pour in the milk and heat until it is warm, then gradually beat this into the eggs.

Use a rectangular or square baking dish a little smaller than the sheets of filo. Open the sheets only when you are ready to use them and keep them in a pile so that they do not dry out.

Lay a sheet in the greased baking dish, pressing it into the corners with a pastry brush and letting the edges come up the sides of the dish. Pour a little of the milk, butter and egg mixture – about 80 ml or a little less than a standard ladleful – all over the sheet. (You will need a similar amount to pour between each sheet and a larger amount for the last one on top.) Sprinkle on a little of the grated *kaşar* or Cheddar. Lay a second sheet on top and repeat with the milk, butter and egg mixture and then the grated cheese.

Continue until you have used about half the sheets, then spread the spinach filling evenly on top. To do this, press lumps of the spinach and feta mixture between the palms of your hands to flatten them and lay them side-by-side.

Continue layering sheets of filo, pouring over each the milk mixture and sprinkling with cheese until you are left with 2 last sheets. With a sharp or fine serrated knife, trim the edges of pastry around the sides of the dish. Lay the remaining 2 sheets on top of the pie, sprinkling the milk mixture and cheese between them and tucking them down the side of the dish. If there is too much to tuck in, trim with scissors. Pour any remaining milk mixture over the top.

Bake the pie in an oven pre-heated to 180°C/350°/Gas 4 for 30–45 minutes until the top is golden brown. It puffs up and falls again. Serve hot, cut into pieces.

VARIATION
For an all-cheese filling instead of the spinach, blend 200g feta cheese with 200g cottage cheese and mix in about 50g chopped parsley or dill.

PUFF PASTRY SPINACH ROLL
Ispanakli Börek

For 6–8 people, use the same filling of spinach and feta cheese as in the Creamy Filo Spinach Pie on p.186.

   Cut 300g puff pastry in half and roll each half into a long rectangle about 23cm x 30cm. Roll it out on a floured surface with a floured rolling pin. Keep turning the sheet of pastry over and over and dusting it with flour each time until it is very thin. Put the filling in the middle in a band 23–24cm wide to about 2.5cm from the short ends at the top and bottom. Fold one side of the pastry over the filling, then fold the other side over the first, making a long parcel. Press the ends firmly to seal them. Place the two parcels on a baking dish, folded side down, brush with an egg yolk mixed with a drop of water, and bake in an oven pre-heated to 180°C/375°/Gas 4 for 35 minutes until puffed up and golden. Serve hot.

LITTLE CHEESE FILO ROLLS
Peynirli Sigara Böreği

These dainty little rolls or 'cigars' make ideal appetizers and canapés. The cheese used is beyaz peynir or 'white cheese' which is salty and much like feta cheese. Use large sheets of filo measuring about 48cm x 30cm, cut into strips, but if the filo sheets are too thin, the pastry is liable to tear and the filling to burst out during the cooking. In that case, use 2 strips together, brushing with butter in between. You will then need double the number of sheets. I prefer using only one strip if possible – it makes for a lighter pastry. (See p.15 for information about filo.) Serve the rolls hot. They can be made in advance and reheated.

MAKES 16 ROLLS

        200g feta cheese, mashed with a fork
        1 egg, lightly beaten
        3 tablespoons chopped mint or dill
        8 large sheets of filo
        75g butter

For the filling, mix the mashed feta with the egg and herbs.

Take out the sheets of filo only when you are ready to use them since they dry out quickly. Cut them into 4 rectangles measuring about 30cm x 12cm and put them in a pile on top of each other. Brush the top strip lightly with melted butter. Take a tablespoon of filling. Place it at one short end of the strip in a thin sausage-shape along the edge – about 2cm from it and 2cm from the side edges. Roll up the filo with the filling inside, like a cigarette. Fold in the ends about one-third of the way along to trap the filling and then continue to roll.

Do the same with the remaining strips of filo and cheese filling. Place the cigars, seam side down, on a baking sheet and brush the tops with melted butter. Bake in an oven pre-heated to 150°C/300°F/Gas 2 for 30 minutes or until crisp and golden.

BARLEY SOUP with YOGHURT
Yoğurtlu Çorbasi

This Anatolian peasant soup with its delicate flavour of mint and saffron is magnificent. I make it when I have a roast chicken carcass or, better still, when I have two, and have remembered to retain their cooking juices and the melted fat.

SERVES 8 OR MORE

1–2 chicken carcasses
salt and white pepper
1 large onion, chopped
2 tablespoons vegetable oil
130g pearl barley
good pinch of saffron threads
2 tablespoons chopped flat-leaf parsley
4 tablespoons chopped mint
500g natural (full-fat) yoghurt

Put the chicken carcass or carcasses into a large pan with about 2.5 litres water. Add salt and pepper and boil for 1 hour or longer. Strain, and put back any little bits of chicken into the stock.

In the washed and dried pan, fry the onion in the oil until soft. Add the stock and any cooking juices and melted fat left over from the original roasting of the chicken. Bring to the boil, then add the barley. Crush the saffron threads with the back of a spoon on a little plate and stir them in. Simmer over a low heat for about 30 minutes until the barley is swollen and tender. Add the parsley and mint and adjust the seasoning but remember the yoghurt will add a little needed sharpness.

Just before serving, beat the yoghurt in a bowl with a few ladles of the soup. Then pour the yoghurt mixture into the soup, beating vigorously, and heat to just below boiling, stirring constantly. Do not allow the soup to boil, or it will curdle.

COLD YOGHURT SOUP with CHICKPEAS and BULGUR
Yoğurtlu Nohut Çorbasi

I made notes about this recipe and a few others at Haci Abdullah's restaurant in Istanbul. It is a cool summer soup using rural staples and it takes only minutes to make.

SERVES 6

150g bulgur
salt
1kg natural (full-fat) yoghurt
2 tablespoons crushed dried mint
2 garlic cloves, crushed (optional)
1 x 400g tin of chickpeas, drained

Put the bulgur into a pan with 250ml water and a little salt. Bring to the boil and cook, covered, over a very low heat for about 10 minutes until the water has been absorbed and the grain is tender.

Pour the yoghurt into a serving bowl, beat in a further 250ml cold water, add the mint and garlic (if using), season with salt, and mix well. Stir in the drained chickpeas and the bulgur and serve.

PUMPKIN SOUP
Kabak Çorbasi

This is the simplest pumpkin soup ever where the pure sweet taste of pumpkin is married with the slightly sharp one of yoghurt. The large orange-fleshed pumpkins are winter vegetables, but you can find them throughout the year in Asian and Middle Eastern stores, sold by the slice, with their seeds and fibres removed, and wrapped in cling film.

SERVES 4

1.25kg pumpkin
1 litre chicken stock (or use 2 stock cubes)
1–2 teaspoons sugar
salt and black pepper
To serve with: 250g natural (full-fat) or strained Greek Style yoghurt

Remove the peel and any seeds and fibre from the pumpkin and cut the flesh into pieces. The peel is extremely hard and you have to cut it away by laying the slices or chunks cut side down, and pressing down with a large heavy knife.

Put the pieces into a large pan with only about 350ml stock (it will not cover the pieces), and simmer, covered, for 15 minutes or until the pumpkin is tender.

Blend to a purée in a food processor and return to the pan, or mash it with a potato masher. Add the remaining stock, the sugar and a little salt and pepper, and cook for a few minutes more, adding water, to thin the soup if necessary.

Serve the soup hot, and pass round the yoghurt (which should be at room temperature) in a bowl for people to help themselves.

TOMATO and RICE SOUP
Domatesli Pirinç Çorbasi

For this fresh-tasting soup, I blend the tomatoes to a cream in a food processor without peeling them and only cook them a little. The egg and lemon finish gives it a creamy texture. The rice should be cooked separately and added just before serving as it goes mushy if it stays too long in the soup. Spearmint is commonly used but you can use other types of mint.

SERVES 4–6
- 75g basmati or long–grain rice
- 2 chicken stock cubes
- 1kg ripe tomatoes
- salt and black pepper
- 3 teaspoons sugar, or to taste
- 2 sprigs of spearmint, finely chopped
- 1 egg
- juice of $1/2$ lemon

First cook the rice. Wash it in a bowl of cold water, then drain and rinse under the cold tap. Pour it into plenty of boiling salted water and cook for about 20 minutes until just tender. (Some brands that claim not to be parboiled or pre-cooked now take as little as 8–10 minutes, so read the information on the packet.) Drain and keep it on one side until you are ready to serve.

In a large pan bring to the boil 300ml water with the crumbled chicken stock cubes.

Without peeling them, cut the tomatoes into quarters and remove the hard white bits near the stem end. Blend to a light cream in a food processor and add to the pan. Season with salt, pepper and sugar and add the mint. Mix well and simmer for 5 minutes.

Just before serving, stir in the rice, adding a little water if the soup is too thick, and bring to the boil. In a little bowl, beat the egg with the lemon juice. Add a ladle of the soup to the egg, beat well, then pour it into the soup, stirring vigorously, for a few seconds only until it becomes creamy, then quickly take off the heat. Do not let it boil again or the egg will set.

Main Courses

Meat – lamb or mutton – cooked in a variety of ways, is the prestige food of Turkey. Chicken comes second. Fish and seafood was always appreciated in the coastal cities, especially in Istanbul and Izmir but, apart from a few esteemed fish, it was considered poor man's food and was bought from vendors and eaten in the street. At night at the top of the Bosphorous, a thousand lights glittered on the sea from the little boats of menfolk fishing for their families. It is only in the last twenty years, since fish restaurants have proliferated in response to demand by foreign tourists, that they have become enormously popular with the local population. It seems surprising in a country surrounded by three large seas – the Black Sea, the Aegean and the Mediterranean, as well as the smaller Sea of Marmara – that fish does not enjoy equal status to meat, even though it is more expensive. One suggestion is that for a people with atavistic tastes born in the steppelands of Central Asia, it was not easy to incorporate the produce of the sea in their culinary traditions.

Many years ago I asked the head of the Association of Turkish Chefs why meat was so important in Turkey. He replied that in Ottoman times, Islamic law allowed men to have four wives, they were obliged to satisfy them all equally and that required a great deal of strength and energy so they had to eat a lot of meat! A certain sultan, he said, was reputed to have habitually eaten a whole lamb at one sitting. I suspect he was pulling my leg.

Meat is the food cooked when people entertain, but the majority of the population can rarely afford it and lives mainly on bulgur, rice, pulses and vegetables. Rice pilaf is eaten almost every day in the cities, sometimes for both lunch and supper, either as an accompaniment or as a substantial main course. As well as being a staple meal, it has always been considered a grand dish of celebration. There is no wedding without a rice pilaf. Bulgur pilaf is more common than rice in rural homes since Anatolia is wheat country.

SMOKED MACKEREL
with WALNUT SAUCE
Taratorlu Uskumru

This can be served as a first course or as a cold main course with pickles, sliced red onions and a green salad. Cold-smoked mackerel is soft and moist and more of a delicacy than the hot-smoked variety. Hazelnuts, almonds or pine nuts can be used as an alternative to walnuts for this classic sauce which is called tarator. In that case, white bread should be used. The sauce can be served with poached or grilled fish and also with cold vegetables cooked in olive oil.

SERVES 4

2 cold-smoked mackerel
1 lemon, cut in quarters

FOR THE SAUCE
100g walnut halves
75g or 3 slices wholemeal bread, crusts removed
2 garlic cloves, crushed
6 tablespoons olive oil
3 tablespoons white wine vinegar
salt

Make the sauce first. Grind the walnuts in a food processor, then add the bread, previously soaked in water and squeezed dry, and the garlic, and blend together. Add the oil and vinegar, a little salt, and blend with just enough water – about 4 tablespoons – to produce a creamy consistency.

Skin and fillet the fish, and serve with the sauce and lemon quarters.

GRILLED SEA BASS FLAMBÉED
with RAKI
Raki Soslu Levrek

Raki, the Turkish national spirit, gives the grilled sea bass a faint anis aroma. Arak, ouzo and even Pernod can be used instead. Other fish such as bream, turbot and red mullet can be prepared in the same way.

SERVES 4

4 sea bass fillets (weighing about 900g), skin on
4 tablespoons extra virgin olive oil
salt and black pepper
4 tablespoons raki

Brush both sides of the fillets with 2 tablespoons of the oil and season lightly with salt and pepper. Arrange the fish on a piece of foil in a heatproof dish, skin side up, and place them under a pre-heated grill. Cook for about 4 minutes or until the skin is crisp and brown and the flesh just beginning to flake when you cut into the thickest part with a pointed knife.

Take the fish from under the grill, pour over the raki and set light to it. Serve immediately the flames have died down, sprinkling on the remaining oil.

DEEP-FRIED RED MULLET
with GARLIC and PARSLEY
Barbunya Tavasi

Deep-frying is the most popular way of cooking small to medium-sized whole fish, and red mullet (barbunya) are among the most prized. Garlic and parsley enhance their sweet flesh. Ask the fishmonger to clean the fish, but to leave the head on. Serve them with salad or the Mashed Potatoes with Olive Oil and Spring Onions on p.174.

SERVES 4

4 red mullet (weighing about 275–350g each)
5 garlic cloves, crushed
salt and black pepper

large bunch of flat-leaf parsley, chopped
flour
olive oil for frying
To serve with: 1 lemon, cut in quarters

Rub the fish with about a quarter of the crushed garlic mixed with salt and pepper, then stuff them with 5 tablespoons of the parsley mixed with the remaining garlic and a little salt and pepper.

Roll the fish in flour until they are well covered and deep-fry in sizzling oil for about 4–5 minutes. Then lift them out and drain on kitchen paper.

Serve sprinkled with the remaining parsley, accompanied by lemon quarters.

SEARED TUNA with LEMON DRESSING
Izgara Orkinoz

Olive oil and lemon with parsley or dill is the standard dressing in Turkey for all grilled and fried fish. The best way to eat tuna is rare – simply seared, with the flesh inside still pink, almost raw. Serve it with a salad or the mashed potatoes with olive oil and spring onions on p.174.

SERVES 4

juice of 1 lemon
salt and black pepper
6 tablespoons extra virgin olive oil
2 tablespoons finely chopped flat-leaf parsley or dill
4 thick tuna steaks

For the dressing, mix the lemon juice, salt and pepper and 4 tablespoons of the oil, then stir in the herbs.

Heat the remaining 2 tablespoons oil in a large, preferably non-stick, frying pan. Put in the tuna steaks and cook them over a high heat for less than 1 minute on each side, sprinkling them lightly with salt. Cut into one with a pointed knife to test for doneness; the time depends on the thickness of the steak. It should be uncooked and red inside. If you prefer it less rare, cook it for only a tiny bit longer. You can easily spoil tuna by overcooking it.

Serve the tuna steaks with the dressing poured over.

CHICKEN with PLUMS
Erikli Tavuk

This is a dish of Georgian origin. Georgia, which borders on north-west Turkey, is famous for its plum trees and plum sauces. Our slightly sour dark red plums will do well.

SERVES 6

6 skinned chicken fillets, breasts or thighs
2–3 garlic cloves, chopped
35g butter
1 tablespoon sunflower oil
salt and pepper
9 plums

FOR THE SAUCE
4 tablespoons plum jam
1 tablespoon red or white wine vinegar
1 garlic clove, crushed
pinch of chilli pepper flakes or ground chilli pepper

In a large frying pan, sauté the chicken fillets with the garlic in a mixture of butter and oil, over a low heat. Cook them for about 10–15 minutes, until they are no longer pink inside when you cut in with a pointed knife. Season with salt and pepper, and turn the pieces over at least once.

Just before serving, cut the plums in half and ease out the stones. Lift out the chicken pieces and put them on one side while you sauté the plums. Cook them for 7–10 minutes, turning them over once, until they soften. Return the chicken pieces to the pan and heat through.

For the sauce, heat the plum jam with the vinegar in a small saucepan, stir in the garlic and chilli flakes or ground chilli pepper and cook for a few moments longer.

Serve the chicken pieces with the sauce poured over, and garnished with the plums.

RICE PILAF
Pilav

This is the basic recipe for the plain rice that accompanies grills and stews. Although long-grain rice is more commonly used, basmati is today preferred by gourmets. It is my preferred rice for pilaf. It has an appealing taste and aroma, and the grains stay light, fluffy and separate. You can use water or stock: it is best to use real chicken stock if possible but stock made with stock cubes will do very well, too. Use $1^1/2$ cubes with 750ml water.

SERVES 6–8

500g long-grain or basmati rice
750ml water or chicken stock
75g butter
salt

Wash the rice (American long-grain does not need washing). Pour cold water over it in a bowl, stir well and leave it to soak for a few minutes, then strain and rinse in cold running water.

Bring the water or stock to the boil in a pan. Put in the butter, cut into pieces, and when it has melted, pour in the drained rice. Stir well, bring to the boil, then cook gently over a very low heat, tightly covered and undisturbed, for 18–20 minutes until the rice is tender, the water has been absorbed and little holes have appeared on the surface. Add a little extra water if it becomes too dry. (Some brands that claim not to be parboiled or pre-cooked now take as little as 8–10 minutes, so read the information on the packet.) Turn out and fluff up the grains with a fork. If you need to reheat the rice, put it, covered, in the oven for 15–20 minutes or until it is really hot.

VARIATION

For rice with chickpeas, *nohutlu pilav*, prepare the rice as above. Fry 1 chopped onion in 2 tablespoons sunflower oil until soft. Add the drained chickpeas from a 400g tin and heat through, then mix into the rice.

This dish has a place in Ottoman folklore. At the Topkapi Palace, in the time of Sultan Mehmet the Conqueror (he captured Constantinople in 1453), a little gold ball in the shape of a chickpea would be hidden in the rice, creating excitement among the guests, each hoping to find it on their plate.

SAUTÉED CHICKEN
with TOMATO PILAF
Tavuk Ve Domatesli Pilav

Sautéed chicken kebabs are more tender and juicy than the grilled ones on skewers which are served in kebab houses. Accompany these with tomato pilaf and a yoghurt and cucumber salad (p.161). The dark wine-red spice called sumac (p.11) lends a sharp lemony taste to the chicken.

SERVES 4

4 boned and skinned chicken fillets, breast or thigh
1 tablespoon sunflower oil
35g butter
salt and black pepper
2 tablespoons chopped flat-leaf parsley
To garnish: 1 lemon, quartered, or sumac

FOR THE TOMATO PILAF
300g long-grain or basmati rice
500g ripe tomatoes, peeled
1 chicken stock cube
2 teaspoons sugar
salt and black pepper
75g butter

Start by making the tomato pilaf. Wash the rice by pouring cold water over it in a bowl, stir well and leave to soak for a few minutes, then strain and rinse under cold water.

Quarter the tomatoes, remove the hard white bits near the stem end, then liquefy in a food processor. Measure the resulting tomato juice and add enough water to make it up to 650ml. Pour it into a pan, add the crumbled stock cube, the sugar and a little salt and pepper and bring to the boil.

Add the rice and stir well. Simmer, covered, over a low heat, for 18–20 minutes until the rice is tender and the liquid absorbed. Do not stir during the cooking, but add a little extra water if it becomes too dry. Fold in the butter, cut into small pieces. Taste and add salt and pepper if necessary.

While the rice is cooking, cut the chicken into pieces of about 3.5cm. Heat the oil and butter in a frying pan and sauté the chicken for 6–8 minutes until lightly browned, turning the pieces over once. Sprinkle the chicken with parsley and serve with lemon quarters or with sumac to sprinkle over, accompanied by the rice.

ROAST CHICKEN with PINE NUT and RAISIN PILAF
Pilavli Ve Tavuk Firinda

Many of the dishes popular in the court kitchens in Constantinople during the Ottoman period spread throughout the Empire. This pilaf is one of the classics that you find in all the cities that were once the outposts of the Empire. It is particularly good as an accompaniment to roast chicken and it also often forms a stuffing for the bird.

SERVES 4–6

1 large chicken
2 tablespoons extra virgin olive oil
salt and pepper

FOR THE PILAF
400g long-grain or basmati rice
1 large onion, chopped
3 tablespoons sunflower oil
100g pine nuts
750ml chicken stock (or use 1^1/$_2$ stock cubes)
^{1}/$_2$ teaspoon ground allspice
1 teaspoon ground cinnamon
salt and pepper
3 tablespoons currants or tiny black raisins
60–75g butter, cut into small pieces

Rub the chicken with a mixture of oil, salt and pepper. Put it breast-side down in a roasting pan so that the fat runs down, which prevents the breasts from drying out. Add 4 tablespoons of water to the bottom of the pan. Roast for 1 hour in an oven pre-heated to 200°C/400°F/Gas 6, then turn the chicken breast-side up and continue to cook for 15–30 minutes, depending on the size of the chicken, until it is well done and brown.

While the chicken is cooking, prepare the pilaf. Wash the rice by pouring cold water over it, stir well and leave to soak for a few minutes. Strain, then rinse with cold running water.

In a large pan, fry the onion in the oil until soft and golden. Add the pine nuts and stir until lightly coloured. Add the rice and stir over a moderate heat until it is well coated with fat. Then add the hot stock and stir in the allspice, cinnamon, salt (you need to take into consideration the saltiness of the stock), pepper and the currants or raisins. Bring to the boil, then simmer, covered and undisturbed, over a low heat for 20 minutes, or until the rice is tender and the water absorbed. Add a little extra water if it looks necessary.

Stir in the butter, check the seasoning and add salt if necessary. Serve hot with the chicken.

ROAST CHICKEN with BULGUR and WALNUT PILAF
Tavuk Firinda Ve Bulgur Pilav

Bulgur pilaf is an everyday dish in rural Turkey. Bulgur is whole wheat kernels that have been boiled then dried and ground. In the old days in rural areas, before mechanization, and still today in some parts, it is made collectively. The men harvest the wheat, then the women separate the grain from the chaff. They wash the grain and boil it for hours in huge pots until it splits. It is then dried in the sun, spread out on large sheets laid out on the flat roofs of houses or in the fields. When it is dry and hard, it is taken to be ground in a stone mill. Three types of grind — coarse, medium and fine — can be found in Middle Eastern stores in this country. The coarse-ground one is the best for pilaf, but the medium- ground one, which is the most widely available, will also do.

Roast the chickens as described in the recipe for Roast Chicken with Pine Nut and Raisin Pilaf on p.206. You can make the bulgur pilaf in advance and reheat it in the oven before serving.

BULGUR PILAF TO SERVE 8

500g coarse or medium bulgur
1 large onion, chopped
2 tablespoons sunflower oil
1 litre chicken stock (or use 1^1/2 stock cubes)
salt and pepper
1^1/2 teaspoons ground cinnamon
^{1}/2 teaspoon ground allspice
200g walnuts, chopped coarsely
75–100g butter, cut into small pieces

Wash the bulgur – although I find that with the processed qualities of bulgur today, this is not strictly necessary. Pour cold water over it, stir well, then rinse under the cold tap and drain. Fry the onion in the oil until it is soft and golden. Add the bulgur, stir well, then pour in the hot stock. Add salt (taking into consideration the saltiness of the stock), pepper, cinnamon and allspice. Stir and cook, covered and undisturbed, over a very low heat for about 15 minutes or until the liquid is absorbed and the grain is tender. Check the seasoning and add salt if necessary.

Finally, fold in the walnuts and the butter, cut into small pieces.

CHICKEN PILAF in a PIE
Perdeli Pilav

Perdeli pilav means 'veiled pilaf'. The veil is a pastry crust in the shape of a dome. It takes time and care, but if you like artistry and dramatic effects, it is very well worth making. Much of it can be made in advance, but the last bit – encasing the chicken and rice in puff pastry – must be done as close as possible to serving.

SERVES 6

1 chicken
2 tablespoons sunflower oil
salt and black pepper
1 onion
300g long-grain or basmati rice
1^{1}/$_{2}$ chicken stock cubes
50g butter, cut into small pieces
50g pistachio nuts, chopped very coarsely
50g blanched almonds, chopped very coarsely
1 medium onion, quartered
500g puff pastry
1 egg, separated

The chicken is roasted and the carcass is used to make a broth which is served with the pie. Rub the chicken with the oil, salt and pepper. Put it breast-side down in a roasting pan so that the fat runs down, which prevents the breasts from drying out. Add 4 tablespoons of water to the bottom of the pan. Roast for 45 minutes in an oven pre-heated to 200°C/400°F/Gas 6, then turn the chicken breast-side up and continue to cook for a further 20 minutes.

When the chicken is cool enough to handle, cut it up into 6 large pieces and remove the skin and bones (which should be kept for the broth). Cut any remaining meat from the carcass into small pieces. Keep all this covered with cling film so it does not dry out. Keep the chicken juices and the fat from the roasting pan for the rice.

Put the skin, bones and carcass into a pan with the onion, cover with water, add a little salt, and simmer for 1 hour until the broth is reduced and concentrated, then strain it. This will be the 'sauce' to accompany the pie.

Wash the rice by pouring cold water over it, stir, and leave to soak for a few minutes, then strain and rinse in cold running water. Bring 500ml water to the boil with the crumbled stock cubes, add the rice and stir well. Add salt, taking into consideration the saltiness of the stock cubes. Cook, covered and undisturbed, over a very low heat until the rice is only just tender. (Some brands that claim not to be parboiled or pre-cooked now take as little as 8–10 minutes, so read the information on the packet.)

Pour in the chicken juices and the fat from the roasting pan, and add the reserved small pieces of chicken. Fold in the butter, the pistachios and almonds. Taste to see that there is enough salt because rice needs quite a bit. The rice, too, can be prepared in advance.

Assemble the pie not too long before your guests arrive. Roll out the puff pastry so that it is a large square measuring 36–40cm on a floured surface with a floured rolling pin, turning the sheet of pastry often and dusting it with flour. Lift it on to a large flat baking dish or sheet. Put the rice in the centre, and shape it into a dome, with a base of about 25cm in diameter. Arrange the 6 large chicken pieces on top. Bring the pastry up over the rice and chicken mound, bringing up the four corners to meet at the top, and twisting them together. Now comes the artful part. You have to make it look like an Ottoman dome!

Bring the edges of the pastry together to close the side openings, right up to the top of the dome, hugging the filling. Cut away the excess dough and seal the four openings by pinching them firmly together. A little egg white brushed along the edges makes them stick better. By pinching and twisting all the way along the edges, produce a scalloped effect (like the hem of women's lingerie). It is the kind of edging you find along many Middle Eastern pies. Cut a little round about 4cm in diameter from the off-cuts and stick it on the top of the dome, with a little egg white, to cover up the joins.

Brush the whole pastry with the egg yolk mixed with a drop of water, and bake in an oven pre-heated to 180°C/350°F/Gas 4 for 45 minutes or until the pastry is crisp and brown.

Serve with the strained and reheated chicken broth.

VARIATION

If you want the chicken pilaf but do not want to bother with a pastry crust, press the pilaf into a ring- or dome-shaped mould and heat it through in the oven. Turn it out and surround it with the chicken pieces.

PUFF PASTRY MEAT PIES with RAISINS and PINE NUTS
Talaş Böreği

These individual pies are tasty, elegant and very easy to prepare. They make a perfect light meal, accompanied by a salad.

SERVES 4

1 large onion, chopped
2 tablespoons sunflower oil
500g minced lamb or beef
salt and black pepper
$^1/_2$ teaspoon ground cinnamon
$^1/_2$ teaspoon ground allspice
30g pine nuts
2 tablespoons currants or small black raisins
handful of chopped flat-leaf parsley
400g puff pastry
1 egg, separated

First make the filling. Fry the onion in the oil until soft and golden. Add the minced meat, the seasoning and spices. Turn the meat over, and crush it with a fork to break up any lumps. Cook for about 10 minutes until the meat is no longer pink and the juices have been absorbed. Stir in the pine nuts, currants or raisins, and the parsley, then let it cool.

Cut the puff pastry into 4 pieces. Roll each piece out into a square or rectangle, large enough to make an eventual flat parcel of about 18cm x 10cm. Roll out the pastry on a floured surface with a floured rolling pin, turning the sheets often and dusting them each time with flour. Spread a quarter of the meat filling on to one half of one of the sheets of pastry, leaving a 1.25cm margin around the three edges. Brush the edges with egg white to make them stick better. Fold the pastry over to cover the filling. Trim any superfluous pastry from around the pie with a knife and pinch firmly to seal. Place the pies, turned over with the smooth side up, on an oiled flat baking sheet and brush the tops with the egg yolk mixed with a drop of water.

Bake in an oven pre-heated to 180°C/350°F/Gas 4 for 25–30 minutes, until puffed up and golden.

KOFTE KEBAB with TOMATO SAUCE and YOGHURT
Yoğurtlu Köfte Kebabi

This is a mainstay of Turkish kebab houses where it is often dramatically served in a dish with a dome-shaped copper lid, the type that was once used at the sultan's palace. I serve it in a large round clay dish which can be warmed in the oven.

This is a multilayered extravaganza. There is toasted pitta bread at the bottom with tomato sauce poured over. This is topped with yoghurt and sprinkled with fried pine nuts. Grilled minced meat kebabs or shish kebab, or both, are laid on top. It requires organization and must be assembled at the last minute as the pitta should remain a little crisp. The tomato sauce and meat should be very hot while the yoghurt should be at room temperature.

SERVES 4–6

2 pitta breads
750g minced beef or lamb
salt and black pepper
1 medium onion, chopped finely (optional)
bunch of flat-leaf parsley (50g), finely chopped
1 teaspoon sumac + a pinch more (p.11)
500g natural (full-fat) yoghurt
2 tablespoons butter or extra virgin olive oil
2–3 tablespoons pine nuts

FOR THE TOMATO SAUCE
1 small onion, chopped
2 tablespoons extra virgin olive oil
2 cloves garlic, chopped
1 chilli pepper, seeded and chopped
750g tomatoes, peeled and chopped
salt and black pepper
1–2 teaspoons sugar

Make the tomato sauce first. Fry the onion in the oil until soft. Add the garlic and chilli pepper, and stir for a moment or two. Put in the tomatoes, season with salt, pepper and sugar, and cook over a medium heat for 10 minutes until they soften.

Open out the pitta and toast them until they are crisp, then break them into small pieces in your hands.

For the kofte kebabs, season the minced beef or lamb with salt and pepper, and work it into a soft dough with your hands. Add the onion (if using) and the parsley, and work into the meat. Shape into sausages about 2cm thick and 7cm long. Arrange them on an oiled sheet of foil on a baking sheet and cook them under a pre-heated grill for about 8 minutes, turning them over once, until well browned outside but still pink and moist inside.

Spread the pieces of toasted pitta at the bottom of the serving dish and sprinkle over a pinch of sumac. Pour the hot tomato sauce all over and top with a layer of the yoghurt beaten with a fork.

Heat the butter or oil with the pine nuts and stir in the remaining teaspoon of sumac. When the butter or oil sizzles, sprinkle it all over the yoghurt. Arrange the meat on top and serve at once.

VARIATION

For a rural *yoghurtlu* kebab, sauté small pieces of lamb in butter or oil with chopped onion, and salt and pepper. Serve on a bed of toasted and broken pitta bread and pour warmed yoghurt over the top. Mix a little paprika in sizzling butter and dribble over the yoghurt.

STUFFED AUBERGINES
Karniyarik

*These aubergines stuffed with minced meat – the Turkish name, karniyarik, means
'slashed belly' – are served as a hot main dish with rice pilaf (p.203). Use small,
elongated aubergines – at most 14cm long, each weighing about 125g.*

SERVES 6

6 thin and long medium-sized aubergines
salt
sunflower oil
2 onions, chopped
400g minced beef or lamb
1 tablespoons tomato paste
2 large tomatoes
1 teaspoon ground cinnamon
$^1/_2$ teaspoon ground allspice
black pepper
large bunch of flat-leaf parsley, chopped
250ml tomato juice

Trim the caps but leave the stems on the aubergines. Peel 1.25cm strips off the skins
lengthways, leaving 1.25cm strips of peel. Soak the aubergines in water mixed with
1 tablespoon of salt for 30 minutes, then drain and dry them. Fry them very briefly
in hot shallow oil, 2–3 in the frying pan at a time, turning to brown them lightly all
over. Drain them on kitchen paper.

For the filling, fry the onion in another pan in 2–3 tablespoons oil until it is soft.
Add the meat and cook for about 10 minutes, crushing it with a fork and turning it
over until it changes colour. Add the tomato paste and one of the tomatoes, peeled
and chopped, the cinnamon, allspice and salt and pepper. Stir well and simmer
for about 10 minutes until the liquid is reduced.

Place the aubergines side by side in a single layer in an oven-proof dish. With
a sharp pointed knife, make a slit in each one, lengthways, along one of the bare
strips on the top until about 2.5cm from each end. Carefully open the slits and,
with a dessertspoon, press against the flesh on the insides to make a hollow pocket.

Fill each of the aubergines with some of the filling, and place a slice of the
remaining tomato on top. Pour the tomato juice into the dish, cover with foil, and
bake in an oven pre-heated to 180°C/350°F/Gas 4 for about 40 minutes or until the
aubergines are soft.

STUFFED QUINCES
Ayva Dolmasi

This is truly exquisite. Quinces are now available for quite a long period in Middle Eastern and Asian stores. In this recipe, the fruits are stuffed with a meat filling and served hot. Quinces are hard and take a long time to cook in the oven before you can cut them up and stuff them, but you can do this in advance – even the day before. I used very large quinces because those were the ones available at the time, but you can use 4 smaller ones, in which case the baking time will be less.

Serve hot with rice with chickpeas or rice pilaf (p.203).

SERVES 4

2 large quinces (each weighing about 500g)
1 medium onion, chopped
$1^1/2$ tablespoons vegetable oil
3 tablespoons pine nuts
200g lean minced lamb or beef
1 teaspoon ground cinnamon
$^1/2$ teaspoon ground allspice
salt and black pepper

Wash the quinces and rub off the light down that covers their skin in patches. Put them on a piece of foil on a baking sheet and bake in an oven pre-heated to 170°C/325°/Gas 3 for 1–2 hours (the time varies considerably) until they feel soft when you press them.

For the stuffing, fry the onion in the oil until soft. Add the pine nuts and stir, turning them over, until golden. Put the minced meat into a bowl and add the cinnamon, allspice, salt and pepper. Mix and work well to a smooth paste with your hand. Add the fried onions and pine nuts and work them into the paste.

When the quinces are cool enough to handle, cut them open lengthways through the stem end. Remove the cores with a pointed knife and discard them. With a pointed spoon, scoop out about one-third of the pulp and mix it into the meat mixture. Heap a quarter of this mixture into each quince half and press it down.

Return the 4 stuffed quince halves to the baking sheet and bake at 180°C/350°F/Gas 4 for 30 minutes.

LAMB STEW with AUBERGINE SAUCE
Hünkâr Beğendi

One legend surrounding the name of the sauce, hünkâr beğendi, which means 'Her Majesty's delight', places it in 1869 when the Sultan Abdul Aziz entertained Empress Eugénie (my Istanbul grandmother was named after her), wife of Napoleon III, in his white rococo palace of Beylerbey on the Asian side of the Bosphorous. The Empress was so enchanted by the pale creamy aubergine purée that she asked for the recipe to be given to her cooks. The Sultan's cook explained that he could not pass on the recipe because he 'cooked with his eyes and his nose'.

In Turkey, they use mature kaşar or Gruyère cheese in the sauce, but mature Cheddar can be used too. Serve it with rice pilaf (p.203).

SERVES 6

1 large onion, chopped

3 tablespoons sunflower oil

1kg boned leg or neck fillet of lamb

500g tomatoes, peeled and chopped

1 teaspoon sugar, or to taste

salt and black pepper

FOR THE AUBERGINE SAUCE

1.5kg aubergines

75g butter

3 tablespoons flour

500ml hot milk

salt

good pinch of ground nutmeg

50g grated cheese (see above)

For the stew, fry the onion in the oil until soft. Cut the meat into 3cm cubes, add it to the pan and cook, turning it to brown lightly all over. Add the tomatoes, sugar, salt and pepper. Cover with water and simmer, with the lid on, for 1 hour, until the meat is very tender, adding water if it becomes dry, but letting the sauce reduce at the end.

For the purée, prick the aubergines with a pointed knife to prevent them from bursting in the oven. Place them on a large piece of foil on a baking sheet and roast them in a hot oven pre-heated to 240°C/475°F/Gas 9 oven for about 45–55 minutes or until they feel very soft when you press them and the skins are wrinkled. When cool enough to handle, peel and drop them into a strainer or colander with small holes and press out as much of their juices as possible. Still in the colander, chop the flesh with a pointed knife, then mash it with a fork or wooden spoon, letting the juices escape through the holes.

Make a béchamel sauce: melt the butter in a saucepan, add the flour, and stir over low heat for about 2 minutes until it is well blended. Take the pan off the heat and add the milk gradually, beating vigorously all the time to avoid lumps forming. Add salt and nutmeg, and cook over a low heat, stirring constantly for about 15 minutes until the sauce thickens.

Off the heat, mix the aubergine purée into the béchamel sauce, then return to the heat, beating vigorously until it is well blended. Add the grated cheese and stir until it has melted. Add a little salt if necessary.

Serve the meat stew in a shallow dish with the aubergine sauce in a circle around it.

LAMB STEW with SHALLOTS and CHESTNUTS
Kestaneli Kuzu

This is a dish you can prepare well in advance. In Turkey, they may add a little grape molasses called pekmez which you can buy in Turkish stores but, for me, the dish is sweet enough as it is with the onions, chestnuts and sugar.

Serve it hot with plain rice or rice with chickpeas (p. 203).

SERVES 6–8
750g shallots or baby onions
1.5kg boned shoulder or neck fillet of lamb
4 tablespoons sunflower oil
salt and black pepper
1 teaspoon ground cinnamon
$^1/_2$ teaspoon ground allspice
1 teaspoon sugar
500g frozen or vacuum-packed chestnuts

To peel the shallots or baby onions more easily, blanch them in boiling water for 5 minutes. This loosens their skins. When they are cool enough to handle, peel them and trim the roots.

Cut the meat into 6–8 pieces. Remove any skin, and trim off some but not all of the fat.

In a large saucepan, fry the shallots or onions in the oil over a medium heat, turning them, until they are brown all over. Then lift them out and put in the meat. Turn the pieces to brown them on all sides.

Add water to barely cover the meat. Bring it to the boil, remove any scum, then add the cinnamon, allspice, sugar, salt and pepper. Simmer, covered, for about $1^1/2$ hours until the meat is very tender, turning it over and adding a little water so that it does not dry out. Put back the onions and cook for a further 15 minutes. Finally, add the chestnuts and cook for 10 minutes more.

LAMB SHANKS with EGG and LEMON SAUCE
Terbiyeli Kuzu Incik

This dish can be made with lamb shanks, knuckle of veal (osso buco) or with cubed meat such as shoulder of lamb. Butchers sell fresh lamb shanks from the foreleg weighing about 300g and frozen ones from New Zealand from the back leg weighing from 400–500g. Lamb shanks cooked for a long time have a wonderful tenderness and texture without being stringy, and they produce a rich stock. Although they take a long time to cook, they don't need any attention. This is the classic Turkish terbiyeli egg and lemon sauce.

SERVES 6

4 large or 6 small lamb shanks
3 garlic cloves, peeled
salt and black pepper
400g baby onions or shallots, peeled
3 large carrots, sliced
1 celeriac, peeled and cubed
3 medium new potatoes, quartered

2 tablespoons chopped flat-leaf parsley
2 tablespoons chopped dill
2 egg yolks
juice of 1 lemon
1 teaspoon sugar

Put the lamb shanks into a large pan and cover with water. Bring them to the boil, remove any scum, and add the garlic cloves, salt and pepper. Cook, with the lid on, over a very low heat for 2–2^1/$_2$ hours, adding water if necessary to keep the meat covered, until the meat is so tender it can be pulled off the bone. Lift out the shanks and when cold enough to handle, remove the meat from the bones and keep it aside in a bowl with a little stock to keep it moist. Ladle off as much fat as you can. If you are left with too much stock (you only need enough to cover the meat and vegetables), reduce it by boiling down.

Put the vegetables into the stock (to peel the shallots or baby onions more easily, place them into boiling water and poach for a few minutes to loosen their skins; then peel them while still warm) and cook for 20 minutes, until all the vegetables are very tender. Return the meat to the pan and stir in the parsley and dill.

Just before serving, beat the egg yolks with the lemon juice and sugar in a bowl. Pour in a ladle of boiling stock from the stew, beating vigorously. Return this mixture to the stew, stirring constantly, and heat through for a moment or two, without letting the liquid boil again or the eggs will curdle.

NOTE

It sometimes makes sense to start the dish a day ahead because of the time the shanks take to boil. In that case, let them simmer for the 2–2^1/$_2$ hours, then let them cool in their broth and refrigerate. Remove the solid fat which collects on the surface before heating through and continuing as above.

Desserts

A wide range of nutty syrupy pastries, milk puddings and fruit compotes are the most typical and essential part of Ottoman gastronomy. Traditionally served at every festive event, be it a wedding, the birth of a baby, a circumcision, or the inauguration of a new home, sweets are the first item of food that is decided upon when a celebration is planned. They symbolize the hope that a marriage will be happy, that a child will be healthy, that a family will prosper. They also signal that a guest is welcome. Some sweets are famously attached to particular religious festivals.

APRICOTS STUFFED with CREAM
Kaymakli Kayisi Tatlisi

Use large dried apricots for this famous Turkish sweet. You need to soak them in water overnight (even if you are using a semi-dried moist variety). The cream used in Turkey is the thick kaymak made from water buffalo's milk. The best alternatives in this country are clotted cream or mascarpone.

SERVES 4–6
250g large dried apricots, soaked in water overnight
300ml water
250g sugar
1 tablespoon lemon juice
250g clotted cream or mascarpone
3 tablespoons pistachios, chopped finely

Drain the apricots. Make a syrup by boiling the water with the sugar and lemon juice. Add the apricots and simmer for 20 minutes, or until the apricots are soft and the syrup is reduced and thick enough to coat the back of a spoon. Leave to cool.

Enlarge the slit along one side of each apricot and stuff with a little cream or mascarpone. Arrange the apricots on a dish and serve sprinkled with the chopped pistachios.

COMPOTE of FRESH APRICOTS
Kayisi Kompostosu

Compotes of dried or fresh fruits in syrup are popular desserts. At parties in Turkey, they are the last thing to be served, signalling that there is nothing more to follow. This sharp-tasting compote with fresh apricots is especially delicious. I add pistachios for their colour as well as for their taste and they should be peeled for this dish. To do this most easily, poach them in water for 1–2 minutes and drain; when they are cool enough to handle, pull off or squeeze away the skins.

SERVES 6 OR MORE
1kg apricots, washed and stones removed
500ml water

200g sugar
50g blanched almonds or pistachios
50g pine nuts
To serve with: 250g natural (full-fat) yoghurt or cream (optional)

Put the apricots into a wide pan with the water and the sugar. Bring to the boil and simmer for a few minutes until the apricots soften, turning them once if the water does not entirely cover them. Lift them out and put them on one side while you reduce the syrup by simmering it until it is thick enough to coat the back of a spoon. Return the apricots to the pan, add the almonds or pistachios and pine nuts and cook for 1–2 minutes more. Serve it cold, with yoghurt or cream, if you wish.

ORANGE PUDDING
Portakalli Tatlisi

This orange jelly with orange slices can also be made with the juice of freshly squeezed blood oranges or mandarins. Many supermarkets and stores now sell these juices freshly squeezed which makes it an easy pudding to prepare. It is set with cornflour and is not as firm as a jelly set with gelatine.

SERVES 8
1 litre orange or mandarin juice, freshly squeezed
125g sugar
70g cornflour
3 large oranges
seeds of 1 pomegranate
To serve with: 250g double cream, whipped

Bring the orange or mandarin juice to the boil with the sugar. Dissolve the cornflour in 250ml water and pour it into the simmering juice, stirring vigorously. Continue to stir – in one direction only – until the mixture thickens, then cook over a low heat for about 15 minutes.

Peel the oranges, taking care to remove all the white pith. Cut each orange into thick slices and each slice into 4 pieces. Remove the pips.

Let the orange or mandarin mixture cool and pour into a glass serving bowl. Stir in the pieces of orange, cover with cling film and chill in the refrigerator for a few hours.

Sprinkle the pomegranate seeds over the pudding and serve with whipped cream.

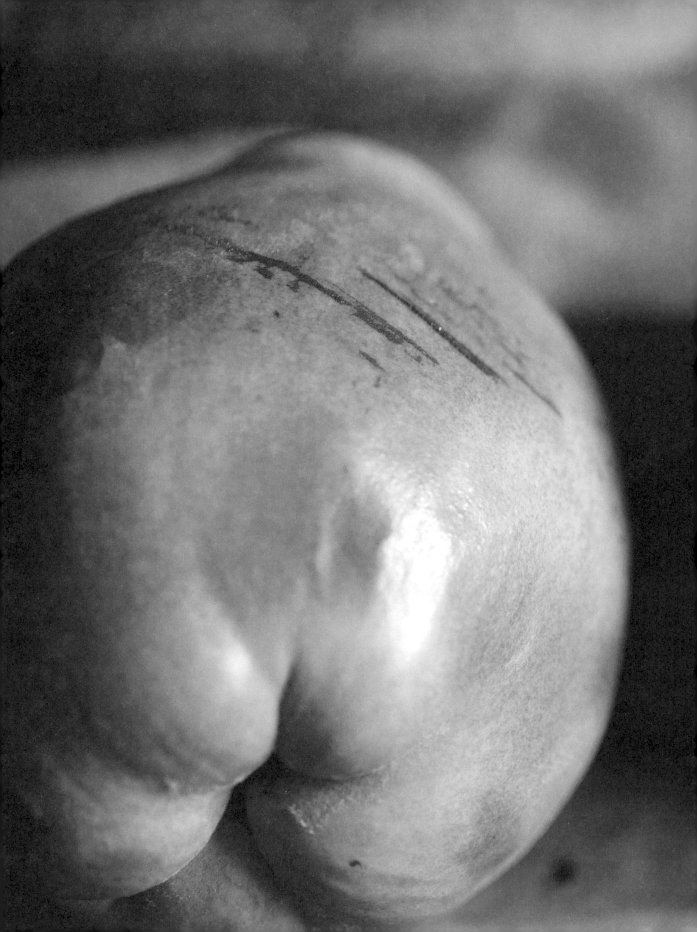

ROAST QUINCES
Ayva Tatlisi

I love these roast quinces even more than the famous quinces in syrup that I have written about in other books, because here the fruits keep their natural and unique taste and perfume. Quinces can be small like an apple, and they can be huge and weigh up to 500g each. You need about 250g per person so a large one is enough for two. Cooking times vary depending on their size and degree of ripeness. Quinces are now available for a much longer period in Middle Eastern stores.

Kaymak (p.226) is the cream served with it in Turkey, but clotted cream or mascarpone will do very well.

SERVES 6

3 or 6 quinces, weighing about 1.5kg
35g unsalted butter
6 tablespoons sugar
To serve with: 150g clotted cream or mascarpone

Wash the quinces, rubbing their skins to remove the light down that sometimes covers them in patches. Roast them whole, in an oven pre-heated to 190°C/375°F/Gas 5, until they feel soft. Depending on their size and ripeness, it can take from 1 hour up to 2 hours for the largest, so watch them carefully. (The three I cooked, weighing 1kg, took 1^1/2 hours.)

When they are cool enough to handle, cut them in half through the core, and cut away the blackened ends and the cores with a pointed knife. Place them, cut side up, on a baking sheet. Put a sliver of butter on top of each half and sprinkle each with 1 tablespoon sugar.

Put them back in the oven for ^{1}/2–1 hour until they are very soft and have turned a rich burgundy colour. If you like, put them under the grill for a few moments until the sugar just begins to caramelize. They fill the kitchen with a sweet smell.

Serve hot with clotted cream or mascarpone.

PUMPKIN DESSERT
Kabak Tatlisi

Pumpkin is frequently used in Turkey in sweet as well as savoury dishes. This is a 'cheese' with an unusual delicious flavour. It is best made the night before and keeps very well for days in the refrigerator. You need the large pumpkins with the sweet orange flesh. They are winter vegetables, but you can now buy them throughout the year in Asian and Middle Eastern stores, where they are sold by the slice, weighing between $^1/_2$kg and 1kg, the seeds and stringy fibres removed. Some British greengrocers also sell them by the slice.

In Turkey, this dessert is served with the very thick cream called kaymak (see p.226) but clotted cream or mascarpone will do very well. It is very rich so serve small portions.

SERVES 10

2kg pumpkin slices
400g sugar
150g walnuts, finely chopped
To serve with: 200g clotted cream or mascarpone

Prepare the pumpkin. Scrape away any remaining seeds or stringy bits. The rind is very thin and hard. It is more easily removed if you first cut the slices into chunks. Lay the chunks, skin side facing you, and cut it away, pressing down with force with a large heavy knife.

Cut the flesh into pieces of about 3–4cm. Put them into a wide saucepan with 250ml water, and cook, tightly covered so that they steam, over a low heat for about 20 minutes or until the flesh is very tender. Drain and mash the flesh with a potato masher. Continue to cook, now uncovered, until most of the liquid has evaporated.

Stir in the sugar and continue to cook until all the water is absorbed, stirring often and making sure that the purée doesn't burn.

Spread the paste on a serving plate, cover with cling film and leave in the refrigerator overnight. Serve cold, sprinkled all over with walnuts, and accompanied by the cream or mascarpone.

YOGHURT CAKE
Yoğurtlu Tatlisi

There are many versions of Turkish yoghurt cake. This one is like a light, airy, fresh-tasting cheesecake. If you wish, you can make a syrup which should be passed round in a jug for people to help themselves. I prefer the cake pure and simple, without the syrup.

SERVES 6

4 large eggs, separated
100g caster sugar
3 tablespoons plain flour
400g strained Greek Style yoghurt
grated zest of 1 lemon, unwaxed
juice of 1 lemon

FOR THE OPTIONAL SYRUP
150ml water
250g sugar
1 tablespoon lemon juice
grated zest of 1 orange, unwaxed

Beat the egg yolks with the sugar to a thick pale cream. Beat in the flour, then the yoghurt, lemon zest and lemon juice until it is thoroughly blended.

Whisk the egg whites until stiff and fold them into the yoghurt mixture. Pour this into a round non-stick, baking tin (about 23cm in diameter), greased with butter. Bake in an oven pre-heated to 180°C/350°/Gas 4 for 50–60 minutes, until the top is brown. It will puff up like a soufflé and then subside.

Turn out on to a serving plate, and serve warm or cold.

If you are making the syrup, boil the water with the sugar, the lemon juice and grated orange zest for 3–5 minutes. Let it cool, then chill in the refrigerator.

MILK and ALMOND PUDDING
Keşkül

Turkey has a very wide range of milk puddings. I once spent much of one night watching specialist milk pudding-makers at work, endlessly stirring creams in giant copper cauldrons. They said they had to work at night because that was when the milk arrived, which was why, they complained, they could not recruit young people to do the job. I don't think I blame them. This pudding, made with ground almonds, is my favourite.

SERVES 6

100g blanched almonds
1 litre full-fat milk
4 tablespoons ground rice
100g sugar
2–3 drops of almond essence
To garnish: 2 tablespoons finely chopped or pounded pistachios

Grind the almonds finely in a food processor. Bring the milk to the boil, preferably in a non-stick pan (which prevents the cream sticking and burning at the bottom), then take it off the heat.

In a small bowl, mix the ground rice to a paste with 4–5 tablespoons of water, making sure there are no lumps. Add this to the milk, stirring vigorously with a wooden spoon, and cook over a low heat, stirring constantly, and always in the same direction to avoid lumps forming, for about 15 minutes or until the mixture begins to thicken. (If lumps form, you can save the cream by beating it with an electric beater.)

Add the ground almonds and continue to cook over the lowest possible heat, stirring occasionally, for 20 minutes or until the consistency is that of a thin porridge. Then add the sugar and continue to cook, stirring, until it has dissolved. Always stir in the same direction. Do not scrape the bottom of the pan; this is in case it sticks and burns a little – you don't want to scrape up any burnt bits.

Stir in the almond essence, let the pudding cool, then pour it into a glass serving bowl or individual bowls. Serve chilled, sprinkled with the chopped pistachios.

NOTE

In Turkey, it is a traditional option to serve a heaped teaspoonful of *kaymak* (p.226) but here you can use clotted cream. Make a little slit in the skin of each portion, and slip through it a heaped teaspoon of clotted cream.

RICE PUDDING with ROSE WATER
Sütlaç

Egg yolks give this version of rice pudding a wonderful creamy texture. It has a delicate taste of rose water and gum mastic (p.10). You must pound and grind the tiny lumps with a teaspoon of sugar to a fine powder in a pestle and mortar (or use a spice grinder). Use very little as otherwise the taste can be quite unpleasant. A few drops of vanilla essence are an alternative flavouring if you cannot get gum mastic.

The pudding is addictive, homely comfort food. A brittle caramel topping turns it into a more glamorous option.

SERVES 6

150g short-grain or pudding rice
350ml water
1.2 litre full fat milk
150g sugar
1–1$^{1}/_{2}$ tablespoons rose water
$^{1}/_{4}$ teaspoon pulverized gum mastic or 3 drops vanilla essence
4 egg yolks
For the caramel topping: 4 tablespoons caster sugar (optional)

Put the rice in a large pan with the water. Bring it to the boil and simmer for 8 minutes, or until the water is absorbed. Add the milk and simmer on very low heat for 30–40 minutes, or until the rice is very soft but there is still quite a bit of liquid left. Stir occasionally with a wooden spoon to make sure that the rice does not stick to the bottom of the pan.

Put in the sugar and stir until it has dissolved. Add the rose water, turn off the heat and sprinkle on the gum mastic, stirring vigorously. If you are using vanilla essence, put it in at the same time as the sugar.

Beat the egg yolks in a small bowl then beat in a ladle of the simmering pudding. Return this mixture to the pan, stirring constantly for a few moments only, until the liquid thickens a little (it becomes creamy), but do not let it boil or the yolks will curdle. Pour the pudding into a serving dish – use a heatproof one if you are making the caramel topping – let it cool and then refrigerate.

If you are going to add the caramel topping, the pudding must be chilled before you add the sugar. Sprinkle the top with the 4 tablespoons sugar and put under a pre-heated grill. The sugar will bubble and gradually turn into dark caramel. If it is too near the grill, burnt spots will appear. If that happens, you can just lift them off when the caramel has cooled and hardened. Refrigerate before serving.

PISTACHIO CAKE

This moist, nutty cake soaked in syrup is a modern pastry. Make it at least 2 hours before you are ready to serve so that the syrup has time to soak in. You can buy unsalted shelled pistachios in Middle Eastern and Asian stores.

SERVES 10–12
5 eggs, separated
200g caster sugar
200g pistachios, ground finely
50g pistachios, chopped very coarsely
To serve with: 250g clotted cream (optional)

FOR THE SYRUP
300g sugar
180ml water
1 tablespoon lemon juice
2 tablespoons rose water

Make the syrup first. Bring the sugar, water and lemon juice to the boil and simmer until the sugar is dissolved, then stir in the rose water. Let the syrup cool, then chill it in the refrigerator.

Beat the egg yolks with the sugar to a pale cream, then add the ground pistachios and mix very well. Beat the egg whites until stiff and fold them in gently. Pour into a greased and floured non-stick cake tin 23–25cm in diameter and sprinkle the coarsely chopped pistachios on top. Bake in an oven pre-heated to 180°C/350°F/Gas 4 for about 45 minutes.

Turn the cake out into a deep serving dish. Make little holes over the top with a fork and pour over the syrup. The holes will let it soak in quickly.

Serve, if you like, with clotted cream.

TEL KADAYIF with CLOTTED CREAM and PISTACHIOS

For this luscious sweet, you need to buy the soft white vermicelli-like pastry called kadayif by the Turks and sold here by its Greek name kataifi in Turkish and Lebanese stores. In Egypt we called it konafa. I saw this version of the pastry being prepared in a large frying pan in a restaurant in Istanbul, but it is easier to bake it in the oven. It is scrumptious both hot and cold. I even like it days after, when the syrup has soaked and softened the pastry – it keeps well in the refrigerator. You can buy loose unsalted shelled pistachios in the same stores as kadayif.

In Turkey they use the cream called kaymak (see p.226) but clotted cream is a very good alternative.

SERVES 12
400g kataifi pastry
200g unsalted butter, melted
400g thick clotted cream
100g pistachios, chopped medium fine

FOR THE SYRUP
400g sugar
250ml water
1 tablespoon lemon juice
2 tablespoons orange blossom water (optional)

Make the syrup first. Bring to the boil the sugar, water and lemon juice and simmer for about 5 minutes, until it is thick enough to coat the back of a spoon, then add the orange blossom water (if using). Let the syrup cool, then chill it in the refrigerator.

Put the pastry into a large bowl. Pull out and separate the strands as much as possible with your fingers. Pour the melted butter over them and work it in very thoroughly with your fingers, pulling out and separating the strands and turning them over so that they do not stick together and are entirely coated with butter.

Spread the greased pastry all over the bottom of a large round pie pan measuring 27–30cm in diameter (or in two smaller pans). Press it down and flatten it with the palm of your hands. Bake it in an oven pre-heated to 180°C/350°F/Gas 4 for about 40–45 minutes, or until it is golden. Then place the pan on the hob over a medium heat and move it around for a moment or two so that the pastry browns slightly.

Run a sharp knife round the pan to loosen the sides of the pastry, and turn it out, bottom side up, on to a large serving dish. Pour the cold syrup all over the hot pastry. Spread the thick clotted cream all over the top and sprinkle generously with chopped pistachios.

Alternatively, you can pour over only half the syrup before serving and pass the rest around in a jug for everyone to help themselves to more.

Lebanon

When I was a child in Egypt, Beirut was the Paris of the Middle East, and the mountain resorts of Lebanon were our Switzerland. People went there to 'recuperate' – at least that was the reason members of my extended family gave – and they came back with fantastic stories of the unending assortments of mezze (appetizers, as in Turkey but with a different spelling) they were offered in the resort cafés. My family was from Àleppo in Syria, which was considered the pearl of the Arab kitchen, so praise from them was special. Today, Lebanese restaurants with their typical menus have come to represent Arab food everywhere around the world. So big is their reputation that when a Syrian restaurant opens in London, it calls itself 'Lebanese', and when hotels in Egypt put on a special Egyptian buffet, the dishes are Lebanese. How did that come about? One reason is that the Lebanese are famously bons viveurs who know how to make the best of their culinary heritage. They are also great entrepreneurs and they were the first in the Middle East to develop a restaurant trade. That trade spread to Europe and elsewhere when the civil war forced many to seek their fortunes abroad in the 1970s and '80s.

A Cuisine that Reflects the Past

The cooking of Lebanon has much in common with that of Turkey, and is also similar to that of Syria, Palestine and Jordan, countries that share with it a long history of constant change of foreign rule. These countries were all part of the Ottoman Empire until the early twentieth century when Lebanon was part of historic Syria. National borders here are recent – since the 1940s when the countries became independent nation states – but the culture Lebanon shares with her neighbours is very old and has absorbed a wide range of influences.

The Lebanese like to attribute their famous worldliness and entrepreneurial acumen to the Phoenicians who dominated the Mediterranean and colonized their coast around 2,500 BC, creating cities along the shore and opening trade routes across the sea. Egyptian, Persian, Greek and Roman civilizations have left their traces in the form of monuments and artefacts. In the fourth century, the area became part of the Byzantine Empire, and Hellenic culture and strict Christian religious orthodoxy were introduced. The influence of the Christian religion on the food today can be felt through a wide repertoire of meatless vegetarian and Lenten dishes.

A distinctive Levantine Muslim cuisine began to develop with the arrival of Islam and the establishment of the first great dynasty of the Muslim Empire, the Umayyads, in Damascus in 658. The Umayyads were overthrown after 100 years, and a new dynasty, the Abbassids, moved their capital to Baghdad where Persian cooking traditions dominated in the court kitchens. By the ninth century, historic Syria, including the part which is now Lebanon, was ruled by a succession of small Egyptian-based dynasties. In 1095 the Crusaders joined the Byzantine army in a thrust to liberate the Holy Land and established themselves on the Syrian and Lebanese coast. They were finally pushed out in the late thirteenth century. The Mameluks, originally slave soldiers who took over from their masters based in Egypt, ruled Syria and Egypt for 300 years until the Ottoman Turks seized the area in the sixteenth century.

Each occupation left a legacy in architecture – there are palaces, mosques, *khans* (*caravanserais*) and *hamams* (baths) – and each also brought something to the kitchen. A few of the dishes in this book, such as the meat cooked in vinegar with onions and aubergines, could have come out of a thirteenth-century Baghdad culinary manuscript. Falafel and broad bean salad came through the early association with Egypt. The Ottoman Turks kept control of the region by co-opting local feudal lords (emirs) as governors, but their influence was powerful, and in the kitchen it was also lasting. After the collapse of the Ottoman Empire, the League of Nations awarded France the mandate for Syria and Mount Lebanon in 1920, and in 1946 Lebanon became an independent state. European missionary schools in the mountains and the American University in Beirut had already, by the late nineteenth century, opened Lebanon up to Western cultural influences; the French added a certain style and elegance to the table.

Extraordinary Culinary Diversity in a Tiny Country

The standard Lebanese restaurant menu is set in stone with items that never change, but at home in the cities and villages there is extraordinary culinary diversity. You might wonder how in a tiny country less than half the size of Wales, the cooking could be so varied, but when you visit Lebanon it becomes clear. It is a land of high mountains and a long narrow sea coast with three different climate zones. Roads into the previously inaccessible interior are as recent as the 1960s, and access is still difficult, so villages nestling in the mountains and valleys have remained isolated from one another, retaining the individuality of their cooking which is based on local produce. Communities have been further separated in this Muslim-Christian country by their division into many religious and sectarian groups, most of them living in their own villages or in separate quarters in the cities. There are Shiite, Sunni and Druze Muslims. The Maronites are the largest Christian group – theirs is a Roman Catholic Church of Eastern origin. It is followed by Greek Orthodox, Greek Catholic, Syrian Catholic, Chaldean Catholic, Protestant and Armenian Churches.

I am nevertheless forever surprised and fascinated when I discover a new dish or variation of a dish. When I was invited by my friends Mai Ghoussoub and her husband Hazim Saghie to watch Hazim's mother cook for a party when she came to stay with them in London, every dish she made was new to me, and each one was delicious. Khalida Saghie comes from the village of Beino, in the region of Akkar, which is close to the Syrian border; originally all the people in the village were Greek Orthodox but now they have been joined by a few Maronite and Muslim families. Khalida had arrived with her home-made pomegranate syrup, her fermented cheese, and her freshly milled, fine-ground bulgur (called burghul in Lebanon). She went to work and never stopped until all the guests had arrived and then she quickly went to change into beautiful silks.

Hazim, a columnist for *Al Hayat*, the Arabic daily newspaper, gave me a little background to the food in Lebanon. The country is extremely fertile – together with Syria, Palestine, Jordan and Iraq, it is known as 'The Fertile Crescent' – and most of the population used to live off the land. It is a peculiarity of Lebanon that it is the only place in the Middle East where a classic type of feudalism exists. Elsewhere, it is a case of absentee landlords, but in Lebanon, from the Middle Ages onwards, the land was divided into fiefs, and the feudal lords lived among their peasants.

Families like the Maan and the Chehabs established feudal principalities and built themselves palaces in the mountains. This has meant that the countryside was sustainable and that a rich rural culinary tradition developed in the mountain villages. They grew wheat in the valleys, and olive trees, vines, mulberry trees for silk worms, and fruit trees on terraces. Some of the villages, such as Zahlé, Beit Chehab and Mashgara grew into towns and cities.

Beginning in the late nineteenth century, when Beirut became a mini cosmopolitan city and a commercial and intellectual centre, there was a Christian migration from the mountains to Beirut and the coastal cities where the inhabitants were mainly Sunni Muslims and Greek Orthodox. (Christians, like other minorities, had moved high up into the mountains to ensure their survival and independence.) It is through the meeting of the Ottoman cooking of the main cities along the coast and the cooking of the mountains, between the urban rice culture and the rural burghul (bulgur) culture, that the classic Lebanese cuisine of today took shape.

An all-important part of rural tradition is the preservation of food. The provisions made in the summer to last over the winter form the basis of Lebanese cooking and provide its distinctive flavours. These traditions, called the *mune*, were originally a means of survival in a country whose seasons alternated dramatically with short periods of great abundance and long ones of scarcity. Figs, apricots and tomatoes were laid out on trays in the fields to dry in the sun. Grains, pulses and nuts were dried on roof tops. Meats were slowly cooked and preserved in their fat. The juice of sour pomegranates was boiled down to syrupy molasses; tomatoes were reduced to paste. Yoghurt was drained to make a soft cheese which was rolled into balls and preserved in olive oil. Butter was clarified to last. Fruit and vegetables were made into jams and pickles. Olives were preserved in salt or crushed for their oil. Distilled rose and orange blossom waters were produced by boiling petals in alembics. Nowadays, all these things are made commercially and in the cities they are considered delicacies, but there are still those who make them at home, and peasants in their rural hinterland still live off their produce. Every country dwelling once had a special store-room for the *mune* (many still do) and the woman of the house held the key to the supplies she had laboured to produce, usually with the help of neighbours. During the last long civil war when routes were barred and people were afraid to travel, the *mune* became important again.

The Lebanese are famously great emigrants and emigration abroad, mainly to Africa and the Americas, was a Christian phenomenon that began in the late nineteenth century. It is said that there are more Lebanese living abroad than in Lebanon – but

many of them return home. When families returned, they brought with them the quality of life to which they had grown accustomed. They built beautiful houses (you can see big cars outside) and began to spend money on eating well. They were no longer cooking like the local 'peasants' with clarified butter and sheep's tail fat, but took to lighter cooking with fresh butter and oil. They saw themselves as neither mountain nor coastal people, but in the middle, and having a touch of worldliness.

Social and economic contrasts have also contributed, along with the country's geography, to culinary diversity and are a reason why you can find many versions of every dish. Prosperity is concentrated in Beirut and on the coast. Apart from the mountain 'aristocracies' and the rich villages of returnees from Africa, Latin America and elsewhere, the hinterland is in the main poor and has traditionally subsisted on agriculture.

The Mezze Tradition

One important factor in the development of a sophisticated Lebanese cuisine was that drinking was not banned in this pluralistic country. The Church owned vineyards, and monasteries produced wine. The role of wine and especially *arak*, a powerful distilled spirit made from sweet white grapes flavoured with aniseed, was crucial in refining Lebanese food.

The drinking of *arak* (it is *raki* in Turkey and *ouzo* in Greece) is behind the whole philosophy and practice of the *mezze* tradition. The *mezze*, a national institution, represents an art of living where socialising is all-important. The tradition developed as a way of soaking up the national drink, affectionately called 'lion's milk' because it turns cloudy when water is added. It is mixed with cold water (one part *arak* to two of water, but this can vary) and served with a large piece of ice.

According to legend, the special character of the Lebanese *mezze* was born in the Bekaa Valley where *arak* is produced and where the Lebanese vineyards such as Kefraya and Ksara are situated. The Bekaa Valley is a high valley, cradled between two parallel high mountain ranges, the Mount Lebanon and the Anti-Lebanon. Renowned for its fresh air, its natural springs and the river Bardaouni which cascades down the mountain, it is a major agricultural region. It is also the stopping place for travellers on their way from Damascus in Syria.

Zahlé, the resort where Lebanon's favourite riverside restaurants are situated, acquired a mythical reputation for gastronomy. In 1920, the first two cafés opened by the river. They gave away assorted nuts, seeds, olives, bits of cheese and raw vegetables with the local *arak*. Gradually, the entire valley became filled with open-air cafés, each larger and more luxurious than the next, each vying to attract customers who flocked from all over the Middle East with ever more varied *mezze*. The reputation of the local mountain village foods they offered spread far and wide, both at home and abroad. It is on these *mezze* that the ubiquitous menu of Lebanese restaurants around the world is based. While in the countryside, hands cross amicably over the table to pick at the foods even when individual plates are offered; in the cities you are given plates to help yourself and you only select foods from your corner of the table. That, Hazim says, is a less sociable way, not quite in the original spirit of the *mezze*.

Whereas restaurant food is based on *mezze* and grilled meats, family meals in the home revolve around a main dish, usually a meat and vegetable stew or stuffed vegetables such as courgettes, served with burghul or rice and sometimes also yoghurt. It is accompanied by radishes, little cucumbers, spring onions, and pickled turnips or by a salad, and followed by fruit, and it ends with Turkish coffee. Desserts and pastries are not always served at the end of the meal but to visitors who may turn up during the afternoon.

Hospitality and convivial socializing are an all-important part of Lebanese life. I am used to high Middle Eastern standards of hospitality, but I have never experienced anything like the gracious, warm and joyful way in which I was entertained in Lebanon. Everybody is always out and about, meeting friends and enjoying themselves. I wondered how they could ever get any work done in this famously entrepreneurial part of the Middle East. People entertain constantly and *mezze* are the favourite way of entertaining. If you visit a home unexpectedly, you are invariably asked to stay for a drink, and a colourful assortment of *mezze* appears as if by magic. A modest assortment may comprise such items as roasted pumpkin seeds or chickpeas, pistachios, olives, pickled turnips and pickled cucumbers, tomatoes, baby Cos lettuce hearts, radishes, spring onions, *labneh* (yoghurt cheese), feta and haloumi cheese.

Extended family reunions always turn into gargantuan feasts that begin with mezze. There will be *kibbeh* (see p.323), small savoury pies, little meat pizzas, a variety of stuffed vegetables, tiny omelettes, grilled quails, *bottarga*, and a variety of dips and salads. They will be served with Arab flat breads or pieces of the very thin large Lebanese *markouk* (see p.253), used for picking up morsels of food. The *mezze* is followed by main dishes and pastries.

It was during the 1960s, between the civil war of 1958 and that of 1975, during the seventeen years of relative calm, when roads were built and communications became easy, that a unified Lebanese cuisine came into its own and the restaurant trade flourished. Unlike some other Middle Eastern countries at that time, such as Syria and Egypt, Lebanon did not have a socialist or military regime. It encouraged private enterprise and attracted money and investment, creating a prosperity unprecedented in that part of the Middle East. The opportunities also created the broadest middle class in the region that could patronize a restaurant trade. Many restaurants were opened during this time, and when the last civil war broke out, many restaurateurs left and opened establishments abroad. That is when Lebanese restaurants mushroomed in Britain and elsewhere.

The Important Role of Vegetables

Vegetables and pulses are extremely popular in Lebanon and appear in both everyday and celebratory dishes – mezze, pickles, salads, main and side dishes. The Arabs introduced the cultivation of certain vegetables such as spinach and aubergines to the country at an early point, while the crops from the New World of the Americas arrived late in the Arab world – some as late as the nineteenth century. The tomato, for instance, was introduced in Syria in 1851 when it was labelled 'franji', which means French, as everything that came from Europe was then called.

Vegetables are always considered important anywhere where much of the population is composed of peasants who can rarely afford meat, but in Lebanon they have a particularly vital role. Many vegetarian dishes are associated with the Christian communities because of the fasts prescribed by the Eastern Orthodox, Catholic and Armenian Churches. Until a few decades ago, Christians from these Churches felt compelled to abide by the strict rules that obliged them to either partial abstinence, when meat could be taken only once a day at the principal meal, or complete abstinence from meat. All foods derived from animals, including sometimes eggs and dairy products, were prohibited for forty days before Christmas, fifteen days before the Assumption of the Virgin Mary, during Lent, which begins seven weeks before Easter, as well as on every Wednesday and Friday in the year. Nowadays, although restrictions have generally been dropped, many of the traditional meatless dishes of grain, vegetables and pulses have been adopted by the general population in the cities where they represent the trendy healthy diet that city people now aspire to.

On a recent visit to Lebanon I spent much time in the kitchen with someone who is a genius with vegetables. Kamal Mouzawak, a food writer and TV chef, teaches vegetarian and gourmet healthy eating. He is the Lebanese co-ordinator of the Slow Food movement and has started a farmers' market in Beirut. He lives with his fashion designer partner, Rabih Kayrouz. They are celebrated for their dinner parties (Rabih is in charge of the dramatic décor) that they hold in their fabulous old-style apartment and on their roof garden. On one occasion, I helped with the cooking when they were entertaining sixty people. Kamal also took me to meet his mother, Fariba, at her village. Several of the dishes in this book are inspired by him and by his mother.

I was a guest on the Lebanese TV programme presented by Kamal and Mariam Nour which is popular all over the Arab world. Mariam is famously dedicated to spreading her ideas on the healing power of vegetarian and macrobiotic foods which she intermingles with ideas about spirituality, philosophy, the art of living, self-knowledge, identity, meditation and similar therapies. We were joined by two women who brought baskets full of produce such as lentils still on the plant, and wild endive and herbs from their peasants' co-operative in the south of the country. They made for us a salad of burghul and tomato paste and a porridge of wheat and yoghurt.

About Bread

Bread is used for picking up morsels of food, for dipping into purées or soaking up a sauce. People also roll up pieces into small cornets and fill them with food. A common Lebanese bread is like a very thin round pitta, called *khobz halabi* (Àleppo bread) which comes in varying sizes. Another more typical bread, called *markouk*, is made on a curved metal *saj* and is like a very large, very thin giant pancake. There is also a sesame bread called *ka'ak bil semsum* which is sold in the street and looks like a handbag with a ring handle. It is eaten with za'tar, a mix of dried thyme, sumac, sesame seeds and salt.

About Beverages

Beverages are much like those in Turkey – the cool yoghurt drink *ayran*, the heartwarming thick, milky drink *sahlab* (*salep* in Turkey – see p.157), Turkish coffee, mint tea and cinnamon tea, infusions such as *karkade* (made with hibiscus), syrups such as apricot, date, tamarind and liquorice. A typically Lebanese after-dinner drink that is offered as an alternative to Turkish coffee is 'white' coffee, which is boiling water with a drop of orange blossom water. You should try it.

Starters and Mezze

The tradition of the *mezze* – the little appetizers and hors d'œuvre served with drinks – goes right across the Mediterranean, but Lebanon beats every country by the sheer quantity and variety that is offered in restaurants, with some serving as many as forty and even fifty different ones. At home, some of these little dishes appear on the Sunday lunch tables when extended families get together (everybody goes to visit their parents in the mountain villages on Sunday) and no buffet table could be without a familiar selection.

I went to Zahlé, the 'world capital' of the Arab *mezze* (see p.249). My father and many of my cousins in Egypt had been regular visitors to the mountain resort and their descriptions were the basis of an idyllic rural image I had formed in my imagination. It is now the main city of the Bekaa Valley, full of concrete housing and, in season, a tourist trap of the Arab world. But the rows of open-air restaurants along the river are still immensely appealing with their *mezze* menus rooted in the local rural traditions.

Mezze are the best part of a Lebanese meal. Picking at a variety of delicious foods with different flavours and textures is a wonderful way to eat. But the convivial aspect of the tradition is equally important. The highlight of a recent stay in Lebanon was a wedding party near the ancient city of Baalbek in the Bekaa Valley. Nadim Khattar, an architect based in London, and Andrea Kowalski, a Venezuelan working at the BBC, had organized a sumptuous feast for their guests who came from all over the world; it was held in a field in the middle of the countryside. The lunch went on for hours as little dish upon little dish arrived at the long tables, one more exquisite than the other, each jostling for space, while baby lambs roasted on fires and musicians played. It was pure joy – better than the scenes imagined in my childhood. The wedding party went on for two days. The spirit of fun and conviviality attached to the lingering over *mezze* is something everyone should try to emulate.

Start a dinner party with a carefully chosen variety of *mezze* (it could be just two or three). Serve them with warm bread – the thin round Lebanese pitta-like bread called *khobz halabi* or the very thin sheets called *markouk* (see p.253) or with pitta bread – and put olives and raw vegetables, radishes, tomatoes, cucumbers, spring onions, on the table.

All the dishes in this chapter, except the soups, can be served as part of a *mezze* selection. Some make good finger-food and, with the dips, can be served with drinks at a party. Some can make a wonderful first course or even a light snack on their own.

CHEESE and YOGHURT DIP
Jibne Wa Labneh

This dip is quick to make. Serve it with crisp toasted flat bread and, if you like, black olives, cucumbers cut into little sticks, plum tomatoes cut in wedges, and spring onions. You can now find labneh, the very thick Lebanese strained yoghurt, in Middle Eastern stores.

SERVES 6–8

250g feta cheese
250g thick Lebanese or strained Greek Style yoghurt
4 tablespoons extra virgin olive oil

Crush the feta cheese with a fork, then add the yoghurt and mash together. Spread the dip in a shallow serving dish and dribble over the olive oil.

AUBERGINE and TAHINI DIP
Baba Ghanouj

This version of the famous dip – an unusual one with added yoghurt – is particularly delicious and creamy. Serve with pitta or Lebanese bread.

SERVES 6–8

2 aubergines (weighing about 650g)
3 tablespoons tahini
juice of 2 lemons
125–200g strained Greek Style yoghurt
2 garlic cloves, crushed, or to taste
salt
2 tablespoons extra virgin olive oil
2 tablespoons chopped flat-leaf parsley

Prick the aubergines in a few places with a pointed knife to prevent them from exploding. Turn them over the flame of the gas hob or a hot barbecue, or under the grill, until the skin is charred all over (this gives them a distinctive smoky flavour) and they feel very soft when you press them. Alternatively, place them on a sheet

of foil on an oven tray and roast them in the hottest oven (pre-heated to
240°C/475°F/Gas 9) for 45–60 minutes until the skins are wrinkled and they
are very soft.

When cool enough to handle, peel and drop them into a strainer or colander
with small holes. Press out as much of their juices as possible. Still in the colander,
chop the flesh with a pointed knife, then mash it with a fork or wooden spoon,
letting the juices escape through the holes. Adding a tiny squeeze of lemon juice
helps to keep the purée looking pale and appetizing.

In a bowl, beat the tahini with the lemon juice (the tahini stiffens at first then
softens), then beat in the yoghurt. Add the mashed aubergines, garlic and some
salt. Beat vigorously and taste to adjust the flavouring.

Spread the purée on to a flat serving dish and garnish with a dribble of olive
oil and a sprinkling of parsley.

VARIATION
My friend Kamal, whom I watched in his kitchen in Beirut, adds the juice
of a bitter orange. In this case, omit the yoghurt.

HUMMUS
CHICKPEA and TAHINI DIP
Hummus Bi Tehine

Hummus is very popular in Britain now. It is the kind of thing you make to taste, adding a little more lemon, garlic, salt or tahini as you go along. Serve it with warmed pitta bread.

SERVES 6

250g chickpeas, soaked in water overnight
3–4 tablespoons tahini
juice of 2 lemons
3 cloves garlic, crushed
salt
4 tablespoons extra virgin olive oil

Drain the soaked chickpeas and put them into a pan with plenty of fresh water. Bring to the boil, remove the scum and simmer for $1^1/2$ hours, until they are very soft. Drain, reserving the cooking water.

Blend the chickpeas to a purée in a food processor. Add the remaining ingredients, except the oil, and a little of the cooking water, just enough to blend to a soft creamy paste. Taste and adjust the seasoning.

Pour the hummus into a shallow dish and dribble over the oil.

OPTIONAL GARNISHES

Sprinkle on plenty of finely chopped parsley; or make a star design with lines of paprika and ground cumin; or sprinkle with sumac (p.11) and a little chopped flat-leaf parsley; or garnish with a few whole boiled chickpeas, or with pine nuts lightly fried in butter.

VARIATIONS

For a hot version, pour the hummus into a shallow baking dish and bake for 15–20 minutes in an oven pre-heated to 200°C/400°F/Gas 6. Lightly fry 100g pine nuts in 4 tablespoons of butter or extra virgin olive oil and sprinkle them, with the melted butter or oil, over the dish.

Balila is a warm chickpea salad. Boil the soaked and drained chickpeas in plenty of water for $1^1/2$ hours. Turn them out into a serving bowl with just a little of their reduced cooking water and crush them only slightly with a fork. Stir in, to taste, plenty of extra virgin olive oil, a generous amount of crushed garlic, a pinch of chilli pepper (optional) and some finely chopped mint.

TABBOULEH

There is a mystique around the preparation of this famous salad. I watched my friend Kamal make it in Beirut, and his main tip was that you must slice, not chop, the parsley, so that it does not get crushed and mushy. Use the fine-ground bulgur which is available in Middle Eastern stores. These stores and Asian ones also sell parsley in tied bunches that weigh between 200 and 300g with stems. Mix and dress the salad only when you are ready to serve.

SERVES 6

large bunch of flat-leaf parsley (about 250g)
bunch of mint (about 50g)
75g fine-ground bulgur
juice of 2 lemons
400g firm ripe tomatoes, diced finely
6 spring onions, sliced thinly
5 tablespoons extra virgin olive oil
salt and black pepper
1 Cos or 2 Little Gem lettuces

Keeping the parsley in its bunch, wash it by plunging the leaves in a bowl of water. Shake the water out and leave it to dry on a cloth. Holding the bunch tightly with one hand on a chopping board, slice the leaves with a very sharp knife as finely as you possibly can. Wash and slice the mint leaves in the same way and add them to the parsley.

Rinse the bulgur very briefly in a strainer under the cold tap then press out the excess water. About 20 minutes before you are ready to serve, mix the bulgur with the lemon juice and chopped tomatoes so that it softens in their juices.

Just before serving, mix all the ingredients gently together. The traditional way of eating tabbouleh is to scoop it up with Cos lettuce leaves cut in half or the leaves of Little Gem lettuces. Serve the leaves separately or stick them in the bowl around the salad.

الربيع
AL-RABIH
الرمّان
Mélasse de gren
Pure pomegran
0181-4520707
BEST
10 FL. OZ

WALNUT and POMEGRANATE SALAD
Muhammara

This is a version of a surprising paste that you also find in Turkey. Pomegranate molasses give it an intriguing sweet-and-sour flavour (p.10). Some like it peppery hot with chilli flakes or purée (see variation below); personally I like it with only a touch of ground chilli pepper.

SERVES 6

100g shelled walnuts
50g brown bread, crusts off
1 tablespoon pomegranate molasses
$^1/_4$–$^1/_2$ teaspoon ground cumin
pinch of ground chilli pepper
salt
4 tablespoons extra virgin olive oil
40g pine nuts (optional)

Grind the walnuts in a food processor. Soak the bread in water, squeeze it dry, and put it into the food processor with the walnuts. Add the pomegranate molasses, cumin, chilli pepper, a little salt, the olive oil and 3 tablespoons of water, and blend to a soft paste. If it is too stiff, add another tablespoon or so of water.

Serve spread on a flat plate, sprinkled, if you like, with the pine nuts fried in a drop of oil until they only just begin to colour.

VARIATIONS

If you want it hot, add 1 teaspoon or more of *harissa*, the North African chilli purée that you can buy in jars or tubes in Middle Eastern and North African stores. A few stores sell an 'artisan' brand that is particularly good.

Another version of *muhammara* is a 50/50 blend of walnuts and pine nuts.

BULGUR and CHICKPEA SALAD
Safsouf

This rustic salad from the Bekaa Valley does not feature on the standard restaurant menu. It began originally as the leftover meatless filling for vine leaves. Make it with fine-ground bulgur.

SERVES 6

200g fine-ground bulgur
2 garlic cloves, crushed
juice of 2^{1}/$_{2}$–3 lemons
salt and black pepper
7 tablespoons extra virgin olive oil
1 x 400g tin of chickpeas
large bunch of flat-leaf parsley (about 250g), chopped
large bunch of mint (about 90g), chopped

Soak the bulgur in plenty of cold water for 20 minutes until tender, then drain and squeeze out the excess water. In a bowl, mix the garlic, lemon juice, salt, pepper and oil. Soak the drained chickpeas in this for 10 minutes, then stir in the bulgur.
   Chop the herbs finely and mix them in when you are ready to serve.

MINT and PARSLEY SALAD
with RICE
Tabbouleh Bi Roz

This is a very green and appealing herby salad, also born as the leftover filling of vegetables cooked in oil. It is meant to be very sharp, but start with one lemon and add more, if you wish, after tasting.

SERVES 4

100g basmati rice
large bunch of flat-leaf parsley (about 150g), chopped
5 sprigs of mint, chopped
7 spring onions, sliced thinly
juice of 1–1$^{1}/_{2}$ lemons
5 tablespoons extra virgin olive oil
black pepper
5 ripe and firm tomatoes, diced finely
salt
1 Little Gem lettuce (optional)

Cook the rice in plenty of boiling salted water for about 10–20 minutes. (Some brands that claim not to be parboiled or pre-cooked now take as little as 8–10 minutes, so read the information on the packet and watch the rice carefully so it does not overcook.) When it is just tender, drain quickly. Set on one side to cool.

Just before serving, mix the rice with the parsley, mint and spring onions. Dress with a mixture of lemon juice, oil, salt and pepper, and mix well. Serve on a flat plate, topped with the diced tomato lightly seasoned with salt.

Garnish, if you like, with a ring of lettuce leaves stuck around the edges of the salad.

BREAD SALAD with SUMAC
Fattoush

This bread salad is the favourite everyday Lebanese salad. Sumac (p.11) gives it a distinctive sharp flavour. The old traditional way was to moisten the toasted bread with water and a little lemon juice before soaking it further with the dressing, which made it deliciously soft and soggy. Nowadays, the toasted bread is broken into pieces and added to the salad at the end while it is crisp. You can buy purslane and small cucumbers (they have a better flavour than our large ones) in Middle Eastern stores.

SERVES 6–8

1^1/$_2$ pitta breads
1 Cos lettuce, cut into 1.5 cm ribbons
about 100g purslane leaves or lamb's lettuce
4 firm ripe tomatoes, cut into medium pieces
4 small cucumbers, peeled and cut into thick slices
1 green pepper, seeded and cut into small slices
1^1/$_2$ mild onions or 8 spring onions, chopped
large handful of chopped flat-leaf parsley
4–5 sprigs of mint, shredded
100ml extra virgin olive oil
juice of 1 lemon
salt and black pepper
1 tablespoon sumac

Cut around the pitta and open them out. Toast them under the grill or in the oven until they are crisp; turn them over once. Break them into small pieces in your hands.

Put all the vegetables and herbs into a large bowl. For the dressing, mix the oil with the lemon juice, salt, pepper and sumac.

Just before serving, sprinkle the toasted pitta over the salad, then toss the salad well with the dressing.

AUBERGINE and TOMATO SALAD
Batinjan Raheb

This salad is delicious and beautiful to look at.

SERVES 6–8

2–3 aubergines (weighing about 1kg)
juice of $1/2$–1 lemon
3 garlic cloves, crushed
4 tablespoons extra virgin olive oil
salt and black pepper
large handful of chopped flat-leaf parsley
4 sprigs of mint, chopped
4 spring onions, sliced thinly
4 plum tomatoes (unpeeled), diced
handful of fresh pomegranate seeds (optional)

Prick the aubergines in a few places with a pointed knife to prevent them from exploding. Turn them over the flame of the gas hob or a hot barbecue, or under the grill, until the skin is charred all over (this gives them a distinctive smoky flavour) and they feel very soft when you press them. Alternatively, place them on a sheet of foil on an oven tray and roast them in the hottest oven (pre-heated to 240°C/475°F/Gas 9) for 45–60 minutes until the skins are wrinkled and they are very soft.

When cool enough to handle, peel and drop them into a strainer or colander with small holes. Press out as much of their juices as possible. Still in the colander, chop the flesh with a pointed knife, then mash it with a fork or wooden spoon, letting the juices escape through the holes.

Mix the aubergine purée with the lemon juice, garlic, olive oil, salt, pepper, parsley and mint. Spread the purée on a large flat serving plate. Sprinkle all over with the spring onions, tomatoes and (if using) the pomegranate seeds.

AUBERGINE SLICES with POMEGRANATE, YOGHURT and TAHINI
Batinjan Bil Rumman Wal Laban

The dressing of pomegranate molasses and vinegar gives the aubergine slices a sweet-and-sour flavour. Serve them hot or cold, with the yoghurt topping at room temperature.

SERVES 6

4 aubergines (1.2kg)
extra virgin olive oil
salt
1¹/₂ tablespoons pomegranate molasses (p.10)
1¹/₂ tablespoons red or white wine vinegar
500g natural (full-fat) yoghurt
1 garlic clove, crushed
2 tablespoons tahini
50g pine nuts

Cut the aubergines into slices (lengthways or across) about 1.25cm thick. Place them on an oiled sheet of foil on a baking sheet or tray. Brush both sides of the aubergine slices with oil and sprinkle lightly with salt. Place in a very hot oven pre-heated to 240°C/475°F/Gas 9 for about 30 minutes, until they are soft and browned, turning the slices over once. Arrange on a shallow serving dish.

Mix the pomegranate molasses, vinegar and 2 tablespoons of oil, and brush the aubergine slices with this dressing. Beat the yoghurt with the garlic and tahini and spread over the slices. Fry the pine nuts very briefly in ¹/₂ tablespoon of oil, stirring to brown them very lightly all over, and sprinkle over the yoghurt.

VARIATION
Instead of the pine nuts, garnish with the shiny pink seeds of a fresh pomegranate.

CURLY ENDIVE with CARAMELIZED ONIONS
Hinbeh

Wild chicory is used for this Lebanese mountain salad. The sweetness of the caramelized onion topping is a contrast to the slightly bitter leaves. You can sometimes find bunches of wild chicory, which has long, dark green leaves, in Middle Eastern stores, but ordinary curly endive — what the French call chicorée — will do very well. The salad can also be made with dandelion leaves.

SERVES 4–6

about 1kg curly endive
2 large onions, sliced
6 tablespoons extra virgin olive oil
4–6 garlic cloves, crushed
salt and black pepper
2 lemons

Trim the stem ends of the endive and remove any discoloured bits, then wash the leaves. Boil in salted water for a couple of minutes or until it is soft, then drain and press out the excess water. Cut up the leaves into pieces 4–6cm long.

Fry the onions in the oil in a large pan over a medium heat until brown and caramelized, stirring often. Remove about three-quarters of the onions to use as the topping, draining them on kitchen paper. Add the garlic to the onions remaining in the pan and as soon as the aroma rises put in the endive. Add salt and pepper and the juice of $1/2$ lemon, and cook, stirring, for a minute or so.

Serve cold on a flat serving dish with the caramelized onions sprinkled all over the top, accompanied by the remaining lemon cut into quarters.

VARIATION

To the onions remaining in the pan, add 1 x 400g tin of chickpeas or haricot beans, well drained, at the same time as the endive.

AUBERGINES with TOMATOES and CHICKPEAS
Mussaka'A Menazzaleh

This dish can be served cold as a salad or hot as a side dish to accompany meat or chicken. It has a delicate sweet-and-sour flavour.

SERVES 6

2 aubergines
extra virgin olive oil
salt
2–3 garlic cloves, crushed
500g tomatoes, peeled and chopped
2 teaspoons sugar
black pepper
$1^1/_2$ tablespoons pomegranate molasses (p.10)
1 x 400g tin of chickpeas, drained
2 tablespoons chopped flat-leaf parsley

Cut the aubergines in half lengthways, then into 1.25cm slices. Brush them generously with oil, sprinkle lightly with salt, and cook them under the grill for 15 minutes, or on an oiled griddle, turning them over once. They do not need to be cooked through as they will be stewed further in the sauce.

In a large saucepan, heat the garlic in 1 tablespoon of oil for seconds only, stirring, until it just begins to colour. Add the tomatoes and squash them gently in the pan. Add, sugar, salt and pepper and cook for 15 minutes. Add the pomegranate molasses, put in the aubergines and simmer for 20–30 minutes or until the aubergines are very soft. Add the chickpeas towards the end.

Serve sprinkled with chopped parsley.

ROAST POTATOES with LEMON and CORIANDER
Batata Bel Lamoun Wal Cosbara

These potatoes are normally deep-fried or sautéed in olive oil but they are equally good roasted. They are served cold, although I admit I like them hot, too.

SERVES 6

1kg new potatoes, peeled or not
salt and black pepper
5–6 tablespoons extra virgin olive oil
4 garlic cloves, crushed
juice of 1^1/$_2$ lemons
large handful of chopped coriander

Boil the potatoes in salted water for about 10 minutes, then drain and transfer to a wide baking dish. Cut them into 1.25cm pieces, sprinkle over some salt and pepper, the oil and the garlic. Mix and turn the pieces of potato so they are coated all over with the oil.

Roast the potato pieces in a very hot oven, pre-heated to 240°C/475°F/Gas 9, for 30 minutes or until they are crisp and brown. Take them out, sprinkle evenly with the lemon juice and coriander, and mix well, being careful not to break the potatoes.

CHEESE OMELETTE
Ijjit Al Jibne

This simple herby omelette can be served as a light main dish accompanied by a salad. It can be served hot or cold. To serve it as a mezze, cut it into small wedges, or make tiny pancakes (see variation).

SERVES 4–6

175g feta cheese, mashed with a fork
8 eggs, lightly beaten
6 spring onions, sliced thinly
handful of chopped mint
large handful of chopped flat-leaf parsley
white pepper
3 tablespoons olive oil

Lightly beat the eggs with the rest of the ingredients, except the oil, in a bowl.

Heat 2 tablespoons of the oil in a large non-stick frying pan. When it begins to sizzle, pour in the egg mixture. Cook over a low heat for about 10 minutes or until the bottom sets. Dribble the remaining oil over the top of the omelette and cook under the grill for a few minutes until lightly browned. Serve it cut in wedges like a cake.

VARIATION

Drop small amounts of the egg mixture in batches – by the half ladle – in a non-stick frying pan filmed with oil and turn them over as soon as the bottom becomes detached.

COURGETTES with VINEGAR, MINT and GARLIC
Koussa Bil Khal

These courgette slices are usually fried but they are just as good grilled. They can be prepared hours before serving, even a day ahead.

SERVES 6

5 large courgettes (weighing about 1kg)
salt
extra virgin olive oil
2 tablespoons white wine vinegar
2 teaspoons crushed dried mint
2–3 garlic cloves, crushed

Trim the ends of the courgettes and cut them lengthways into slices about 0.75cm thick. Arrange them side by side on a baking sheet lined with foil and brushed with oil. Brush the slices generously with oil and sprinkle lightly with salt.

Cook under a pre-heated grill until lightly browned, then turn over, brush the other side with oil and return to the grill until browned. Mix the vinegar with the mint and garlic and brush a little on to each slice. Serve at room temperature.

VARIATIONS

Instead of using raw garlic, heat it in 2 tablespoons oil in a small frying pan until the aroma rises, but do not let it colour.

Serve the grilled slices topped with strained Greek Style yoghurt.

SPINACH and BEANS with CARAMELIZED ONIONS
Sabanekh Bi Loubia

Use black-eyed beans or haricot beans for this dish. You can use frozen spinach (defrost it thoroughly). If using fresh, wash it well and remove the stems only if they are very thick.

SERVES 4–6

1 large onion, sliced
6 tablespoons extra virgin olive oil
3 garlic cloves, chopped
250g fresh spinach
salt and black pepper
1 x 400g tin of beans, drained
juice of $^1/_4$ –$^1/_2$ lemon

Fry the onion in 2 tablespoons of the oil, stirring often, until brown and caramelized.

In a large saucepan, heat the garlic in 2 tablespoons of the oil for moments only until the aroma rises. Add the spinach, put on the lid and cook, without adding water, for a minute or two until the leaves crumple to a soft mass. Add salt and pepper.

Stir the beans and the fried onions into the spinach; add lemon juice and cook through. Add the remaining oil and serve cold.

VARIATION
Chickpeas can be used in the same way instead of beans.

LENTILS with PASTA and CARAMELIZED ONIONS
Rishta Bi Addas

Rishta bi addas can be eaten hot or at room temperature, like a pasta salad. The tagliatelle is usually cooked in the same water as the lentils which gives the pasta a pleasant earthy colour and flavour, but you can also boil them separately.

SERVES 4–6

1 large onion, sliced
6–7 tablespoons extra virgin olive oil
100g large green or brown lentils
100g dry tagliatelle nests
salt and black pepper
large handful of chopped flat-leaf parsley

Fry the onion in 2 tablespoons oil until brown and caramelized, stirring often. It is a good idea to start with the lid on – this allows it to soften more quickly.

Rinse the lentils and boil them in plenty of water until they are only just tender. Some brands take as little as 10–15 minutes, others take much longer. You should read the instructions on the packet and watch the cooking carefully.

Break the tagliatelle into pieces by crushing the nests in your hand and drop the pieces into the pan with the lentils – there should be enough water to cover them. Add salt, stir and boil vigorously until the pasta is cooked *al dente*.

Drain quickly, and toss gently with the remaining olive oil, a little salt and pepper, the fried onions and the parsley.

CHICKPEAS with TOASTED BREAD and YOGHURT
Fattet Hummus Bi Laban

A layer of chickpeas, spread over toasted bread soaked in their cooking broth, smothered in yoghurt with an elusive taste of tahini, and a pine nut topping may sound heavy but it is surprisingly light and delicate in the eating, and the mix of textures, temperatures and flavours is a joy. The bread must be the very thin flat bread known as khobz halabi which is sold by Lebanese bakeries in London. You need either 1 large one measuring about 30cm in diameter, or 2 smaller ones; or 1 pitta bread could be used instead.

SERVES 6–8

250g chickpeas, soaked for 2 hours or overnight
salt
2 garlic cloves, crushed
1 large or 2 small very thin Lebanese flat breads (see above)
$2^1/2$ tablespoons tahini
1kg natural (full-fat) yoghurt, at room temperature
100g pine nuts
$1^1/2$ tablespoons extra virgin olive oil

Drain the chickpeas and put them into a pan with water to cover, then simmer, covered, for $1^1/4$–$1^1/2$ hours until they are very soft. Add water so that the level remains about 1cm above the chickpeas throughout. Add salt when the chickpeas have begun to soften, and the crushed garlic towards the end of the cooking.

Toast the bread in an oven pre-heated to 200°C/400°F/Gas 6 until it becomes crisp. Then place it in the bottom of an ovenproof dish and break it up into smallish pieces by pressing down on it with the palm of your hand. Pour the hot chickpeas and enough of their cooking liquid over the pieces of bread so that they are well soaked. If you are not ready to serve, you can reheat this in the oven when you are.

Before serving, beat the tahini into the yoghurt, and pour it over the chickpeas. Quickly fry the pine nuts in the oil, stirring, until lightly browned, and sprinkle over the dish.

※ Fry the pine nuts in 3 tablespoons butter until lightly coloured, then add 2 tablespoons crushed dried mint and ¹/₂ tablespoon wine vinegar.

※ In a version called *tasseia*, the chickpeas are crushed and mixed with 2–3 tablespoons tahini, the juice of ¹/₂ lemon and 1 crushed garlic clove. You can put these into a blender with a little of the cooking water. Squeeze a little lemon juice into the chickpea water before sprinkling it over the bread, spread the mashed chickpea purée over the top and cover with yoghurt, and garnish as above.

※ Instead of toasting the bread, some people cut it into triangles and deep-fry them in hot oil. Drain the pieces on kitchen paper.

PRAWNS with GARLIC and CORIANDER
Kreidess Bi Cosbara

Use raw king prawns for this dish; they are grey and turn pink when they are cooked. Some supermarkets sell them ready-peeled.

SERVES 4

16 large raw king prawns
3 tablespoons extra virgin olive oil
3 garlic cloves, chopped finely
handful of chopped coriander
1 lemon, cut in quarters

If the prawns need peeling, pull off the heads and legs, then peel off the shells, but leave the tails on. If you see a dark thread along the back, make a fine slit with a sharp knife and pull it out.

Heat the oil in a large frying pan, add the prawns and cook for a minute. Turn them over, add the garlic and the coriander and cook for a minute more, until the prawns turn pink. They should not need any salt. Serve them hot with lemon quarters.

OKRA with BABY ONIONS and TOMATOES
Bamia Bi Banadoura

Cooked in this way, in olive oil, the dish is normally served cold as a salad, but I also like it hot with rice or as a side dish with meat or chicken.

SERVES 4–6

500g medium-sized okra
250g baby onions or shallots
5 tablespoons extra virgin olive oil
6 whole garlic cloves, peeled
500g tomatoes, peeled and chopped
salt and black pepper
1 teaspoon sugar
bunch of flat-leaf parsley, chopped

Wash the okra and, with a small sharp knife, carefully pare the conical stem ends without cutting through the pods. To peel the baby onions or shallots more easily, put them into boiling water and simmer for 5 minutes. Drain, and peel them when they are cool enough to handle.

In a large pan over a low heat, gently fry the onions and garlic cloves in 3 tablespoons of the oil, shaking the pan to colour them very lightly all over. Add the okra and sauté gently for about 5 minutes, turning the pods around in the pan.

Add the tomatoes, season with salt, pepper and sugar, and simmer for 15 minutes or until the okra are tender and the sauce is reduced. Taste and adjust the seasoning, stir in the coriander and cook a minute more. Stir in the remaining oil and serve at room temperature.

VARIATION

Add the juice of ½ lemon or 1 tablespoon pomegranate molasses (p.10) towards the end of the cooking time. If adding molasses, omit the sugar.

GRILLED CHICKEN WINGS
with LEMON and GARLIC
Jawaneh

Chicken wings are a very popular mezze item. They should be quite lemony and garlicky. You eat them with your fingers.

SERVES 4

3 tablespoons extra virgin olive oil
juice of 1 lemon
salt and black pepper
2–4 garlic cloves, crushed
16 chicken wings
2 tablespoons chopped flat-leaf parsley

Mix the oil, lemon juice, salt, pepper and garlic, and place the chicken wings in this marinade. Leave for 1 hour, covered with cling film, in the refrigerator. Place the chicken wings on a piece of foil on a baking tray, pour the marinade over them, and cook them under a pre-heated grill for 7 minutes, turning them over once. Or barbecue them over glowing embers for the same amount of time. Serve them sprinkled with chopped parsley.

GRILLED QUAILS
Siman Meshwi

Quails are part of the mezze tradition. Use your hands to eat them.

SERVES 4

4 quails
2 tablespoons extra virgin olive oil
salt and pepper
1 tablespoon chopped flat-leaf parsley

Lay each quail breast-side down. Cut along one side of the backbone, then along the other side, and remove the bone. Open out the bird and turn it over. Cut the wing and leg joints just enough to pull them a little apart, then press down hard with the palm of your hand to flatten the bird.

Place the quails on a sheet of foil on an oven tray. Rub them with the oil and sprinkle with salt and pepper. Cook the birds under a pre-heated grill for about 8 minutes, turning them over once. Serve sprinkled with the chopped parsley.

SPINACH PIES
Fatayer Bi Sabanikh

These little pies are a famous Lenten speciality; they are deliciously sharp and lemony. A good commercial puff pastry will do very well for the dough. The pies are wonderful eaten hot and also good cold.

You may use frozen leaf spinach instead of fresh spinach. Defrost it and squeeze out the liquid.

MAKES ABOUT 24 PIES

500g fresh spinach leaves
1 large onion, chopped
4 tablespoons extra virgin olive oil
salt and pepper
$^1/_2$ teaspoon ground allspice
juice of 1 lemon or 1 tablespoon sumac (p.11)
400g puff pastry
flour

Wash the spinach and remove any thick stems (you can leave the thin stems of very young spinach). Put the leaves into a large saucepan (without water – there is enough that clings to the leaves) and steam with the lid on for a minute or two until the spinach crumples to a soft mass. Strain in a colander, then squeeze all the liquid out with your hands. Chop the spinach coarsely.

In a large frying pan, fry the onion in 3 tablespoons of the oil, stirring occasionally, until golden. Add the spinach, salt and pepper, the allspice and the lemon juice or sumac, and mix well, leaving the pan on the heat for a few moments so any excess liquid can evaporate.

Cut the puff pastry in half to make rolling out more manageable. Lightly dust the rolling surface and the rolling pin with flour. Roll out each half into a thin sheet, turning the sheet over a few times and dusting it each time with a little flour. Cut it into rounds with a pastry cutter 10 cm in diameter. Off-cuts can be rolled into a ball and rolled out again so you do not waste any part of the dough. Put the rounds in a pile and wrap it in cling film. Do the same with the remaining pastry.

Take a round of pastry, lay it flat on one hand and put a tablespoon of stuffing in the middle. To make the traditional Lebanese three-sided pie, lift up two sides and pinch the neighbouring edges together, making a thin-ridged joint. Lift up the third side and join its two edges to the other two to make a small three-sided pyramid with a rounded base. Seal the openings by pinching the edges firmly all the way to the top. Don't worry if the pies open a little at the top to reveal the filling. Repeat with the remaining pastry circles and filling.

Place the pies on sheets of foil on baking trays, brush the tops with the remaining oil and bake in an oven pre-heated to 180°C/350°F/Gas 4 for 25–30 minutes or until golden.

VARIATION

Add 75g pine nuts to the fried onions, and stir until they begin to colour, before adding the spinach.

LITTLE MEAT PIZZAS
Lahma Bi Ajeen

The dough given here is one of a variety used to make the famous Arab 'pizzas' variously called lahma bi ajeen and sfiha. It contains yoghurt and olive oil and is soft and moist. Small pizzas make good finger-food; large ones make an excellent snack. They can be made in advance and reheated.

Do also try the different toppings given in the variations below.

MAKES ABOUT 20 SMALL PIZZAS

FOR THE DOUGH
about 250g warm yoghurt
2 teaspoons dried yeast
pinch of sugar
50ml warm water
500g strong white bread flour
1 teaspoon salt
4 tablespoons extra virgin olive oil

FOR THE MEAT AND TOMATO TOPPING
1 large onion
600g minced lamb
3 large garlic cloves, crushed
$1/2$ teaspoon ground allspice
salt and black pepper
2 tablespoons pomegranate molasses (p.10)
500g tomatoes (unpeeled), chopped finely
50g pine nuts (optional)

To warm the yoghurt, put the pot into a bowl or pan of hot – not boiling – water for about 1 hour. Dissolve the yeast with the sugar in the water and leave for about 10 minutes until it froths. In a large bowl, mix the flour with the salt and oil, add the yeast mixture and just enough of the yoghurt to make the dough hold together in a ball. Begin by mixing with a fork, then work with your hand. Knead for about 10 minutes until the dough is smooth and elastic. Add a drop of oil to the bowl and roll the dough around in it to grease it all over and prevent a dry skin forming.

Cover the bowl with cling film and leave in a warm place for 1^1/$_2$ hours until it has doubled in bulk.

Punch down the risen dough and knead for 1 minute. Take lumps the size of a large walnut if making mini pizzas, or the size of an egg if making large ones, and roll out on a clean surface with a rolling pin. Do not flour these as the dough is very greasy and will not stick. Roll out thinly into rounds about 3mm thick and place on oiled sheets of foil on baking trays.

For the topping, finely chop the onion in the food processor and drain it of its juices. Put the meat, onion, garlic, allspice, salt, pepper, and pomegranate molasses into a bowl. Mix well and work with your hand into a soft paste. Then work in the tomato and the pine nuts (if using). Take lumps of the mixture and spread thickly over each round of dough; go right up to the edges as the topping tends to shrink while the dough expands as it cooks.

Bake one tray at a time in an oven pre-heated to 200°C/400°F/Gas 6 for 15 minutes, placing each on the top shelf. Serve the pizzas hot.

VARIATIONS

✴ Meat and yoghurt topping: Mix 600g minced lamb, 1 large onion (finely chopped in a food processor and drained of its juices), 100g natural (full fat) yoghurt, the juice of ^{1}/$_2$ lemon, salt and pepper, ^{1}/$_2$ teaspoon allspice, and 50g pine nuts.

✴ Meat and Tomato with Chilli: Work together to a paste 1 large onion (very finely chopped in the food processor and drained of its juices) ^{1}/$_2$–1 finely chopped chilli pepper, 600g minced lamb, 4 tablespoons concentrated tomato paste, 2 tablespoons pomegranate molasses, salt and pepper.

OUED SOUSS
OLiVE OiL
1·L: £ 3.50
9·) = FOR: 6

LITTLE PUFF PASTRY CHEESE PIES
Sambousek Bi Jibne

These melt-in-the-mouth cheese sambousek make good party food. They can be eaten hot or warm. You can make them in advance and heat them through before serving. Use fresh or frozen and defrosted puff pastry.

MAKES 32 PIES

> 500g puff pastry
> flour
> 40g butter, melted

> FOR THE FILLING
> 250g mozzarella cheese
> 250g feta cheese
> 2 eggs, lightly beaten

It is important to roll out the puff pastry as thinly as you possibly can. It is easier to do this if you cut it into 4 equal pieces and roll out each one separately. Dust the rolling surface and the rolling pin with flour. Roll out the first sheet of pastry, turning it over and dusting with flour, until you can cut 6 rounds with a 10cm pastry cutter. Make a ball out of the off-cuts, roll this out and make 2 more rounds. Put the 8 rounds in a pile and wrap it in cling film. Do the same with the remaining pastry.

For the filling, blend the mozzarella in a food processor. Mash the feta cheese with a fork and mix it and the mozzarella well together in a bowl, then mix in the eggs.

Put a tablespoon of the filling on one half of each round of pastry. Dip your finger in water and slightly dampen the pastry edges (this is to make them stick better), then fold the pastry over the filling to make a half-moon shape. Seal the pies by pinching the edges very firmly together. A traditional way is to finish by twisting the edges, making a scalloped effect; another is to press down with the prongs of a fork.

Arrange the pies on sheets of foil in baking trays. Brush the tops with melted butter and bake them in an oven pre-heated to 200°C/400°F/Gas 6 for about 15–20 minutes or until they are puffed up and lightly golden.

VARIATIONS
✷ Instead of baking, deep-fry the pies in vegetable oil, turning them over once. Drain them on kitchen paper.
✷ For a shiny golden colour, instead of brushing with melted butter, brush the pies with egg yolk mixed with a drop of water.

RED LENTIL and RICE SOUP
Makhlouta

Serve this creamy soup with thin Lebanese flat bread cut into triangles, opened out, brushed with olive oil and toasted in the oven until crisp.

SERVES 6–8

2 large onions, sliced
2 tablespoons extra virgin olive oil
1.75 litres chicken stock (made with 2 stock cubes)
200g red lentils
100g Italian or round rice
black pepper
2 teaspoons ground coriander
salt
1 teaspoon ground cumin
2 lemons

Fry the onions in the oil. Cover the pan and cook over a low heat, stirring occasionally, until they soften. Then cook over a high heat, stirring often, until they are very brown and caramelized. Drain on kitchen paper and put them to one side.

Bring the stock to the boil, then put in the lentils and rice. Add pepper and the coriander, and simmer for about 35–45 minutes, until the lentils and rice fall apart and the soup has a creamy texture. Add a little salt towards the end of the cooking time, taking into account the saltiness of the stock cubes, and a little water if necessary to thin the soup to a light creamy consistency.

Serve, sprinkling each plateful with a pinch of cumin and garnishing each with a topping of fried onions. Pass around lemon quarters.

GREEN VEGETABLE SOUP

This spring soup is green and aromatic. It becomes more substantial if served over rice. Other vegetables such as artichoke bottoms (frozen ones will do: p.95), cut into pieces, peas and broad beans can also be added.

SERVES 6–8

200g long-grain or basmati rice
2 litres chicken or vegetable stock (made with 2 stock cubes)
2 leeks
1 small head of celery with leaves
salt and white pepper
3–4 garlic cloves, crushed
juice of 1 lemon
1 teaspoon sugar, or more to taste
200g courgettes
2 tablespoons crushed dried mint

To cook the rice, add it to plenty of boiling salted water and simmer for 10–18 minutes (the time varies depending on the type of rice) or until tender, then drain quickly. Keep it on one side until you are ready to serve.

Heat the stock in a large pan. Cut the leeks and celery into slices about 0.75cm thick and add them to the pan. Simmer for about 30 minutes until they are tender.

Add salt (taking into account the saltiness of the stock), pepper, the garlic, lemon juice and sugar, then add the courgettes, trimmed of their ends and cut in half lengthways then into 0.75cm slices. Cook for 5 minutes, then add the mint and cook 5 minutes more. Taste and adjust the flavourings.

Serve in soup bowls over the rice.

Main Courses

Everyone in Lebanon appreciates the old traditional dishes that now make up the national cuisine. The repertoire is mainly represented by the refined sophisticated dishes of the old Greek Orthodox and Sunni *grande bourgeoisie* of Beirut and those of the Maronite *grands seigneurs* of the mountains, combined with simple rural dishes and with the festive dishes associated with religious holidays. There are the traditionalists; the modernizers who may simply lighten the cooking and present the food in a novel way; and there are those who allow themselves to be creative.

SEA BREAM with SAFFRON RICE
Samak Wal Roz Bil Zafaran

Ask the fishmonger to clean and scale the fish, and remove the fins and gills, but to leave the heads on. This rice – which is cooked with olive oil instead of the usual butter – is the traditional rice to accompany fish in Lebanon. Turmeric is sometimes used instead of saffron. Start cooking the rice first.

SERVES 4

4 sea bream (weighing about 400g each)
salt and black pepper
2 tablespoons extra virgin olive oil
1 lemon

FOR THE RICE

6 tablespoons extra virgin olive oil
$1/2$ teaspoon saffron powder or threads
300g American long-grain rice
550ml boiling water
salt and black pepper
2 medium onions, sliced
75g pine nuts

For the rice, heat 2 tablespoons of the oil in a pan. Stir in the saffron and add the rice. Stir well until the rice acquires a transparent yellow glow. Add the boiling water, stir in the salt and pepper, and simmer over a low heat, covered and undisturbed, for between 10 and 20 minutes, until the rice is tender and the water has been absorbed (the time depends on the type of rice). Then stir in another 2 tablespoons oil.

Fry the onions in the remaining 2 tablespoons oil, stirring occasionally, until brown. Add the pine nuts, and stir until they are lightly coloured.

Make 2–3 slashes about 0.75cm deep in the thickest part of the fish so that they cook evenly. Put them side by side in a baking dish, sprinkle with salt and pepper and rub them generously with oil. Bake in an oven pre-heated to 220°C/ 425°F/Gas 7 for 15 minutes.

Serve the fish with lemon quarters, and the rice separately, shaped in a mound, and garnished with the pine nuts and onions.

PAN-FRIED RED MULLET
with TAHINI SAUCE
Sultan Ibrahim Makli Bi Tehine

The most popular item on the menu in the fish restaurants along the long Lebanese coast are the deep-fried red mullet that come accompanied by a tahini sauce and very thin, crisp, deep-fried bread. They are fried whole, coated with flour, but at home I find it easier to pan-fry red mullet fillets.

SERVES 4

8 red mullet fillets (weighing about 80g each), skin on
salt and black pepper
2–3 tablespoons extra virgin olive oil
1 lemon

FOR THE TAHINI SAUCE
75ml tahini
juice of 1 lemon
75ml cold water
salt
$1/2$–1 clove garlic (optional)

First make the sauce. Stir the tahini in the jar before using. With a fork, beat the tahini with the lemon juice. It will thicken to a stiff paste. Add the water, beating vigorously until you get the consistency of a pale runny cream. Then add a little salt and the garlic (if using) and pour into a serving bowl.

Season the red mullet fillets with salt and pepper and fry in the hot oil, preferably in a non-stick frying pan, for about 2 minutes on the skin side, then turn and cook the other side for half a minute more.

Serve the fish at once and let people pour the tahini sauce on the side.

VARIATION
Season 4 fish fillets (150g–200g), such as cod or haddock, with salt and white pepper and $1/2$ teaspoon ground cumin. Dip the fillets in flour to coat them all over, and shallow-fry in sizzling olive oil, turning over once. Drain on kitchen paper and serve with the tahini sauce.

FISH with RICE and ONION SAUCE
Sayyadieh

The distinctive feature of this famous Arab fish and rice dish is the flavour of caramelized onions in the brown broth which suffuses the rice and colours it a pale brown. Use skinned fillets of white fish such as bream, turbot, haddock or cod.

SERVES 4

600g onions, sliced
4–5 tablespoons extra virgin olive oil
2 fish or chicken stock cubes
salt and black pepper
$^1/_2$ teaspoon ground cumin
$^1/_2$ teaspoon ground allspice
300g long-grain or basmati rice, washed
4 fish fillets (each weighing 150–200g)
$^1/_2$–1 lemon

In a large saucepan, fry the onions in $2^1/_2$ tablespoons of the oil over a low heat, with the lid on, until they are soft and transparent, stirring occasionally. Then take off the lid and let them get very dark brown and caramelized. Blend them to a cream in a food processor and return this to the pan.

Add about 1 litre boiling water and the crumbled stock cubes; season with salt, pepper, cumin and allspice, and simmer for about 10 minutes.

Pour out the onion stock to measure the quantity you need for cooking the rice. Return 550ml to the pan, and put the rest on one side to use as the sauce. Add the rice and some salt, stir well, and cook, covered, over a low heat, for about 10–18 minutes until the rice is tender. (Some brands that claim not to be parboiled or pre-cooked now take as little as 8–10 minutes, so read the information on the packet.) Drain and keep it on one side until you are ready to serve.

Pan-fry the fish fillets, seasoned with salt and pepper, in the remaining oil, for 2–3 minutes on each side, until the flesh just begins to flake. Squeeze a little lemon juice over them. Fry the pine nuts in a drop of oil until lightly browned. Reheat the onion sauce, adding a little lemon juice to taste.

Serve the rice heaped in a mound with the sauce poured over. Arrange the pieces of fish on top or around the rice and sprinkle with the pine nuts.

 (❀) A way of preparing the dish in advance is to layer it in a deep oven dish
– pine nuts first, then fish, then rice – and heat it through in the oven.
Turn it out upside down just before serving and serve the sauce separately.

 (❀) You can accompany the dish with the tahini sauce on p. 302 as well
as its brown sauce.

 (❀) For a 'white' version of the same dish, the onions should be meltingly
soft but should not be allowed to brown.

COD with PINE NUT SAUCE
Samak Bil Tarator Bi Senobar

*This is a dish which is served cold and is especially good for a buffet party. It is
beautiful and dramatic. Get a large white fish – sea bass would be great but is
expensive; cod or haddock will do very well. (Although salmon is not a fish used in
Lebanon, and not a fish of the Mediterranean regions, it is good to serve in this way.)
Have the fish skinned – and also filleted, if you like – and ask for the head and tail.
Cooked in foil, the fish steams in its own juice and the flesh remains moist. The pine
nut sauce, tarator bi senobar, has a very delicate flavour.*

SERVES 8–10   2 tablespoons extra virgin olive oil

1 whole cod weighing about 2.5kg

salt

1 lemon, cut into thin slices

To garnish: 3 tablespoons pine nuts or 4 tablespoons chopped
flat-leaf parsley, and 2 lemons, sliced

FOR THE PINE NUT SAUCE

3 slices good white bread

250g pine nuts

juice of 2 lemons

2 garlic cloves, crushed

salt

Brush a large sheet of foil with a little of the oil. Place the fish in the middle (if
using fillets place them on top of each other), sprinkle lightly with salt and rub with
the remaining oil. Sprinkle the cavity of the fish with a little salt and put in the

lemon slices. Wrap in a loose parcel, twisting the foil edges together to seal it. Wrap the head and tail separately in another piece of foil.

Bake the fish in an oven pre-heated to 200°C/400°F/Gas 6 for 30–45 minutes or until done. To test for doneness, cut into the thickest part and check that the flesh flakes and has turned white right through. The head and tail should come out of the oven after 20 minutes.

For the sauce, cut away the crusts from the bread (it should now weigh about 70g) and soak the slices in water. Blend the pine nuts to a paste in a food processor. Then add the bread squeezed dry, the lemon juice and garlic, and blend well. Add a little salt and about 3–4 tablespoons of fish juices or cold water – just enough to blend to the consistency of thick cream.

Serve the fish cold, covered with the sauce and with the head and tail in place. Decorate the fish with a pattern using pine nuts fried gently in a drop of oil until slightly coloured, or with parsley and lemon slices cut into half-moon shapes.

CHICKEN PIE with ONIONS and SUMAC
Musakhan

This pie with a beguilingly flavoured filling is a refined interpretation of musakhan which is of Bedouin origin and is baked in thin Arab bread. It is delicious and you must try it. It can be made in advance and reheated before serving. Use the large size sheets of filo (about 48cm x 30cm) that are sold frozen, and defrost for 3 hours; see p.15 for information about using filo.

SERVES 6

600g onions, sliced

2^1/$_2$ tablespoons sunflower oil

6 boned chicken thighs (without skin)

1^1/$_2$ tablespoon sumac (p.10)

1 teaspoon ground cinnamon

^{1}/$_2$ teaspoon ground cardomom

^{1}/$_2$–1 lemon

salt and black pepper

7 sheets of filo pastry (about 200g)

60g butter, melted

For the filling, fry the onions in the oil until soft and beginning to colour. Cook over a low heat, with the lid on to start with, stirring occasionally, until they soften, then remove the lid and cook over a medium high heat. Cut the chicken into pieces sized around 2–2.5cm and add them to the onions. Cook, turning the pieces, until they are lightly coloured all over. Add the sumac, cinnamon and cardomom, and the lemon juice, salt and pepper, and mix well.

Be ready to assemble the pie quickly so that the filo does not dry out. Brush a large round baking pan, about 28cm in diameter, with melted butter. Place the first sheet of filo in the pan so that it nestles in the bottom, and the two ends hangs over the side. Brush the sheet quickly with melted butter, pressing it into the corners with the brush. Repeat with four more of the sheets so the sides of the pan are completely covered.

Spread the filling evenly in the pan over the sheets and fold the overhanging filo back over the filling to enclose it, again brushing each bit with melted butter. Cover the surface with the remaining two sheets of filo, brushing each with melted butter. Tuck them into the sides of the pan, trimming them with scissors to make this easier.

Bake the pie in an oven pre-heated to 180°C/350°F/Gas 4 for 25 minutes or until browned. Turn it out, upside down, on to a large platter and serve hot. Use a finely serrated knife to cut it up into wedges.

VARIATIONS
For a more homely snack, fill pitta bread with the hot filling and heat through in the oven.

CHICKEN and CHICKPEAS
with YOGHURT
Fattet Djaj

A number of dishes that go under the general name of fatta all have in common a bed of toasted bread soaked in stock and a topping of yoghurt. The name denotes the manner of breaking up crisp toasted bread with your hands. To me, they recall a special person, the late Josephine Salam. Many years ago I received a letter from her from Beirut saying that she had a number of recipes she thought I would like. On our first meeting at Claridges tea room, where a band played Noël Coward tunes, she offered to come to my house and show me how to make fatta with chicken. We made that and many more meals together. It was the time of the civil war in Lebanon and as she came and went from the country, I received an ongoing account of everyday life in the ravaged city. Her daughter, Rana, has become an artist and designer. For her thesis at the Royal College of Art in London, she asked me to give a lecture on the history of Middle Eastern food. She had ten portraits of me painted on cloth by a poster-painter in Egypt (he used photographs I gave Rana) and hung them around the college to publicize the event. She laid out foods and spices out as in a souk, put on a tape of sounds and music recorded in an Egyptian street, and passed around Arab delicacies. When she visited me a few years later with her husband and new baby, I offered her the fatta with stuffed aubergines on p.312.

SERVES 8

1kg natural (full-fat) yoghurt

200g strained Greek Style yoghurt

2 garlic cloves, crushed

1^1/$_2$ tablespoons crushed dried mint

salt

1 large chicken

1 large onion, cut in half

1 large carrot, cut into pieces

2 bay leaves

1 cinnamon stick

6–8 cardamom pods

white pepper

3 very thin Lebanese breads or 2 pitta breads

3–4 tablespoons white wine vinegar

1 x 400g tin of chickpeas, drained

100g pine nuts

2 tablespoons extra virgin olive oil

Mix the two types of yoghurt in a bowl and beat in the garlic and mint with a little salt. Let it come to room temperature.

Put the chicken into a large saucepan and cover with water. Bring it to the boil, and remove any scum. Add the onion and the carrot, the bay leaves, cinnamon stick and cardomom pods, and salt and pepper. Simmer, covered, for 1–1^1/2 hours, until the chicken is very tender and almost falls off the bone.

Open out the Lebanese or pitta breads. Toast them in the oven or under the grill until they are crisp and only lightly browned. Then break them up into pieces in your hands and spread them at the bottom of a wide baking dish. Mix the wine vinegar in about 300 ml of the strained chicken stock, and pour over the bread, adding more if necessary, so that the bread is thoroughly soaked and soggy. Sprinkle the chickpeas over it.

Lift out the chicken and cut the meat into pieces, removing the skin and bones. Spread the chicken over the soaked bread and chickpeas and cover the dish with foil. Heat through in the oven 20 minutes before you are ready to serve – it should be very hot.

Just before serving, pour the yoghurt evenly all over the dish. Briefly fry the pine nuts in the olive oil until lightly golden and sprinkle over the top.

VARIATION

Instead of adding mint to the yoghurt, beat in 3 tablespoons of tahini.

GRILLED POUSSINS with SUMAC
Farrouj Meshwi Bil Sumac

Poussins in this country tend to have a somewhat bland flavour but with lemon, sumac and olive oil they are a treat.

SERVES 2

2 poussins
$^1/_2$ lemon
2 tablespoons extra virgin olive oil
salt and black pepper
1 teaspoon sumac (p.11)

Cut the poussins down both sides of the backbone with poultry shears or kitchen scissors and remove the bone. Cut the wing and leg joints just enough to pull them a little apart, then open the poussins out and flatten them by pressing down hard with the palm of your hand. Rub them with a mixture of lemon juice, oil, salt and pepper. Leave in a cool place for 30 minutes to absorb the lemon juice.

Cook the poussins on a sheet of foil under a pre-heated grill or on a barbecue, flesh side to the heat for 10 minutes, then turn and cook the skin side for 5–10 minutes. Cut into a thigh with a pointed knife to check for doneness; they are ready when the juices no longer run pink but the meat is still juicy. Sprinkle with sumac and serve with pitta or Lebanese bread.

OPTIONAL ACCOMPANIMENT

Slice 1 large red or white onion thinly and sprinkle generously with salt. Leave for 30 minutes until the juices run out and it loses its strong flavour. Then rinse and drain the onion and mix it with 4 tablespoons chopped flat-leaf parsley.

STUFFED AUBERGINES, TOASTED BREAD, TOMATO SAUCE and YOGHURT

Fattet Batinjan

This dish is complex and it requires time, but it has dramatic appeal and it is quite delicious with layers of different textures and flavours. I like to add two ingredients which are optional: pomegranate molasses (p.10) which give a brown colour and sweet-and-sour flavour to the tomato sauce, and the tahini which gives a nutty flavour to the yoghurt. Look for small aubergines, 10–11cm long, which can usually be found in Middle Eastern and Asian stores.

SERVES 6

- 2–3 tablespoons vegetable oil
- 350g lean minced beef or lamb
- salt and black pepper
- 1 teaspoon ground cinnamon
- $^1/_2$ teaspoon ground allspice
- 75g pine nuts
- 6 small aubergines (weighing about 800g)
- 1 kg tomatoes, peeled and chopped
- 2 teaspoons sugar
- $1^1/_2$ tablespoons pomegranate molasses (optional)
- 2 pitta breads
- 500g natural yoghurt, at room temperature
- 2 tablespoons tahini (optional)
- 2 garlic cloves (optional)

For the aubergine stuffing, heat 2 tablespoons of the oil in a frying pan. Put in the meat and add salt, pepper, the cinnamon and allspice. Cook, crushing the meat with a fork and turning it over, for about 8 minutes until it has changed colour and the liquid has evaporated.

In another small frying pan, fry the pine nuts in a drop of oil, shaking the pan to brown them slightly all over. Stir half the pine nuts into the meat.

Wash the aubergines, cut a slice off at the stem end and, using an apple corer, hollow out the flesh. Insert the corer, digging it in while gently turning it, then give a sharp, quick twist as you reach near the end, and pull out the flesh. Repeat this action with the corer, or scrape the sides with a sharp knife, to leave a shell with walls about 5mm thick, being careful not to pierce the skin. Fill the cavities with the meat and pine nut mixture.

Put the tomatoes into a wide pan with the sugar, a little salt and pepper and (if using) the pomegranate molasses. Stir well and simmer for 5 minutes. Put in the aubergines, and simmer over a low heat for 45 minutes or until the aubergines are very soft, turning them over once.

Open out the pitta breads by cutting around them with scissors or a serrated knife, and toast them under the grill until they are crisp and lightly browned. Mix the yoghurt with the tahini and garlic (if using).

Just before serving, assemble the different components in a wide, deep serving dish. Break the toasted pitta breads into small pieces with your hands into the bottom of the dish. Take the aubergines out of the tomato sauce and pour the sauce over the toast which will become soft and swollen. Pour the yoghurt all over the sauce and arrange the stuffed aubergines on top. Finally, sprinkle with the remaining pine nuts.

NOTE

You can use up the extracted aubergine flesh in a salad or an omelette. So that it does not discolour, put it into a bowl of water with salt and a squeeze of lemon juice. Then drain and sauté in olive oil before dressing with lemon juice or mixing with eggs to make an omelette.

STUFFED COURGETTES
in TOMATO SAUCE
Koussa Mahshi Bi Banadoura

This makes a satisfying, homely meal and is especially good when served with vermicelli rice (p.316).

SERVES 4–6

1 kg small courgettes (10–12cm long)

1 large onion, chopped

2 tablespoons sunflower oil

3 garlic cloves, crushed

1 kg tomatoes, peeled and chopped

salt and black pepper

1 tablespoon tomato paste

1–2 teaspoons sugar

1–1^1/$_2$ lemons

1 teaspoon crushed dried mint

FOR THE FILLING

150g lean minced lamb

50g round Italian rice

salt and pepper

^{1}/$_2$ teaspoon ground cinnamon

^{1}/$_2$ teaspoon ground allspice

Wash the courgettes, slice off the stem end and shave off the brown skin on the other end. With a long apple corer, make a hole at the stem end of each vegetable and scoop out the flesh, being careful not to break the skin and nor to break through the other end which must remain closed. This is done by digging in gently while gently turning the corer, then giving a sharp quick twist as it reaches near the end, before pulling out the flesh. It is a skill that is acquired with a little practice. With the corer or a small sharp knife, cut out a little more of the flesh if necessary, but the shell must be left intact.

Put the filling ingredients together into a bowl and knead well by hand until thoroughly blended. Fill each courgette, packing in the filling to within 1cm of the end to allow for the expansion of the rice.

For the sauce, fry the onion in the oil until golden. Use a pan that will hold the courgettes in one or two whole layers. Add the garlic and stir until the aroma rises, then add the tomatoes. Season with salt and pepper and stir in the tomato paste, the sugar and the juice of half a lemon.

Place the stuffed courgettes side by side in one or two layers in the sauce. Add more water if necessary to cover them and simmer very gently, with the lid on, over a low heat for about 45 minutes, until the courgettes are soft.

Carefully lift the courgettes out of the pan and place them in a serving dish. Stir the mint and the juice of the remaining lemon into the sauce, and continue cooking for a moment or two, then pour over the courgettes.

NOTE

Use the extracted courgette flesh for a salad: simmer in a little water for a minute or two, then drain and dress it with olive oil, lemon juice, salt and pepper.

STUFFED COURGETTES
in YOGURT SAUCE
Koussa Mahshi Bi Laban

Prepare the stuffed courgettes as in the recipe above. Arrange them in a wide pan, only just cover with lamb or chicken stock (use $1^1/2$ stock cubes), and simmer gently, covered, for about 25 minutes, until the water is absorbed and the courgettes are nearly done.

In another saucepan, beat 1kg of natural (full-fat) yoghurt with a little salt until it is liquid. Mix 1 tablespoon cornflour with 2–3 tablespoons water to make a creamy paste, add it to the yoghurt and beat well. This will 'stabilize' the yoghurt and prevent it from curdling when it is cooked. Bring to the boil slowly over a low heat, stirring constantly with a wooden spoon *in one direction only* (this is important), then reduce the heat as low as possible and let the yoghurt barely simmer, *uncovered* (this, too, is supposed to be important), for about 10 minutes until it has thickened.

Pour the yoghurt over the courgettes and simmer for about 20 minutes. Before serving, crush 3 garlic cloves with a little salt, add 2 teaspoons crushed dried mint, and mix well. Fry this mixture in 1 tablespoon butter for moments only, and stir into the yoghurt.

VERMICELLI RICE
Roz Bil Shaghrieh

Roz bil shaghrieh is the everyday rice that accompanies stews, stuffed vegetables and grills in Lebanon. People also eat it by itself with yoghurt poured over. The short-grain rice from Egypt is the traditional rice used but today basmati is preferred. Middle Eastern stores sell Italian 'cut' vermicelli called filini but otherwise you can buy vermicelli nests and break them in your hand into 2cm pieces.

SERVES 4

250g basmati rice
100g filini or broken vermicelli nests
30g butter
about 450 ml boiling water
salt

Wash the rice briefly in cold water, then rinse under the tap in a strainer and drain. Toast the filini or broken vermicelli in a dry frying pan over a medium heat or in a tray under the grill until they are lightly browned, stirring so that they brown evenly. Watch them as they brown very quickly.

Heat the butter in a saucepan over a medium heat, add the rice and stir until the grains are coated. Pour in the boiling water, add the browned vermicelli and some salt and stir well. Then simmer, covered, over a low heat until the rice is tender and the water absorbed. Some brands of basmati now cook in 10 minutes only while others can take up to 20 minutes, so do read the instructions on the pack and be ready to turn off the heat after 10 minutes.

STUFFED ARTICHOKE with MEAT and PINE NUTS
Ardishawki Mahshi

Look for the frozen artichoke bottoms in Middle Eastern stores. There are about 9 in a 400g packet. Serve the dish hot with vermicelli rice (p.316).

SERVES 4

1 large onion, chopped
3 tablespoons sunflower oil
300g minced lamb or beef
salt and black pepper
$^1/_2$ teaspoon ground allspice
50g pine nuts
400g frozen artichoke bottoms, defrosted
1 tablespoon flour
$^1/_2$ lemon

Fry the onion in 2 tablespoons of the oil until golden. Add the meat, salt, pepper and allspice, and stir, turning the meat over and crushing it with a fork until it changes colour. In a small pan, fry the pine nuts in the remaining oil, stirring, until lightly coloured, then add them to the meat.

Place the artichoke bottoms side by side in a shallow baking dish and fill them with the meat mixture. Mix the flour with lemon juice and blend well, then gradually stir in about 200ml water, and pour into the dish. Cover with foil and bake in an oven pre-heated to 180°C/350°F/Gas 4 for 25 minutes or until the artichokes are tender.

'NEW-STYLE' SHISH BARAK

Shish barak are tiny tortellini-like pies with a meat filling that are first baked, then cooked in a yoghurt sauce. This 'new-style' version of large individual coiled pies is inspired by Kamal Mouzawak (for his vegetarian alternative, see the variation). It is an exciting mix of flavours, textures and temperatures and makes a beautiful presentation. Called rakakat, the pastry used in Lebanon is different from filo – it is softer and more pliable, like a paper-thin pancake – but filo will do very well. Use the large sheets measuring about 48cm x 30cm that are normally sold frozen; see p.15 for hints on using filo.

SERVES 12 AS A FIRST COURSE, 6 AS A MAIN DISH

FOR THE FILLING

2 large onions, chopped

3 tablespoons sunflower oil

75g pine nuts

500g lean minced lamb or beef

salt and black pepper

2 teaspoons ground cinnamon

$^{1}/_{2}$ teaspoon ground allspice

$^{1}/_{2}$ teaspoon ground nutmeg

1–2 tablespoons pomegranate molasses (p.10)

FOR THE PASTRY

6 sheets of filo (about 170g)

85g butter, melted

FOR THE SAUCE AND GARNISH

1kg natural yoghurt, at room temperature

salt

2–3 cloves garlic (optional)

4 tablespoons extra virgin olive oil

1 tablespoon crushed dried mint

For the filling, fry the onions in the oil until golden, stirring occasionally. Add the minced meat, salt and pepper, cinnamon, allspice and nutmeg. The filling needs to be well seasoned and strongly flavoured as it is balanced with the filo pastry and yoghurt which are bland. Stir, turning over the meat and crushing it to break up any lumps, until it changes colour and the juices have been absorbed. Then stir in the pomegranate molasses and cook for 1–2 minutes more. In a small pan, fry the pine nuts in a drop of oil, stirring, for moments only, until they just begin to colour. Stir them into the meat and let it cool.

Cut the sheets of filo in half, into 2 rectangles that measure about 30cm x 24cm and pile them on top of each other with the long sides nearest to you. Brush the top sheet with melted butter. Put a line of filling – about 3–4 tablespoons – along the long edge, to reach to about 2cm from either end, and roll up into a long thin roll. Then shape the roll into a tight coil, creasing it a little as you do, so that the pastry does not tear, and place it on a piece of foil (you do not need to grease it) on a baking sheet. Repeat with the remaining sheets of filo and the filling, placing the coils next to each other so that they are held tight. Brush the tops with melted butter.

About 30 minutes before you are ready to serve, bake the pies in an oven pre-heated to 200°C/400°F/ Gas 6 for about 25 minutes until golden.

For the sauce, beat the yoghurt with a little salt and the garlic (if using). For the garnish, mix the olive oil and the dried mint.

Serve the pies as they come out of the oven. Pour about 3 tablespoons yoghurt over each, and dribble a little of the minty olive oil (about a teaspoon) over the top.

VARIATION

For Kamal's vegetarian filling, fry 4 large sliced onions in 4 tablespoons oil until brown, add 150g pine nuts, salt, pepper, 3 teaspoons of ground mixed spices (cinnamon, allspice, nutmeg, ginger, cloves, cumin) and 1^1/$_2$ tablespoons pomegranate molasses.

MINCED MEAT KEBAB
Kafta Meshwiyeh

The minced meat for this kebab – I usually buy shoulder of lamb – should have a good amount of fat so that it remains moist and juicy. Most of it will melt away in the heat of the grill. You will need skewers with a thick wide blade to hold the meat and prevent it from rolling around. Alternatively, it is easier and equally good to shape the meat into burgers. Serve them with Arab flat breads or the very thin Lebanese markouk (p.253), and accompany them with a salad and a choice of mezze.

SERVES 4

2 medium onions
60g chopped flat-leafed parsley
750g lamb, taken from the shoulder with some fat
salt and black pepper

Grate or finely chop the onion in a food processor, then drain and turn it into a bowl. Chop the parsley and add it to the onion. Cut the meat into chunks, then blend it in the food processor to a soft paste, adding salt and pepper. Mix with the parsley and onion and knead with your hand until well blended.

Divide the meat into 8 balls and wrap each one around a skewer, pressing it firmly so that it holds together in a long flat sausage shape. Alternatively, flatten the balls into burgers. Place the skewers or burgers on the oiled grill of a barbecue, over the embers of a charcoal fire or on a rack under the grill, and cook for 5–8 minutes, turning them over once, until browned outside but still pink inside.

Kafta Yoghurtliya

Using the recipe above, roll the meat into little balls the size of a large walnut. Sauté in batches in a little oil in a large frying pan, turning them until they are browned all over but still a little pink inside. You can do this in advance, if you wish, and heat them through, covered with foil, in the oven when you are ready to serve.

Open out a pitta, toast it under the grill and break it into small pieces in the bottom of a serving dish. Just before serving, pour 1kg natural (full-fat) yoghurt, which should be at room temperature, over the toast and drop the meatballs on top. Fry 3 tablespoons pine nuts very briefly in 25g butter and sprinkle them over the dish with their butter.

MEATBALLS with PINE NUTS in TOMATO SAUCE
Daoud Basha

This dish takes its name from the governor who administered Mount Lebanon between 1861 and 1868 in Ottoman times. Serve it with plain or vermicelli rice (p. 316).

SERVES 6

2 medium onions, grated or chopped finely
750g lean minced lamb
salt and pepper
1$^1/_2$ teaspoons ground cinnamon
$^1/_2$ teaspoon ground allspice
100g pine nuts
vegetable oil
1kg tomatoes, peeled or not
2 teaspoons sugar
3 garlic cloves (optional)

Grate or finely chop the onions in a food processor, then drain and turn into a bowl. Add the minced lamb with salt and pepper, cinnamon and allspice, and work to a paste with your hand. Roll the paste into small walnut-sized balls. Make a hole in each ball with your finger, stuff the cavity with a few pine nuts and close the hole.

Alternatively, and more easily, work the pine nuts into the meat paste, then roll it into balls.

Put a little oil in a soup plate and roll the meatballs in it. Then put them into an ovenproof dish and bake in an oven pre-heated to 200°C/400°F/Gas 6 for 15–20 minutes until their colour changes.

For the sauce, cut up the tomatoes and liquidize them in a food processor or blender. Add a little salt and pepper, the sugar and garlic (if using), and pour over the meatballs. Bake them for a further 35 minutes, turning the meatballs over once.

VARIATION
Add the juice of 1 lemon and a good pinch of chilli flakes to the sauce.

BAKED KIBBEH with ONION and PINE NUT TOPPING
Kibbeh Saniyeh

Kibbeh forms a major part of the national dishes of Lebanon. There are countless versions, from a raw meat paste to little oval shells stuffed with a minced meat filling and deep-fried or cooked in yoghurt or bitter orange juice, as well as vegetarian kibbeh with pumpkin, tomato paste or potato, and one with fish – each version having a number of regional variations. One thing they all have in common is bulgur (burghul in Lebanon). Since most are labour-intensive and require skill and application, they are not the kind of thing you undertake if you are not part of the culture.

So I was very happy to discover a traditional kibbeh that was truly delightful and relatively easy, with only one layer of kibbeh and a flavoursome onion and pine nut topping. I found it in a little restaurant in Beirut called Kibbet Zaman (Yesterday's kibbeh). It can be served hot or cold (I prefer it hot) as a main dish or cut up small as a mezze. It is really worth doing – I guarantee you will surprise your guests. Accompany it with baba ghanouj (p.256), hummus (p.258) and a salad.

SERVES 6

FOR THE KIBBEH BASE
125g fine-ground bulgur
1 medium onion, quartered
500g lean lamb, taken from the leg
1/2 teaspoon salt
black pepper
1 teaspoon ground cinnamon
2 tablespoons vegetable oil

FOR THE TOPPING
500g onions, sliced
3 tablespoons extra virgin olive oil
50g pine nuts
salt and black pepper
1/2 teaspoon ground cinnamon
pinch of ground allspice
1/2–1 tablespoon pomegranate molasses (p.10) (optional)

For the *kibbeh* base, rinse the bulgur in a fine sieve in cold running water and drain well. Purée the onion in a food processor. Add the meat, salt, pepper and cinnamon, and blend to a paste. Add the bulgur and blend to a smooth soft paste.

With your hand, press the paste into the bottom of an oiled round shallow ovenproof dish or tart dish about 11cm in diameter. Flatten and smooth the top and rub with 2 tablespoons oil. With a pointed knife, cut the flattened *kibbeh* paste into 6 wedges through the centre, and run the knife round the edges of the dish. Bake in an oven pre-heated to 190°C/375°F/Gas 5 for about 30 minutes until browned.

While the *kibbeh* base is cooking, prepare the topping. Fry the onions in the oil until they are golden brown, stirring often. Add the pine nuts and stir until lightly coloured. Then add a little salt and pepper, the cinnamon and allspice and, if you like a slightly sweet-and-sour flavour (I do), the pomegranate molasses. Cook, stirring, for a minute or so.

Serve the *kibbeh* with the topping spread over.

VARIATIONS

※ Instead of pine nuts, use 75g shelled walnuts, broken into pieces and, if you like, 2 tablespoons raisins soaked in water for 15 minutes and drained. (If you are using raisins, omit the pomegranate molasses.)

※ Add 1 tablespoon sumac (p.11) to the onion topping and omit the pomegranate molasses.

LAMB STEW with VINEGAR and AUBERGINES
Lahma Bi Khal

This dish does not look very nice – it is a muddy brown – but the flavours are deliciously rich and strong, and the meat is meltingly tender. Serve it with plain or vermicelli rice (p. 316).

SERVES 6–8

500g baby onions or shallots
1kg boned shoulder of lamb
sunflower oil
8 whole garlic cloves
salt and pepper
1 teaspoon ground cinnamon
$^1/_2$ teaspoon ground allspice
1 teaspoon sugar
3 medium aubergines
4 tablespoons red or white wine vinegar
1 tablespoon crushed dried mint

To peel the baby onions or shallots, drop them into boiling water and poach for 5 minutes to loosen the skins, then drain and peel them while still warm.

Cut the meat into 8 large pieces and trim off only some of the fat. Heat 2 tablespoons oil in a large pan, put in the meat and turn to brown it all over, then lift it out. It will have released quite a bit of fat. In this, fry the baby onions or shallots and the whole cloves of garlic, stirring until golden. Lift them out and keep them on one side.

Pour off the fat and return the meat to the pan, then cover with water and bring to the boil. Remove the scum, then add the garlic, salt and pepper, cinnamon, allspice and sugar. Simmer, covered, for about $1^1/_2$ hours until the meat is very tender, adding water as necessary to keep it covered.

Cut the aubergines into rounds 1.5cm thick. Brush them with oil and cook them under the pre-heated grill or in a grill pan, turning them over once, until browned. They do not need to be cooked through.

Put the onions in with the meat, add the vinegar and mint and simmer, covered, for 10 minutes. Add the aubergines and cook for a further 20 minutes.

LAMB SHANKS COOKED in YOGHURT
Laban Ummo

The name of this dish, which means 'his mother's milk', implies that the meat of a young animal is cooked in its own mother's milk. It can be made with small lamb shanks or with knuckle of veal (osso buco) or slightly fatty cubed meat. I have used lamb shanks. Serve it with plain or vermicelli rice (p.316). The yoghurt makes a wonderful soupy sauce so provide spoons, too.

SERVES 6

6 lamb shanks (each weighing 300–400g)
salt and white pepper
500g shallots or baby onions, peeled
2kg natural yoghurt
2 tablespoons cornflour
3 garlic cloves (optional)
To serve with: crushed dried mint

Put the lamb shanks into a large pan and cover them with water. Bring to the boil, remove any scum, and add salt and pepper. Cook them with the lid on for 2 hours, adding water to keep them covered. Peel the shallots or baby onions: drop them in boiling water and poach them for 5 minutes to loosen the skins, then drain and peel them while still warm. Add them to the meat and cook for 30 minutes more, until they are soft and the meat is so tender that it falls off the bone.

You need to prepare or 'stabilize' the yoghurt to prevent it from curdling during cooking. Pour it into a large saucepan and beat well until it is liquid. Mix the cornflour to a light paste with 3–4 tablespoons water and add this to the yoghurt, beating vigorously until well mixed. Now bring the yoghurt to the boil slowly, stirring constantly in one direction only, then reduce the heat to as low as possible and let it barely simmer, uncovered, for about 10 minutes. Do not cover the pan with a lid: they say that a drop of steam falling back into the yogurt could ruin it. I am not sure that is true.

Drain the cooked shanks – you can remove the bones or not, as you wish – and the onions and add them to the yoghurt. Stir in a little salt and the garlic (if using) and simmer gently, uncovered, for 10–15 minutes.

When serving, pass round a little bowl of dried mint so people can stir a teaspoonful or so into their sauce if they wish.

ROAST LAMB with RICE, MINCED MEAT and NUTS
Ouzi

A central part of every grand Arab feast is lamb – shoulder or leg – cooked à la cuillère to such tenderness that you can eat it 'with a spoon', accompanied by rice with minced meat and nuts.

This recipe comes from the caterer Nazira Bitar who is the queen of wedding cakes all over the Arab world. She prepared a banquet in Stockholm that was hosted by the King of Jordan for King Carl Gustav and Queen Silvia.

SERVES 6–8

1 leg of lamb (weighing about 2.25kg) or 2 shoulders (2 x 1.7kg)

1 teaspoon ground cinnamon

$1/2$ teaspoon ground allspice

$1/2$ teaspoon ground cumin

$1/2$ teaspoon ground cardamom

salt and black pepper

2 tablespoons sunflower oil

1 onion, cut in quarters

1 head of garlic, cut in half

FOR THE RICE

500g long-grain or basmati rice

1 large onion, chopped

3 tablespoons sunflower oil

250g minced beef

salt and black pepper

1 teaspoons ground cinnamon

$1/2$ teaspoon ground allspice

$1/2$ teaspoon ground nutmeg

$1/2$ teaspoon ground cloves

1 litre lamb or chicken stock (use 2 stock cubes)

50g split almonds

50g pistachios

50g pine nuts

Rub the leg of lamb all over with the spices, salt and pepper and the oil. Put it in a large roasting pan into an oven pre-heated to 220°C/425°F/Gas 7. After 20 minutes, take the pan out of the oven, pour in 1 litre water, and add the onion and garlic. Cover the meat with a large sheet of foil and put it back in the oven. Lower the heat to 150°C/300°F/Gas 2 and cook for 3 hours.

While the meat is cooking, prepare the rice. Wash the rice in cold, water then rinse in a strainer under the tap and drain. In a large pan, fry the onion in 2 tablespoons of the oil until it is soft and beginning to colour. Add the minced beef and cook, stirring, turning it over and crushing it with a fork to break up any lumps, until it has changed colour. Add salt and pepper and all the spices: cinnamon, allspice, nutmeg and cloves. Stir well and add the rice, then stir again.

Pour in the boiling stock, mix well and simmer, covered, for about 10–20 minutes until the rice is tender. (Some brands that claim not to be parboiled or pre-cooked now take as little as 8–10 minutes, so read the information on the packet.) Add a little stock or water if it becomes too dry. Drain and keep it on one side until you are ready to serve.

Fry the almonds, pistachios and pine nuts separately in the remaining oil until they just begin to colour. When the leg of lamb is ready, place it on a serving dish with the rice: you can cut the meat off the bone into slices, if you wish. Sprinkle the fried nuts all over the rice. Serve with a sauce which is the flavoursome meat broth produced at the bottom of the roasting pan. Heat it through and serve it in a jug, first pouring off as much of the fat from the top as you can.

Desserts

In Beirut and other cities in Lebanon, people do not make any of their pastries at home – they buy them in – apart from those attached to religious festivals, and even then, they make them only during those festivals. Pastry-making is one of the legendary trades of the country and the great pastry capital of Lebanon is the city of Tripoli. I was allowed into the kitchens of one of the celebrated pastry-makers there, Abdul Rahman Hallab and Sons, where I saw dozens of different types of pastries being made. I was also taken by a local man, Abdel Karim al Chaar – a friend of the friends who took me to Tripoli – around the souks of the old city to taste yet more pastries made by small artisans. Abdel Karim is a famous singer who sings verses from the Koran in mosques and holds concerts of the classic Arab-Andalusian mode called *tarab*. He came with his daughter Ranine who was at that moment a finalist in the inter-Arab singing competition 'Superstar' on Future TV. Abdel Karim was greeted by all the old men in the souk while young girls with headscarves clustered round Ranine and assured her that they would be voting for her. And we got special treatment in the pastry shops.

In the centre of the *khan* that specialized in perfumed soaps we saw rose water, *mai ward*, and orange blossom water, *mai zahr*, being made in a row of primitive alembics (see p.10). The waters lend a delicate perfume to many Lebanese puddings and pastries. Here, even out in the open, the perfume was intoxicating.

In Beirut, I went to see a pastry-maker called Nazira Bitar whose wedding cakes are famous all over the Arab world. She showed me photograph albums of her fantastically elaborate cakes with edible flowers, birds, butterflies, fruits, shells, and jewels. Her latest are chandeliers that reach from the ceiling to the floor.

MILK PUDDING
Muhallabiya

Muhallabiya is the most popular Lebanese dessert. In restaurants it is usually made with cornflour. At home, ground rice is used or a mixture of both. It is a special refinement to pour a little honey syrup over the top and to garnish it with a large amount of chopped nuts. It is very easy to make but it requires attention and patience during the long time it needs stirring.

SERVES 6

2 tablespoons cornflour
50g ground rice
1 litre milk
100g sugar, or more to taste
1 tablespoon orange blossom water (p.10)
$1^1/2$ tablespoons rose water (p.11)
3 tablespoons clear honey
50g blanched almonds, chopped coarsely
50g pistachio nuts, chopped coarsely

Mix the cornflour and ground rice with about 100ml cold milk, and beat well, making sure that you break up any small lumps. Bring the rest of the milk to the boil in a large, preferably non-stick, pan. Add the cornflour and ground rice mixture, stirring vigorously with a wooden spoon.

Keep over a low heat, and stir constantly, until you feel a slight resistance. Continue to cook gently over a low heat for 15–20 minutes or until the cream thickens further, stirring occasionally. Be very careful not to scrape the bottom of the pan; the cream burns slightly at the bottom, and if it is scraped it will give a burnt taste to the pudding. Add the sugar towards the end.

Stir in the orange blossom water and 1 tablespoon of the rose water, and cook for a few moments more. Let the cream cool a little before pouring into a glass serving bowl. Let it cool, then chill in the refrigerator, covered with cling film.

When the pudding is cold, prepare a honey syrup in a small pan by bringing to the boil the honey with about 125ml water. Stir well and add the remaining $1/2$ tablespoon of rose water. Let it cool and pour over the cold, firmed cream. It will seep in a little.

Serve sprinkled with a pattern of chopped almonds and pistachios.

Instead of garnishing with chopped nuts, serve topped with rose petal jam which is available from Middle Eastern stores.

MILK ICE CREAM with GUM MASTIC and ROSE WATER
Bouza Bi Halib

A brilliant white milk ice cream with a chewy texture made with sahlab (called salep in Turkey), the ground-up root tuber of a member of the orchid family, is very difficult to make successfully at home, so here is a modern version that I also love. It is without sahlab, so not chewy, but the traditional flavourings of mastic and rose water give it the special appeal.

You should pound the tiny lumps of gum mastic (p.10) with a teaspoon of sugar to a fine powder in a pestle and mortar (or use a spice grinder). Use very little as otherwise the taste can be quite unpleasant.

SERVES 4–6

4 egg yolks
100g sugar
300ml single cream
1–2 tablespoons rose water (p.11), to taste
$1/4$ teaspoon pulverized gum mastic
300ml double cream

Beat the egg yolks with the sugar to a thick pale cream in a bowl. Bring the single cream to the boil and gradually pour over the yolk mixture, beating all the time.

Put the bowl into a pan of boiling water or in the top part of a double saucepan and stir constantly until the mixture thickens into a custard. Add the rose water, take off the heat, and sprinkle the gum mastic over the whole surface (if it falls in one place it sticks together in a lump) and stir in vigorously.

Beat the double cream until firm and fold this into the cooled custard.

Pour the mixture into a mould lined with cling film and cover with more cling film. Freeze overnight. Take out of the freezer 5–10 minutes before serving, remove the cling film and turn the ice cream out of its mould.

RICE PUDDING with
APRICOT COMPOTE
Roz Bi Halib Wal Mishmish

This is a moreish homely pudding. Topped by a fruit compote such as stewed apricots, it becomes elegant dinner party fare. It is also good served with the rose petal jam that you can buy in Middle Eastern stores. Gum mastic gives the pudding an intriguing, and to me, very delicious flavour, but it is optional. Serve the pudding cold.

SERVES 6

200g round Italian or pudding rice

350 ml water

1 litre milk

150g sugar, or to taste

2 tablespoons orange blossom or rose water (pp.10 and 11)

$^1/_2$ teaspoon pulverised gum mastic (p.10) (optional)

APRICOT COMPOTE

1kg apricots

400 ml water

150g sugar

1 lemon

Boil the rice in the water for 8 minutes or until the water is absorbed. Add the milk and simmer over a very low heat for about 30 minutes, stirring occasionally to make sure that the bottom does not stick and burn.

When the rice is very soft and the milk not entirely absorbed, add the sugar and stir until dissolved. If it is a bit dry, add a little more milk. Add the orange blossom or rose water or a mix of the two and cook for a minute longer. Turn off the heat, sprinkle on the mastic (if using) and stir very well before pouring into a serving bowl. There should still be quite a bit of liquid. It will be absorbed as the pudding cools. The result should be creamy. Pour into a wide serving dish and chill in the refrigerator, covered with cling film.

For the apricot compote, wash, cut in half and stone the apricots. Put them into a large heavy-bottomed pan with the water, sugar and lemon juice. Cook, covered, over a low heat for 10 minutes or until the apricots fall apart. Let the fruit cool, then chill in the refrigerator before spreading over the rice pudding.

OSMALIYAH with a CREAM FILLING
Kataifi with Cream Filling

Osmaliyah has been known for generations in my family in Egypt as konafa and I have featured it before. I include it here again because, of all the Lebanese pastries that are good to make at home and to serve at a dinner party, this is one of the best; it is my mother's recipe. It is meant to be served hot but it is also good cold.

   You can buy the soft white vermicelli-like dough frozen in Lebanese, Turkish and Greek stores. In Lebanon, it is called knafe but in the UK it is sold by its Greek name kataifi in 400g packets; it should be defrosted for 2–3 hours. The quantities below will make one large pastry to serve 10 but you can also make two half the size, one to serve fewer people and one to put into the freezer to bake at a later date. It freezes well uncooked.

SERVES 10

FOR THE SYRUP

400g sugar

250ml water

1 tablespoon lemon juice

2 tablespoons orange blossom water (p.10)

FOR THE CREAM FILLING

125g ground rice

950ml milk

120ml double cream

4 tablespoons sugar

FOR THE PASTRY

400g kataifi (knafe) pastry, defrosted

200g unsalted butter, melted

To garnish: 100g pistachios, chopped finely

Make the syrup first. Boil the sugar with the water and the lemon juice over a low heat for 5–10 minutes, until it is just thick enough to coat the back of a spoon. Another way to test it is to pour a drop on to a cold plate and if it does not spread out like water, it is ready. Stir in the orange blossom water and cook for a moment more. Let it cool, then chill in the refrigerator. (If you have overcooked the syrup and it becomes too thick to pour when it is cold, you can rescue it by adding a little water and bringing it to the boil again.)

For the filling, mix the ground rice with enough of the cold milk to make a smooth creamy paste. Bring the rest of the milk with the cream to the boil. Add the ground rice paste, stirring vigorously with a wooden spoon. Leave it on a very low heat and continue to stir constantly for 15–20 minutes until the mixture thickens, being careful not to let it burn at the bottom. Then add the sugar and stir well.

Put the *kataifi* pastry in a large bowl. With your fingers, pull out and separate the strands as much as possible. Melt the butter and when it has cooled slightly, pour it over the pastry and work it in very thoroughly with your fingers, pulling out and separating the strands and turning them over so that they do not stick together, and are entirely coated with butter.

Spread half the pastry in the bottom of a large round pie pan, measuring 28–30cm in diameter. Spread the cream filling over it evenly and cover with the rest of the pastry. Press down firmly and flatten it with the palm of your hand. Bake in an oven pre-heated to 180°C/350°F/Gas 4 for about 45 minutes. Some like to brown the bottom – which comes out on top when the pastry is turned out – by running it over heat on a hob for a brief moment only. Others prefer the pastry to remain pale.

Just before serving, run a sharp knife round the edges of the *osmaliyah* to loosen the sides, then turn it out on to a large serving dish. Pour the cold syrup all over the hot pastry and sprinkle the top lavishly with the chopped pistachios.

Alternatively, you can pour only half the syrup over the pastry and pass the rest around in a jug for everyone to help themselves to more if they wish.

OSMALIYA *with* CHEESE FILLING

This is another wonderful dessert that I strongly recommend. It is quicker and easier to make than the previous one with cream. Make the pastry as on p.336 but instead of the cream filling, use 500g mozzarella cheese blended in a food processor with 250g ricotta, 2 tablespoons sugar and 2 tablespoons orange blossom water. Bake as above and pour the cold syrup over the hot pastry as it comes out of the oven, just before serving. Serve hot or at least warm while the cheese is soft.

BELLAWRIEH

This is made with *kataifi* pastry in the same way as the recipe for *Osmaliyah* with a Cream Filling (p.336). Instead of the cream filling, use 500g whole pistachios or chopped walnuts mixed with a few tablespoons of the sugar syrup to bind them together. Serve this pastry cold.

PANCAKES STUFFED
with WALNUTS
Atayef Bil Jawz

To make these spongy pancakes stuffed with walnuts and dipped in syrup called
atayef takes time (and I should warn you that they are fattening) but they are heavenly
and when you have made them more than once, you will find them not too difficult.
The amount of syrup is more than you need but it is good to serve separately as well
in case anyone would like to pour a little more on their pastry.

MAKES ABOUT 20 PANCAKES

FOR THE BATTER
1 teaspoon active dry yeast
1 teaspoon sugar
350ml lukewarm water
200g plain flour
sunflower or vegetable oil for frying

FOR THE SYRUP
500g sugar
300ml water
1 tablespoon lemon juice
1–2 tablespoons orange blossom or rose water (pp.10 and 11)

FOR THE FILLING
250g walnuts, chopped finely
100g sugar
1¹/₂ teaspoons rose water

For the batter, dissolve the yeast with 1 teaspoon of sugar in about 100ml of the
warm water. Let it stand for 10 minutes or until it froths. Put the flour into a large
bowl. Add the yeast mixture and the remaining water gradually, beating vigorously,
to make a creamy, lump-free batter. Cover the bowl with cling film and leave in a
warm place for about 2 hours until the batter rises and becomes bubbly and elastic.

To make the syrup, bring the sugar and water to the boil in a pan with the lemon
juice and simmer for 5–8 minutes, until it is thick enough to coat the back of a

spoon. Then stir in the orange blossom or rose water and simmer for a few seconds more. Allow to cool, then chill in the refrigerator.

For the filling, mix together the walnuts, sugar and rose water.

When the batter is ready, beat it again vigorously. Using a piece of kitchen paper, rub a non-stick frying pan with oil, ensuring it is thoroughly greased with a very thin film of oil. Heat the frying pan until it is very hot, then reduce the heat and keep it at medium.

In batches of 3, pour one-third of a ladle (about 2 tablespoons) of batter into the pan. Spread the batter a little with the back of a fork (it does not spread by itself) so that it becomes a round, 9–10cm in diameter, or an oval. Cook one side of the pancake only. The other side must remain uncooked and moist so that its edges will stick together. When the pancakes lose their whiteness and tiny holes appear, and as they become detached from the pan, lift them out and pile them up on a plate.

Put a tablespoon of filling in the middle of each pancake, on the uncooked side. Fold the pancake in half over the filling to make a half-moon shape, and close the pastries by pinching the edges very firmly together to seal them.

Deep-fry the pancakes *very briefly* in batches in sizzling but not too hot oil, turning them over once, until they just begin to colour. (They become hard if they are fried too long.) Then lift them out with a slotted spoon and drain on kitchen paper. Dip them, while still hot, on both sides in the syrup so they absorb some, and transfer to a serving plate.

Serve them warm or cold. Pour any remaining syrup into a bowl and offer extra to those who have a sweet tooth.

VARIATION

Instead of deep-frying the pancakes, you can bake them. Arrange them on an oiled baking dish, brush them with oil or melted butter, and bake them in an oven pre-heated to 200°C/400°F/Gas 6 for 15–20 minutes.

TINY OPEN PANCAKES with CREAM and ROSE PETAL JAM
Atayef Bil Ashta

These are easy and a treat. Make the pancakes as in Pancakes Stuffed with Walnuts (p.339), but use just 1 tablespoon batter for each pancake, and turn them to cook the other side. Dip the little pancakes into the syrup and arrange on a flat serving plate. Spread each with a heaped teaspoon of clotted cream (you will need about 250g) and top with a teaspoon of rose petal jam. The quantity of batter will make about 30 little pancakes. Alternatively, instead of the rose petal jam, sprinkle finely chopped pistachios over the cream (you will need about 150g).

PANCAKES STUFFED with CHEESE
Atayef Bil Jibne

Follow the above recipe, and instead of walnuts use the following filling: blend in a food processor 375g mozzarella cheese with 4 tablespoons sugar and 2 teaspoons rose water.

ALMOND PUFF PASTRY PIES
Sambousek Bi Loz

These little pies which are filled with nuts – almonds, pine nuts, pistachios or walnuts – can be served with tea or coffee, either dusted with icing sugar or dipped in syrup. Use commercial fresh or frozen and defrosted puff pastry.

MAKES 24 PIES

> 500g puff pastry
> flour for dusting
> 40g unsalted butter, melted
> icing sugar

250g ground almonds
125g caster sugar
3 tablespoons orange blossom water (p.10)

It is important to roll out the puff pastry as thinly as you possibly can. It is easier to do so if you cut the block into 4 equal pieces and roll out each one separately. Dust the surface and the rolling pin with flour and roll out each sheet of pastry, turning it over and dusting it with flour, until you can cut out 6 rounds with a 10cm pastry cutter. Put the rounds in a pile and wrap the pile in cling film. Do the same with the remaining pastry.

Mix the filling ingredients to a paste. Put a tablespoon of the filling in the centre of each round and bring the edges up together over the filling to make a half-moon shape. Seal the edges by pinching them very firmly together. A traditional way is to twist the edges making a scalloped effect; another is to press down with the prongs of a fork.

Arrange the pies on sheets of foil on baking trays. Brush the tops with melted butter and bake in an oven pre-heated to 200°C/400°F/Gas 6 for about 15 minutes or until they are puffed up and lightly golden. Let them cool before dusting with icing sugar.

VARIATIONS

✽ For a pine nut filling, blend 400g pine nuts in a food processor with 200g caster sugar and 4 tablespoons orange blossom water (p.10).

✽ For a pistachio filling, blend 400g pistachios in a food processor with 200g caster sugar and 4 tablespoons rose water.

✽ For a walnut filling, blend 400g walnuts in a food processor with 200g sugar, the grated rind of 1 orange and 4 tablespoons fresh orange juice

✽ For the pastries in syrup, bring to the boil 300ml water and 500g sugar with 1 tablespoon lemon juice, and simmer for 3–5 minutes or until the sugar is completely dissolved. Let it cool and then chill it in the refrigerator. Make the pastries as in the above recipe, or with any of the fillings in the listed variations. Do not dust them with icing sugar but dip them in the cold syrup immediately they come out of the oven.

PISTACHIO PASTE STUFFED
with CREAM
Bohsalino

I had never come across this pastry before. I tasted it in Beirut where a few pâtisseries claim to have invented it. One, called Bohsali, gave it the name Bohsalino; another calls it Taj el Malek. It involves a little skill – akin to pottery making – that improves with practice. In Lebanon they are filled with the thick cream that rises to the top when rich buffalo's milk is boiled. They do not keep more than a day or two because of the cream.

> 200g shelled pistachios
> 100g caster sugar
> 2 tablespoons rose water (p.11)
> about 100g thick clotted cream
> icing sugar to sprinkle on

Grind the pistachios in a food processor, then add the sugar and rose water (don't be tempted to put any more) and blend until it forms a soft malleable slightly oily paste. The mix will appear at first like wet sand but the oil released by the pistachios will bind it into a workable paste.

Rub your hands with oil so that the paste does not stick. Take little lumps the size of a walnut, roll each into a ball, then make a hole in it with your finger and enlarge it, by pinching the sides and pulling them up to make a little dome-shaped pot.

Fill the hole with about 1 tablespoon of clotted cream. Put the pot down on a plate rubbed with oil so that it doesn't stick and make a lid for it: take a lump of paste the size of a large olive, flatten it between the palms of your hands and lay it over the cream. Stick the edges well together and place the pastry lid-side down in a pastry case.

Alternatively you can line tiny cake moulds with cling film and press the paste around the sides, fill the hollow with the cream and cover with a lid.

Keep the pastries in the refrigerator – the cream needs to be refrigerated and the paste will firm – until you are ready to serve them, sprinkled with icing sugar.

VARIATION
Do the same with almonds and use 2 tablespoons of orange blossom water (p.10) instead of rose water.

Index

Acknowledgements

Over the decades, since devoting my life to researching the foods of the Middle East and North Africa, very many people have given me recipes, advice, bits of information, stories that have finally found their way into this book. I will not thank them all here, but they should know that their contribution was much valued and that I always think of them fondly.

Of those who have helped me most when I was preparing *Arabesque*, I am especially grateful to Nevin Halici who has been a fantastic guide in Turkey. The late Turkish gastronome Tugrul Savkai was extremely helpful and I miss him deeply. Kamal Mouzawak was my all-important, entertaining and gracious guide in Lebanon. I cannot thank him enough, and I also thank his mother Fariba for her hospitality and valuable information. Others who have made me love Lebanon (and love them too) and have helped me with my research are my friends Mai Ghoussoub, her husband Hazim Saghie and their families: Hazim's mother Khalida Saghie, Mai's mother Maggie, her sister Hoda, brother-in-law Kamal, nephew Maher and Natasha his new bride. I am also indebted to the caterer Nazira Hadad Bitar. I owe much to Fatema Hal who is a Moroccan restaurateur, anthropologist, and food writer extraordinary. I met her first in Morocco, then in Sicily, Paris and Barcelona.

Over the years I have accumulated a large collection of Arab, Turkish, North African and Iranian cookery books that I dip into for all kinds of information. When I started writing about food there were only three or four around, now there are very many.

My warmest thanks are to my editor Camilla Stoddart for her vision and her enthusiastic support; Jenny Dereham for her intelligent and painstaking editing; Jason Lowe for the beautiful photographs; my agent Jacqueline Korn for her unceasing encouragement.

I fell in love with Carolinda Tolstoy's ceramics when I first saw them. They are arabesques. A few were used in the photographs, but do go and look at her website: www.carolinda-tolstoy.co.uk.

Penguin would like to thank the people of Goldbourne Road, Stoke Newington, Green Lane and Edgware Road for allowing us to photograph there, especially the following establishments: Mangal on Arcola Street, Urfa Sofrasi and Özantepliler on Stoke Newington Road.